The Secular Madrigals of Filippo di Monte
1521-1603

Studies in Musicology, No. 64

George Buelow, Series Editor

Professor of Musicology
Indiana University

Other Titles in This Series

The Secular Madrigals of Filippo di Monte 1521-1603

by
Brian Mann

UMI RESEARCH PRESS
Ann Arbor, Michigan

Produced and distributed by
UMI Research Press
an imprint of
University Microfilms International
Ann Arbor, Michigan 48106

Library of Congress Cataloging in Publication Data

Mann, Brian.
   The secular madrigals of Filippo di Monte, 1521-
1603.

   (Studies in musicology ; no. 64)
   Revision of thesis—University of California, Berkeley,
1981.
   Bibliography: p.
   Includes index.
   1. Monte, Philippe de, 1521-1603. Madrigals. 2. Madrigals
(Music), Italian—History and criticism.   I. Title. II. Series.
ML410.M755M3 1983   784.1'2'00924   83-1061
ISBN 0-8357-1402-0

Contents

List of Tables

Acknowledgments

My work on the madrigals of Filippo di Monte was first undertaken in a graduate seminar taught by Anthony Newcomb, whose enthusiasm for the Italian madrigal and boundless curiosity about its unexplored territories led me to write the present study.

To the Music Department of the University of California, Berkeley, I express my gratitude for the years of support I enjoyed while at work on this subject. To Vincent Duckles, Ann Basart, and John Emerson of the Music Library I am grateful for many kindnesses. I wish also to thank Mary Ankudowich (Werner Josten Library, Smith College), Milton Steinhardt (University of Kansas), Oliver Neighbour (British Library), Watkins Shaw (Royal College of Music), François Lesure (Bibliothèque Nationale), and Sergio Paganelli (Bologna) for their prompt and helpful replies to my letters. To the many European libraries which responded quickly with microfilm material I also express my thanks.

It would be impossible to record the names of all those personal friends who have contributed much to this study; without slighting those I cannot mention, I must at least thank Gary Tomlinson, Walter Frisch, and Linda Coleman, who typed the tables.

My sons Robbie and Iain sustained me in the darkest hours of this *lunga fatica,* but my deepest debt is to my parents, whose support in innumerable ways made the completion of this study possible.

Preface

"Difficulty of treating such an extensive theme in a concise way. Monte the most prolific of all madrigalists."[1] With these terse remarks, Alfred Einstein began a series of manuscript notes, headed *"Filippo di Monte als Madrigalkomponist."* Most probably jotted down in the late 1920s, these *Notes*[2] eventually took finished form as an article of the same title, which appeared in 1930.[3] Four years later, another article, broader in scope, gave Einstein the opportunity to offer a few more observations on this topic.[4] When he finally came to write a chapter on the madrigals of Filippo di Monte for his monumental study, *The Italian Madrigal*,[5] he relied heavily on these two articles. This brief chapter (a mere fourteen pages), taken together with the few comments concerning Monte's work which appear elsewhere in the book, represents Einstein's last and definitive statement on the subject.

The basis of all of Einstein's perceptions was the music itself. Over many years (beginning early in this century), he transcribed virtually all of Monte's huge madrigalian output.[6] This was only part of his much broader plan to transcribe the works of those masters of the Italian madrigal whose music had not appeared in modern edition.

In the very years in which Einstein's self-appointed task of transcribing Monte's secular music was largely completed, a modern edition of his works was begun, in Belgium.[7] From its inception in 1927 to its abandonment in 1939, thirty-one volumes appeared, under the joint editorship of Charles van den Borren and Julius van Nuffel. These editors' evident bias towards sacred music (van Nuffel was a cleric) led to the almost total exclusion of secular madrigals from the series: of its thirty-one volumes, only one is entirely devoted to a book of secular madrigals. In 1975, a new complete edition of Monte's works was again undertaken, under the general editorship of René Lenaerts.[8] Several volumes of madrigals have now appeared in this series.

Einstein's transcriptions remain an important source and research tool for this music; indeed, his efforts even resulted in saving works whose printed sources have disappeared since he transcribed them.[9] Nevertheless, his many volumes of transcriptions have proven to be quite difficult to use: writing in a tiny and often illegible hand, he retained the original clefs, and sketched no bar lines. The result is a score which defies easy familiarity. It was necessary, then, to make new transcriptions. In preparation for the writing of this study, I copied five books of madrigals in their entirety, as well as numerous single pieces from other volumes.

With his own transcriptions in hand, and from a study of the poetry which Monte set over the years, Einstein gave a concise account of Monte's madrigals, dividing the output into stylistic periods, relating Monte's development to the broader history of the Italian madrigal, and—in his most original contribution to the subject—offering his own rather picturesque interpretation of the final phase of Monte's madrigalian career:

> In the end...he forsakes the lofty muse of Petrarch, Bembo, Bernardo Tasso, and Luigi Tansillo in favor of Guarini and Celiano. He is now sixty-five, and it is little short of tragi-comic to see the old man become an Arcadian—like Don Quixote at the end of his life, after the collapse of his knightly ambitions.... We repeat: all this is little short of tragi-comic, for this gesture toward modernity and toward the latest fashion was made in vain. [10]

This view of Monte's final years, set forth in *The Italian Madrigal,* contradicts the opinions he had expressed earlier in his article of 1930. There, he emphasized the lasting artistic accomplishments of Monte's last period, rather than the composer's capitulation to decadent contemporary taste. Einstein's perceptions had evolved quite strikingly over the years, and it will be one of the tasks of this study to examine these critical issues once again.

Because Monte's stature as a composer has generally been slighted by comparison with that of, say, Lasso, his vast output of madrigals has tended to elicit only perfunctory observations in most historical surveys and handbooks. Doubtless the continuing lack of a complete edition has also discouraged most scholars from attempting to survey so vast a musical terrain. As a result, the few observations offered tend to be as misleading as they are brief.

Gustave Reese devoted three pages to Monte's madrigals in his *Music in the Renaissance.*[11] Unfortunately, he does not consider the more important aspects of Monte's output: its unique pattern of stylistic development, and its broader place in the history of the genre. Instead, he offers a number of observations on the music, as it could be viewed in the works available to him. Without the aid of any historical or stylistic focus, his comments are not of much value, and give no hint of the diversity of style present in Monte's works.

Edward J. Dent's brief account of Monte's madrigals in the *New Oxford History* is not much more enlightening:

> His music is accomplished, well-mannered, and agreeable—the typical conventional classical madrigal; it often has great melodic charm but more good taste than originality or intensity of feeling. [12]

Besides exemplifying the fine art of damning with faint praise, these comments reveal a serious and (coming from Dent) surprising misconception of the Italian madrigal, as there is hardly such a thing as the "typical conventional classical madrigal."

Jerome Roche's recent study, *The Madrigal*,[13] at least takes account of the stylistic divisions in Monte's career, and offers sympathetic, if brief, comments on several pieces available in modern edition.

The principal biographical study of Monte, Doorslaer's *La Vie et les Oeuvres de Philippe de Monte*,[14] while an invaluable source of biographical and bibliographical material, has little to say about Monte's music, sacred or secular. Rather, the author relies entirely upon earlier writers, whom he quotes extensively.

Paradoxically, the only full-length monograph on Monte's madrigals is devoted to his *madrigali spirituali*;[15] Monte's five books of spiritual madrigals, all of which appeared in a twelve-year period towards the end of his career, represent only a fraction of his madrigalian output, as we shall see. Furthermore, their stylistic development is ultimately only a reflection of the broader development of his secular style. On the whole, the statistical rather than critical approach which author Piet Nuten takes towards this music has not provided a useful model for the present study.[16]

This survey of the secondary literature reveals all too clearly that no critical reappraisal of Monte's enormous secular *œuvre* has been undertaken since Einstein's work. His writings and perceptions, then, are the starting point for this study, which has as its main theme a critical examination of Monte's secular madrigals—their place in the life of the composer, their relationship to the broader history of the madrigal, their unique stylistic unfolding, and their ultimate value as works of art.

1

Monte's Life and Madrigalian Works: An Introduction

"Rien sans peine"

Monte's motto at the Imperial Court

The Biography

Filippo di Monte was born in 1521, in Mecheln (or Malines) in what is now central Belgium. The place of his birth was for a long time the subject of some controversy, until discovery of sixteenth-century documents referring to him as "Philippus de Monte von Mechel"[1] put to rest the contention that he was from the town of Mons. It now seems clear that his surname is a family name, perhaps an Italianization of the Flemish "van der Berghe," and not an Italian rendering of his place of birth.

Monte's date of birth poses no such problems: there are three contemporary indications of it, the most important of which is an engraved portrait of the composer dated 1594 with the inscription *AETAT SUAE LXXIII*.[2] We also have Monte's own statement in the dedication of his *Pastor Fido,* signed 1 January 1600, that he was seventy-eight years old.[3] Though this points to 1522 as his year of birth, the dedication was most probably written in the preceding year, and thus confirms 1521 as his date of birth.

Nothing at all is known about Monte's early years. Doorslaer confesses to have found no mention of Monte in the Malines archives of the period.[4] It seems likely that he was trained as a choirboy at the church of St. Rombault, whose *acta capitularia* have disappeared.

The earliest evidence of Monte's activities as a professional musician comes, paradoxically, from late in his life. In the dedication of his Nineteenth Book of Madrigals for Five Voices (1598), Monte refers to his youthful activities as music tutor in a noble Neapolitan household. The dedication, to *"il Signor Don Gieronimo di Ghevara, Cavaliero, & Ambasciatore della Sacra Religione Hierosolomitana appresso Sua Maestà Cesarea,"* reads, in part:

...All the same, I shall not let this opportunity pass to reveal to the world (by this sign of gratitude) my devotion to your most noble house, and the Pinella House, where I spent many years of my youth in the most pleasant service of the most Illustrious and most Excellent Lord the Duke of Cirenza, and the most virtuous and honored Lord Giovan Vincenzo Pinelli, brothers of your Lordship's mother. Therefore, I dedicate this nineteenth book of my madrigals for five voices...[5]

Don Gieronimo, the dedicatee, was the nephew of both Giovanni Pinelli and Galaetio Pinelli, Duca de Cirenza. These are the two men whom Monte tutored when they were adolescents. Don Gieronimo's mother was Lucretia Pinelli, their sister. Monte makes no reference to the specific duties he performed in this noble household, but an early seventeenth century biography of Giovanni Vincenzo Pinelli describes Monte as a *proeceptor,* that is, a kind of tutor.[6]

No dates are attached to either of these references to Monte's service in the Pinelli family. Doorslaer, evidently wishing to fill up the enormous gaps in Monte's early biography, placed him with little supporting evidence in Naples from about 1540 to the early 1550s. In a recent article, however, Craig Wright offers newly discovered evidence that Monte sang in the cathedral choir in Cambrai in the late 1540s.[7] Four entries in Cambrai cathedral archives document his presence there: the earliest is for 19 January 1547, the last for 14 June 1549. These prove that Monte was not continuously in Italy from 1542 until 1554, as Doorslaer believed, and as all subsequent biographers have stated. On the basis of these findings, Wright offers two substantial revisions in Monte's biography for these years. He first writes:

The fact that he was then at Cambrai seriously undermines the supposition that he and Lasso were colleagues in Naples from 1550 to 1552. It is clear that Monte was again in the North at the beginning of 1547; after his service at Cambrai it is probable that he went directly to Antwerp where he says he lived in 1554-5. In any case, the Low Countries played a greater role than has been previously supposed [in Monte's formation].[8]

Wright's suggestion that Monte did not return to Italy after 1549 is a reasonable one, though it must remain a mere supposition until supported by documentation. In a later footnote, however, Wright appears to contradict his own views:

The date 1542, given by Doorslaer (and repeated by Piet Nuten in MGG) as the date of Monte's arrival in Naples is in fact hypothetical, based on indirect evidence. It is not impossible that Monte received his first education in the north of France and the Low Countries, and that he went to Italy *after* his years of service at the Cambrai cathedral, that is to say, after 14 June 1549, but before 1554.[9]

Wright's two hypotheses are incompatible; he seems intent upon reducing Monte's years in Italy during this period to a minimum. His first hypothesis is surely the more plausible one: Monte's own remark that he spent many years of his youth in Naples surely indicates a lengthy stay on the peninsula. Furthermore, the fact that Monte's name appears in its Italian form[10] in these archives is proof that he had already been in Italy.

Monte's whereabouts from June 1549 to some time in 1554 remain mysterious. He may have returned to Italy, or may have remained in the North; there is evidence supporting both views. Doorslaer's suggestion that Monte and Lasso became friends in Naples during this period is a pleasant notion unsupported by any known documents.[11]

In 1554, Monte's First Book of Madrigals for Five Voices appeared in Rome, which Doorslaer took as an adequate indication of Monte's presence there in that year. Othmar Wessely, in his preface to the recent edition of the First Book, makes the same assumption:

> De Monte must have spent some time in Rome during the typesetting, as was customary in his day, but apparently he already left before the printing was completed, since we know from his own testimony that he stayed in Antwerp for a while in that same year 1554.[12]

But both Doorslaer and Wessely have overlooked some evidence bearing on this matter. The dedication of the First Book was not signed by Monte, but rather by a certain Giovan Battista Bruno, who dedicated the work to the Roman nobleman Honofrio Vigili. Bruno refers to the madrigals as "the first and most mature fruits of the compositions for five voices, yet printed, by the excellent musician Philippo di Monte."[13] In his next publication, the First Book of Madrigals for Four Voices (1562), Monte wrote his own dedication, which states:

> Being resolved to publish some of my works, so as to take from others the opportunity of publishing things without my knowledge (as happened with my madrigals for five voices...)[14]

Monte is clearly complaining that his First Book for Five Voices had been printed without his permission; that he would consider the incident worth mentioning eight years later suggests just how disturbed he had been been at the time. Probably, then, Monte was not in Rome in 1554, at least during the period in which these madrigals were prepared for publication. In any case, it was not customary, as Wessely states, for composers to supervise the printing of their music. If this were so, every Italian composer would have been obliged to visit Venice, the principal center of music publishing, every time a book of his was printed.

Though Monte cannot be placed in Rome in 1554 with absolute certainty, the fact that the First Book was printed there, dedicated by one Roman to another, and that one of its madrigals appears to honor the Colonna family,[15] speaks for a Roman period in Monte's career some time prior to 1554.

By Monte's own account, we know that he was in Antwerp in both 1554 and 1555. This information comes, once again, from a letter written much later in life. In the dedication of the First Book of Spiritual Madrigals for Six Voices (1583), Monte writes:

> The great humanity shown me by Your Most Illustrious Lordship, both in Antwerp in 1554 and 1555, and finally last year in Augsburg... [16]

The dedication is addressed to Johann Fugger (or "Gioan Fuccari," as Monte styles him), a member of the prominent German merchant family. Further evidence of Monte's activities in this period comes in a celebrated letter written on 22 September 1555 by Dr. Seld, the Imperial Vice-Chancellor to Duke Albert V of Bavaria. In this letter, Seld speaks enthusiastically of Monte, recommending him for the position of *maestro di capella:*

> Thus, there is a suitable man in England now, in the King's Chapel, Philippe de Monte by name, a native of Malines whom I know very well. He is a quiet, reticent man, as modest as a girl, who has spent the greater part of his life in Italy, speaks Italian like a native and also Latin, French, and Flemish. For the rest he is unquestionably the best composer in the whole country, especially in the field of modern music and the *musica reservata.* I now observe that he has no wish to remain in the Royal Chapel, because the other singers are all Spaniards and he the only Fleming. ... Thus I should have for Your Highness the certainty of providing you with a better composer than His Imperial Majesty, the King of France, the King of England, or any other prince in Germany.... [17]

It is not known whether Monte actively pursued the possibility of a position at Munich; in any case, Seld's recommendations did not result in an appointment. His letter tells us a great deal, though, and offers a rare glimpse of Monte's character, albeit from a friend and benefactor. It documents Monte's presence in England, where he sang in the otherwise exclusively Spanish choir of Philip II of Spain. When and how Monte was engaged as a singer in Philip's chapel remains a mystery. Nor is it known when he left England. Seld's indication that Monte did not wish to remain in England was taken by Doorslaer as proof of his imminent departure. Only Monte's statement that he was in Antwerp both in 1554 and 1555 seems to support the hypothesis that he left England after September 1555 (the date of Seld's letter), and was in Antwerp before the end of the year.

Monte's decision to abandon the Spanish chapel and return to the Continent may have caused him some financial difficulty. In the dedicatory letter of his Third Book of Madrigals for Six Voices (1576), he recalls the liberality shown him by the dedicatee, *"il signor Giovan Grimaldi":*

> In Antwerp, finding myself in some difficulty, in need of help and the favor of friends,... Your Illustrious Lordship, on his account, moved with such promptness to declare his generosity to me... [18]

Doorslaer mentions that an Italian merchant named Giovan Antonio Grimaldi was in Antwerp during the years 1554-1555.[19] Though Monte attaches no date to his reference, his letter most likely refers to the period immediately following his return from England. Lasso's presence in Antwerp at this time led Doorslaer to propose that they renewed the friendship which they had formed in Italy. Yet it can neither be proven that they met in Italy, nor that they renewed such an acquaintance in the North.

In the next dozen years, from 1556 to 1568, we have only traces of Monte's whereabouts, though they suggest that he spent most of the time in Italy. In 1558, his setting of *Dolorosi martir* appeared in an anthology published in Rome, the *Secondo libro delle muse, a quattro voci.* In the same year, the wedding of Paolo Giordano Orsini, Duke of Bracciano, and Isabella Medici took place in Rome. A madrigal celebrating the wedding, *Il più forte di Roma,* was published in Monte's First Book of Madrigals for Six Voices (first edition lost). All this places him fairly securely in Rome in 1558.

In 1562, his First Book of Madrigals for Four Voices was published in Venice, by Antonio Gardano. Monte dedicated it to a Neapolitan nobleman, Colantino Caracciolo, on 20 September 1562, in Naples.[20] This might seem to be convincing enough evidence that Monte was in Naples on the date in question, but in fact the matter must be viewed more cautiously. It may be that Monte was merely in Naples when he wrote the letter, but that the date given is that on which the music was sent to the presses, or some other date connected with the printing. Such conclusions arise from a number of observations. For example, in 1569, Monte's Second Book for Four Voices was published; again the dedication was signed in Naples, and dated 1 March 1569. Yet Monte had recently taken up his new appointment in Vienna and cannot have been in Naples in March 1569. Taken together, these facts suggest that the contents of this book date from before his departure from the peninsula.[21] Another example: the dedications of two madrigal books—the Ninth Book for Five Voices, and the Fourth Book for Six Voices—are both dated 20 September 1580; the former gives Prague, and the latter gives Venice alongside the date.[22] Monte can only have been in Prague at this time. The date may either be the day on which Monte actually signed both dedications, or it may be the day on which these books were prepared for the presses. The purpose of this divagation has been to cast some doubt on the credibility of the place and date of dedications as biographical evidence; we should not accept these indications too hastily.

In 1566, Monte was in Florence, where he sang for Fernando de' Medici, Grand Duke of Tuscany, as we learn from the dedication of his *Musica sopra Il Pastor Fido,* written thirty-four years after the event.[23] But despite the fact that Monte's gifts as a singer and composer were admired and cultivated by a number of patrons in the years from 1556 to 1568, we know of his holding no permanent position, either in a noble household, or as a church musician.

In 1568 occurred the major event in Monte's professional life: at the age of forty-seven, he was appointed *maestro di capella* at the Imperial Court in Vienna, under Maximilian II. Jacob Vaet, Monte's predecessor in this position, had died on 8 January of the preceding year. Giovanni da Palestrina was first offered the position, but negotiations with him broke down when he insisted upon a higher salary than was offered.[24] According to recently presented evidence, Gabriel Martinengo was also considered for the position.[25] Finally, Monte, then in Rome, was approached. After some negotiations, he accepted the position, undertaking his responsibilities officially on 1 May 1568. He held this position until his death in 1603, serving two emperors: Maximilian II, and his son Rudolf II, who succeeded to the throne upon his father's death in 1576.

Soon after his appointment, Monte's productivity as a composer increased enormously. The diligence he displayed in his new position was quickly appreciated; extraordinary payments began to come his way as early as November 1569.[26] In 1570, Monte was entrusted with the responsibility of travelling to the Lowlands in search of talented musicians. He returned with several singers for the chapel, and was also responsible for engaging the services for the Emperor of two scientists, Rembert Dodoens and Charles d'Écluse (Clusius). Later in life, Monte corresponded often with d'Écluse, a botanist; some of this correspondence survives, and has been reprinted.[27]

As a further reward for his continuing energy and accomplishments, Monte was made a treasurer in 1572 at the metropolitan cathedral of Cambrai, a church with which he had been associated much earlier in his career, as we have seen.

In 1574, Monte wrote a letter to Maximilian, the importance of which has been overlooked by previous scholars. The ostensible purpose of the letter is to request that his rent payments, now in arrears for three years (!) be taken over by his employer. Yet the manner in which Monte pleads his case is most revealing: he stresses the enormous quantity of music he has composed since his arrival in Vienna, offering it indirectly as a kind of artistic barter:

> Sacred Imperial Majesty,
>   I have not bothered to present to Your Highness all the things I have composed; this would be far too much, for in six years I have written twenty masses, an infinite number of motets, madrigals, and French chansons. All of these, in time, will be printed for Your Highness, as with this book of motets for five voices. As I present them to you, I would also beg you humbly to favor me by paying my house rent, for which I owe little less than three years' worth at seventy florins per year. Since, furthermore, Your Highness has always (as I understand it) done this favor for my predecessor, I would be infinitely obliged. . . .[28]

Monte's request was honored, as a Viennese archive of 1574 shows.[29] The motet book to which Monte alludes is most probably the Third Book of Motets for Five Voices, printed in 1574.[30] Monte dedicated three other publications to the Emperor as well, including two books of madrigals.[31]

Monte seems to have been most active as a teacher in the first five to ten years after his arrival at the Imperial Court. Among his more accomplished students were Giovanni de Macque[32] (ca. 1550-1614) and Giovanni Battista della Gostena[33] (ca. 1540-1598). Macque sang in the Imperial Choir as a boy, and later attended the Jesuit College in Vienna, after his voice changed. He then studied with Monte. By 1574, he was in Rome; this places his period of study with Monte sometime from 1568 to 1574. On the title page of his first effort, the First Book for Six Voices (1576), Macque styles himself *"discepolo di M. Filippo de Monte,"* and the book contains two poems, *Ahi disperata vita* and Petrarch's *Poi che'l camin,* both of which Monte had also recently set in his Second Book for Six Voices (1569). (The settings are not related.)

Della Gostena likewise calls himself a disciple of Monte's on the title page of his First Book for Four Voices (1582); his period of study with Monte is unclear. Monte chose to include one of his student's efforts, *Ohime lasso,* in his own Third Book for Four Voices (first edition lost; before 1576). For Monte, this was a unique gesture; no other madrigal book of his contains the work of another composer.

In 1576, Maximilian died (aged forty-nine), and was succeeded by Rudolf II, then twenty-four years old. On 1 May 1577, Rudolf appointed Monte canon of Cambrai cathedral, evidence of his continuing prestige. Monte soon dedicated a new work to his young patron, his Seventh Book of Madrigals for Five Voices, of 1578.

In the years around 1580 Monte seems to have cultivated his patrons at the Imperial Court in a particularly energetic fashion. In 1580, he dedicated his Eighth Book for Five Voices to Rudolf, his Ninth Book for Five Voices to Rudolf's brother, the Archduke Ernest, and his Fourth Book for Six Voices to Wolfgang Rumf, an important minister at the court. In 1581, he once again dedicated a book to Rudolf, his Tenth Book for Five Voices.[34]

The two dedications to Rudolf are unusual documents. In them, Monte explicitly expresses his desire to change and improve his madrigals, and gives as a reason the fact that his music has not pleased "those who can and should form a judgment on it."[35] The reference is clearly to his immediate circle of patrons at the Imperial Court. Whether his statements and his music were able to mollify his critics is not known; in any case, his attentions to his patrons were not without an immediate financial result, for in 1581 the archives show a payment to Monte of 200 guilders "for his support, and also in consideration of his many years of loyal and diligent service...."[36] Furthermore, in the following year (1582) the archives record another special payment of 100 guilders for "printed books for five voices presented to His Majesty,"[37] apparently a reference to either the Eighth Book for Five Voices, or the Tenth Book.

In 1583 and 1584, Monte and William Byrd in England sent each other motet settings on texts drawn from Psalm 136, *Super flumina Babylonis.* Monte sent his motet *(Super flumina Babylonis)* to Byrd in 1583; Byrd responded in 1584 with the motet, *Quomodo cantabimus.*[38] Though the only source for this information is an eighteenth-century English manuscript (albeit one made directly from a now lost sixteenth-century source), the authenticity of the exchange has never been doubted. The reasons for the exchange have yet to be fully illuminated, however. Doorslaer suggests that Monte made the acquaintance of Byrd and his father while he was in England in 1554-5, an unproven hypothesis. A more likely explanation for the exchange rests upon an interpretation of the texts of these motets. Monte's *Super flumina Babylonis* can be taken as a reference to the current suppression of Catholicism in England. In this view, Monte's motet for Byrd is a symbol of solidarity and support from one of Europe's most prominent Catholic composers sent to a younger English composer whose religion was under attack. Monte may have conceived of this gesture himself, or he may have been persuaded to make it by exiled Catholics in Vienna or Prague. (A number of English recusants gravitated in these years to these bastions of Catholicism.)[39] In this context, Byrd's *Quomodo cantabimus,* with its startling change of textual emphasis and ringing Ionian mode, sounds like a grand affirmation of faith, an act of defiance.[40]

After the extraordinarily productive years around 1580 (there are three publications in each of the years 1580 and 1581), Monte's energies seem to have briefly waned: from 1582 to 1585 only one publication appeared each year. Towards the end of the decade, his activities increased once again. In 1587, he published three books: the Twelfth Book for Five Voices, the Second Book of Motets for Six Voices, and a *Liber Missarum,* the latter published in Antwerp by Plantin. A number of letters to and from Monte bearing on the subject of this book of masses and on a projected second book of masses survive.[41] (A second book of masses was never printed, as far as is known.)

During this thirty-five years at Vienna and Prague, Monte devoted considerable energy to enlarging and improving the Imperial Choir, enlisting the services of a number of singers and instrumentalists who were also active composers. Of particular relevance to the present study are Alessandro Orologio, Jacques Regnart, and Camillo Zanotti, all composers of madrigals in the last decades of the century.

Monte's responsibilities were many, and in 1588—he was now sixty-seven years old—we find him writing a lengthy report on the state of the organ in Prague.[42] In this report, he deplores its poor condition, and mentions the disastrous effect it makes in accompanying the choir. In 1590, he began to suffer from gout, as we learn from a letter written to his friend Charles d'Écluse from Prague on 16 June: "I have joined company with the gout-sufferers, and this has caused my inability to answer your letter...."[43]

By this time, Monte's wide prestige and venerable age had begun to attract a variety of encomia. Stefano Felis, in the dedication of his Sixth Book of Madrigals for Five Voices, of 1591, refers to Monte as a *"principe della musica."*[44] In the following year, Tiburzio Massaino dedicated his First Book of Motets for Four Voices to Monte; the work was printed in Prague, and the dedication signed there on 31 May.[45] Massaino praises Monte quite lavishly, and like other writers before him, mentions the composer's quiet manners and exemplary life.[46] These aspects of his personality seem to have struck his contemporaries as his most characteristic ones; taken together, a picture of a moderate, perhaps even retiring person emerges.

In 1594, an excellent portrait of Monte was engraved by Raphael Sadeler—another indication of his prestige. At the top of Sadeler's engraving we find Monte's motto, *"Rien sans peine"*: it encapsulates the diligent and uninterrupted labor he expended throughout his career at the Imperial Court.

In 1594, Monte and his choir accompanied Rudolf to the Reichstag at Regensburg. Lodovico Zacconi is responsible for the story that Monte and Lasso met on this occasion and discussed musical matters. But Zacconi's story, related in his *Prattica di musica,*[47] has a major flaw: he gives 1593 as the date of the *Reichstag.* Horst Leuchtmann, in his recent biographical study of Lasso, points out that Lasso died on 14 June 1594, and concludes: "Lasso, then, was not present at the Regensburg *Reichstag* of 1594, and the meetings and discussions with Philippe de Monte . . . can certainly not have taken place there at that time."[48] Zacconi's picturesque image of these two eminent and elder figures lamenting the decline in modern music (repeated by Einstein)[49] loses its flavor of authenticity, though it is still possible that Zacconi, writing many years later, was able to recall a conversation he had heard, but was confused about the place and time.

In 1596, a Latin ode in Monte's honor was published in Ingolstadt in a collection of Latin poetry written by Philip Menzelius, a professor of medicine at the University.[50] Titled *In Effigiem Philippi de Monte Musici Caesarei,* the poem is evidently a response to Sadeler's engraving published two years earlier.

As Monte approached his eightieth year, his compositions continued to flow quietly from the Venetian presses of Angelo Gardano. In 1600, in his seventy-ninth year, two books appeared: the *Musica sopra il Pastor Fido,* and his Seventh Book of Motets for Five Voices. Finally, in 1601 and 1602, the stream of publications which had flowed uninterruptedly since his Imperial appointment stopped. A note in the Viennese archives for 1601 mentions his physical weakness.[51] His last work, the Ninth Book of Madrigals for Six Voices, appeared in 1603 (the dedication is dated 1 January).[52]

Sensing that the end was near, Monte wrote his will on 15 January 1603, a long and detailed document in which he carefully settles his financial affairs.[53] He died on 4 July, at the age of eighty-two.

A seeming incongruence exists between Monte's life and his madrigalian output. In the years prior to his Imperial appointment he travelled freely throughout Italy, acquiring many patrons, singing, composing, and perhaps giving instruction to younger composers. Yet in these years, in which he was active almost exclusively as a composer of secular music (or so it appears), he published comparatively little. The importance of his experiences in Italy can hardly be exaggerated, however, for during this time his deep affection for the Italian madrigal was born and nurtured. His entire production of madrigals after 1568 thus takes on the quality of a continual homage to his Italian years. Though his position as *maestro di capella* required only that he compose sacred works, he devoted himself year after year to a kind of music which kept him in touch both with his musical past and with an exciting, ever-changing musical present. After moving to Vienna, with its important new circle of patrons, he continued to dedicate some of his new works to Italian patrons, many of whom he knew from his Italian days.[54]

Yet he also sought out new Italian patrons, right up to the end of his life, and through the dedications of his later books, expressed the hope that his new music would continue to enjoy a role in the culture of the day. To Mario Bevilacqua of the Accademia Filarmonica of Verona, he confides his hope (in the dedication of his Eleventh Book for Five Voices, 1586) that these new madrigals, composed "in a more vivacious and lively manner,"[55] might offer the occasion for some lively singing. Four years later, Monte dedicated his Fourteenth Book for Five Voices to Duke Alfonso d'Este. No doubt aware of the Duke's obsessive love of music, Monte again expresses the desire that his new madrigals might find a place in the Duke's distinguished musical entertainments.[56]

Monte had his circle of admirers in Vienna and Prague as well, to whom he dedicated many books throughout his thirty-five years as Imperial choirmaster. In dedicating his works, he sought out people who were appreciative of his art, and not merely people with political power. In this context, his dedications to Rudolf, with their occasionally timorous and apologetic tone, are exceptional. Evidently, Rudolf's attachment to music was not great: in none of his dedications to Rudolf does Monte refer to any love of music on the Emperor's part. In contrast, Monte's dedications to other figures at Rudolf's court often mention the role which music played in their lives. Thus, in the dedication of his Sixth Book for Six Voices (1591) to Jakob Kurz von Senftenau, described therein as *"Consiglier secreto di S. M. Ces. & Vice-cancelliere dell'Imperio,"* Monte mentions the pleasure which Kurz takes "not only in composing something for his own amusement (when his occupation permits) but also in hearing and judging the compositions of others."[57] Similarly, in his dedication of his Fifteenth Book for Five Voices (1592) to Camillo Caetano, the Papal nuncio, Monte writes: "I could do nothing but send them forth under your most honored name, since Your Most Illustrious

Lordship showed such pleasure a few months ago in playing these madrigals on the viola da gamba."[58]

Monte wrote his madrigals not out of some *horror vacui*, then, but with a clear purpose: to give pleasure and delight to a circle of patrons and admirers which he had attracted early in his career and which he sought to maintain and expand throughout the rest of his life. The list of patrons and dedicatees (not necessarily the same thing) is a long, distinguished, and international one.

Yet the extent to which Monte succeeded over the decades in sustaining and renewing his contemporaries' admiration for his work is another matter. The evidence suggests quite vividly that with a broader and more fickle public his madrigals became less and less popular. To understand this development, his entire madrigalian output must now be scrutinized.

The Sources of Monte's Secular Madrigals

The Integral Publications

The length of Monte's life, coupled with an innate industry and his considerable enthusiasm for the Italian madrigal, had as their result a madrigalian *œuvre* unsurpassed in sheer volume by any other composer of the time. Monte composed thirty-five (possibly thirty-six) books of secular madrigals, and saw them published right up to the year of his death. Table 1.1 gives a complete list of all of Monte's secular books.[59]

Most of this music survives: complete sets of partbooks are extant for twenty-nine of the thirty-five known publications. The following list gives the incomplete books and indicates which partbooks are missing.

VI.6	1591	Canto, Sesto, Basso lost
VII.6	1591	Entirely lost
VIII.6	1594	Quinto, Sesto lost
XVIII.5	1597	Alto, Tenore, Basso, Quinto lost
XIX.5	1598	Quinto lost
IX.6	1603	Entirely lost

The Ninth Book for Six Voices,[60] unknown to Vogel, nevertheless survived into this century in a unique and complete set of partbooks, once in the collection of Wilhelm Heyer of Cologne.[61] Their present whereabouts are unknown; they are presumed to be lost. Einstein transcribed this book in its entirety from this exemplar; with the disappearance of these partbooks, his transcription becomes a precious source for this otherwise lost work.[62] Einstein also transcribed the isolated Basso parts of both the Seventh Book for Six Voices and the Eighteenth Book for Five Voices; these partbooks, once in Berlin, are also now lost.

Table 1.1   Monte's Secular Madrigal Publications

SHORT TITLE, AS IN *RISM:A*	*RISM:A* NUMBER	VOGEL–EINSTEIN NUMBER	*NEW VOGEL* NUMBER	COMMENTS
1. 1554. *Madrigali a cinque voci . . . libro primo.* Roma, Valerio & Lodovico Dorico fratelli, 1554.	M3327	21	743	
REPRINTS:				
1560. Venezia, Girolamo Scotto.	M3328	22	744	
1570b. Venezia, Girolamo Scotto.	M3329	23	745	
1576b. Venezia, erede di Girolamo Scotto.	M3330	24	746	
1580d. Venezia, erede di Girolamo Scotto.	M3331	25	747	
2. 1562. *Il primo libro de madrigali a quattro voci.* Venezia, Antonio Gardano, 1567.	M3332	57	736	
REPRINT:				
1586b. Venezia, erede di Girolamo Scotto.	M3380	58	737	The entry for this reprint in *RISM:A* mistakenly says, "1. Auflage nicht nachweisbar."
3. 1567. *Il secondo libro de madrigali a cinque voci.* Venezia, Antonio Gardano, 1567.	M3333	26	748	

Table 1.1 (cont.)

SHORT TITLE, AS IN *RISM:A*	*RISM:A* NUMBER	VOGEL-EINSTEIN NUMBER	*NEW VOGEL* NUMBER	COMMENTS
REPRINTS:				
1570c. Venezia, Girolamo Scotto.	M3334	27	749	
1576c. Venezia, erede di Girolamo Scotto.	M3335	28	750	
1580e. Venezia, erede di Girolamo Scotto.	M3336	29	751	
1586c. Venezia, erede di Girolamo Scotto.	M3337	--	752	This edition does not exist. (Communication from Sergio Paganelli, Bologna.)
1598b. Venezia, erede di Girolamo Scotto.	M3338	30	753	
4. 1569a. *Il primo libro de madrigali a sei voci*. Venezia, Claudio da Coreggio, 1569.	M3339	3	781	This *RISM:A* short title does not indicate the fact that the title page reads further, "nuovamente et con ogni diligentia ristampato."
REPRINTS:				
1570d. Venezia, Girolamo Scotto.	M3339	4	782	
1574b. Venezia, erede di Girolamo Scotto.	M3341	5	783	
1582b. Venezia, erede di Girolamo Scotto.	M3342	6	784	

Table 1.1 (cont.)

SHORT TITLE, AS IN *RISM:A*	*RISM:A* NUMBER	VOGEL-EINSTEIN NUMBER	*NEW VOGEL* NUMBER	COMMENTS
1583.	--	--	785	This edition does not exist. The *New Vogel* cites only an Alto partbook in Paris; this is in fact an Alto partbook dated 1582 (communication from François Lesure).
1592. Venezia, Angelo Gardano	M3343	7 / 8	786	*Vogel* 8 gives an edition dated "1592"; this is a misreading of the reprint of 1574.
5. 1569b. *Il secondo libro delli madrigali a sei voci.* Venezia, Girolamo Scotto, 1569.	M3344	9	787	
REPRINTS: 1571b. Venezia, Girolamo Scotto.	M3345	--	788	
1576c. Venezia, erede di Girolamo Scotto.	M3346	10	789	
1582c. Venezia, erede di Girolamo Scotto.	M3347	11	790	

Table 1.1 (cont.)

SHORT TITLE, AS IN *RISM:A*	*RISM:A* NUMBER	VOGEL-EINSTEIN NUMBER	*NEW VOGEL* NUMBER	COMMENTS
6. 1569c. *Il secondo libro delli madrigali a quattro voci.* Venezia, Girolamo Scotto, 1569.	M3348	59	738	
REPRINTS: 1585b. Venezia, erede di Girolamo Scotto.	M3349	60	739	
1607. Venezia, Apresso l'Herede di Girolamo Scotto.	--	--	--	This is a hitherto unknown reprint of this book, preserved in a single Basso partbook in Berkeley (see accompanying text).
7. 1570a. *Il terzo libro delli madrigali a cinque voci, con uno a sette nel fine.* Venezia, Girolamo Scotto, 1570.	M3350	31	754	
REPRINTS: 1573. Venezia, Girolamo Scotto.	M3350	32	755	
1578b. Venezia, erede di Girolamo Scotto.	M3351	33	756	
1580f. Venezia, erede di Girolamo Scotto.	M3352		757	
1581c. Venezia, erede di Girolamo Scotto.	M3354	34	758	

Table 1.1 (cont.)

SHORT TITLE, AS IN *RISM:A*	*RISM:A* NUMBER	VOGEL-EINSTEIN NUMBER	*NEW VOGEL* NUMBER	COMMENTS
1594?	--	--	--	Einstein's own copy of *Vogel* (now in Berkeley) has the following entry inserted after *Vogel* 34: "34a Madrigali a 5v. Terzo libro. Ven. Amadino. 1594 Pistoia (A.c.) A. T." "A.c." refers to Pistoia's Archivio capitolare. This putative reprint does not appear in *Vogel*, the *New Vogel*, or *RISM:A*; its existence can neither be confirmed nor denied.
8. 1571a. *Il quatro libro delli madrigali a cinque voci.* Venezia, Girolamo Scotto, 1571. REPRINTS: 1576e. Venezia, erede di Girolamo Scotto. 1581d. Venezia, erede di Girolamo Scotto.	M3355 M3356 M3357	35 36 37	759 760 761	

Table 1.1 (cont.)

SHORT TITLE, AS IN *RISM:A*	*RISM:A* NUMBER	VOGEL-EINSTEIN NUMBER	*NEW VOGEL* NUMBER	COMMENTS
9. 1574a. *Madrigali . . . a cinque voci, libro quinto.. Venezia, li figliuoli di Antonio Gardano, 1574.*	M3358	38	762	
REPRINT: 1592c. Venezia, Angelo Gardano, 1592.	M3359	39	763	
10. 1575a. *Il sesto libro delli madrigali a cinque voci. Venezia, Angelo Gardano, 1575.*	M3360	40	764	
REPRINT: 1588b. Venezia, Angelo Gardano, 1588.	M3361	41	765	
11. 1576a. *Il terzo libro de madrigali a sei voci. Venezia, Angelo Gardano, 1576.*	M3364	12	791	
REPRINT: 1585c. Venezia, Angelo Gardano, 1585.	M3365	13	792	

Table 1.1 (cont.)

SHORT TITLE, AS IN *RISM:A*	*RISM:A* NUMBER	VOGEL-EINSTEIN NUMBER	*NEW VOGEL* NUMBER	COMMENTS
12. 1578a. *Il settimo libro delli madrigali a cinque voci.* Venezia, Angelo Gardano, 1578.	M3366	42	766	
REPRINT: 1583. Venezia, Angelo Gardano, 1583.	M3367	43	767	
13. 1580a. *Il quarto libro de madrigali a sei voci, insieme alcuni a sette.* Venezia, Angelo Gardano, 1580.	M3368	14	793	
REPRINT: 1592d. Venezia, Angelo Gardano, 1592.	M3369	15	794	
14. 1580b. *L'ottavo libro delli madrigali a cinque voci.* Venezia, erede di Girolamo Scotto, 1580.	M3370	44	768	
REPRINT: 1586. Venezia, erede di Girolamo Scotto, 1586.	M3371	45	769	

Table 1.1 (cont.)

SHORT TITLE, AS IN *RISM:A*	*RISM:A* NUMBER	VOGEL– EINSTEIN NUMBER	*NEW VOGEL* NUMBER	COMMENTS
15. 1580c. *Il nono libro de madrigali a cinque voci.* Venezia, erede di Girolamo Scotto, 1580.	M3372	46	770	
16. 1581a. *Il decimo libro delli madrigali a cinque voci.* Venezia, erede di Girolamo Scotto, 1581.	M3373	47	771	
17. 1581b. *Il quarto libro de madri- gali a quattro voci.* Venezia, Angelo Gardano, 1581. REPRINT: 1588c. Venezia, Angelo Gardano, 1588.	M3374 M3375	62 63	741 742	
18. 1582a. *Il primo libro de madri- gali a tre voci.* Venezia, Angelo Gardano, 1582.	M3375	64	735	

Table 1.1 (cont.)

SHORT TITLE, AS IN *RISM:A*	*RISM:A* NUMBER	VOGEL-EINSTEIN NUMBER	*NEW VOGEL* NUMBER	COMMENTS
19. 1584-5. *Il quinto libro de madrigali a sei voci.* Venezia, Angelo Gardano, 1584.	M3376	16	795	The Canto, Tenore and Basso partbooks for this publication are dated 1584. The Alto, Quinto, and Basso partbooks, which are otherwise identical as to title page, dedication, index, and contents, are dated 1585. These latter books do not represent an actual reprint, then, which would customarily lack the dedication, and whose title page would typically include the words *novamente ristampati*. Rather, it appears that this book was printed at year's end, which accounts for the change in dates. *Vogel* 17 and *New Vogel* 796 are thus in error.

Table 1.1 (cont.)

SHORT TITLE, AS IN *RISM:A*	*RISM:A* NUMBER	VOGEL-EINSTEIN NUMBER	*NEW VOGEL* NUMBER	COMMENTS
20. 1585a. *Il terzo libro de madrigali a quattro voci . . . novamente ristampate.* Venezia, erede di Girolamo Scotto, 1585.	M3378, also *RISM:B* 158527	61	740	The title page refers to Monte as "maestro di capella" under Maximilian II, who died in 1576, which suggests that the book was first published during his lifetime. Since the Second Book for Four Voices appeared in 1569 (and the Fourth Book for Four Voices in 1581), this book can be dated in the years from 1569 to 1576.
21. 1586a. *L'undecimo libro delli madrigali a cinque voci.* Venezia, Angelo Gardano, 1586.	M3379	48	772	
22. 1587. *Il duodecimo libro delli madrigali a cinque voci.* Venezia, Angelo Gardano, 1587.	M3381	49	773	
23. 1588a. *Il terzodecimo libro delli madrigali a cinque voci.* Venezia, Angelo Gardano, 1587.	M3382	50	774	

Table 1.1 (cont.)

	SHORT TITLE, AS IN *RISM:A*	*RISM:A* NUMBER	VOGEL-EINSTEIN NUMBER	*NEW VOGEL* NUMBER	COMMENTS
24.	1590. *Il quartodecimo libro delli madrigali a cinque voci.* Venezia, Angelo Gardano, 1590.	M3383	51	775	
25.	1591. *Il sesto libro de madrigali a sei voci.* Venezia, Angelo Gardano, 1591.	M3384	18	797	Only the Alto, Tenore, and Quinto partbooks are extant.
26.	1591. *Il settimo libro de madrigali a sei voci.* Venezia, Angelo Gardano, 1591.	--	19	799	This book is now entirely lost. Only Einstein's transcription of the Basso partbook, once in Berlin, survives, at Smith College.
27.	1592a. *Il quintodecimo libro de madrigali a cinque voci.* Venezia, Angelo Gardano, 1592.	M3385	52	776	
28.	1593. *Il sestodecimo libro de madrigali a cinque voci.* Venezia, Angelo Gardano, 1593.	M3386	53	777	

Table 1.1 (cont.)

	SHORT TITLE, AS IN *RISM:A*	*RISM:A* NUMBER	VOGEL-EINSTEIN NUMBER	*NEW VOGEL* NUMBER	COMMENTS
29.	1594. *L'ottavo libro de madrigali a sei voci.* Venezia, Angelo Gardano, 1594.	M3387	20	800	The Quinto and Sesto partbooks are lost.
30.	1595. *Il decimosettimo libro delli madrigali a cinque voci.* Venezia, Angelo Gardano, 1597.	M3388	54	778	
31.	1597. *Il decimottavo libro de madrigali a cinque voci.* Venezia, Angelo Gardano, 1597.	--	55	779	Only the Canto partbook survives. Einstein's transcription of the now missing Basso partbook is at Smith College.
32.	1598a. *Il decimonono libro delli madrigali a cinque voci.* Venezia, Angelo Gardano, 1598.	M3389	56	780	The Quinto partbook is lost.
33.	1599. *La Fiammetta. Canzone . . . insieme altre canzoni et madrigali vaghissimi a sette voci, con un echo a otto . . . libro primo.* Venezia, Angelo Gardano, 1599.	M3390	1	734	

Table 1.1 (cont.)

SHORT TITLE, AS IN *RISM:A*	*RISM:A* NUMBER	VOGEL-EINSTEIN NUMBER	*NEW VOGEL* NUMBER	COMMENTS
34. 1600. *Musica sopra Il pastor fido . . . ove si contengono canzoni, & madrigali vaghissimi . . . libro secondo, a sette voci.* Venezia, Angelo Gardano, 1599.	M3391	2	806	
35. 1603. *Il nono libro de madrigali a sei voci.* Venezia, Angelo Gardano, 1603.	--	--	801	This book, which was preserved in its entirety in the Heyer Collection, is now lost. Einstein's transcription (from this exemplar) of the entire book is now at Smith College.

One book remains a mystery. In a seventeenth-century inventory of music instruments and music books compiled in Innsbruck, there appears an entry for a *third* book of madrigals for seven voices.[63] The relevant entry reads:

> No. 114. No 7 ud No. 1. Il primo et il secondo lib. delli Madrigali a 6 voci di Philippo de Monte. / No. 2 ud no. 1. Il second et il terzo libro a 7 del medesimo.[64]

There has been no trace of this work in modern times. If indeed a third book for seven voices was published, it would number among Monte's final creations: the second book (titled *Musica sopra il Pastor Fido*) appeared in 1600. In any case, the book remains a cipher in Monte's output.[65]

Monte began late as a published composer of madrigals. His First Book for Five Voices appeared in 1554, when he was already thirty-three years old. In the next fourteen years, he produced only three more madrigal books: the First Book for Six Voices (first edition lost), the First Book for Four Voices (1562), and the Second Book for Five Voices (1567).

As we have already observed, his activities as a madrigalist, and indeed as a composer generally, increased considerably after his Imperial appointment; in the remaining thirty-five years of his life he produced madrigal books in an almost uninterrupted stream. Indeed, one comes away from his publication record with the vivid impression that he felt compelled to issue some musical opus every year. Only three years—1577, 1601, and 1602—passed without a publication of some kind. Evidently the debilities of old age kept him from this self-imposed duty in these latter two years. It is unimaginable that Monte was under any constraint from his Imperial patrons to publish so regularly; the impulse must have come from deep within him.

The years around 1580 mark the high point in his devotion to the madrigal. In this year alone he published three books; in 1581, three more appeared, one of them his first essay in the spiritual madrigal. The year 1580 represents not only a high point in Monte's productivity, but also the high-water mark of his popularity and exposure as a madrigalist before a European public. As Einstein stated: "His madrigal books are now infrequently reprinted, and beginning with the ninth book for five voices [1580], the first edition we know is often also the last."[66] Indeed, the situation is more emphatic than Einstein implies. Every madrigal book which Monte produced before 1580 (there are 13) was reprinted at least once; many were reprinted several times. Of the three books printed in 1580, only two were ever reprinted, as far as is known. Only one of the three books of 1581 was reprinted; after this, the first edition of every new madrigal publication is the only known one.

There is nothing fortuitous in these developments. They reflect the waning of his popularity, a decline which coincides with momentous stylistic changes in the madrigal. In the 1580s, Monte gradually attuned himself to these changes; by 1586, his music was significantly different from what it had been in 1580. Yet in spite of Monte's accommodation to contemporary taste, the evidence suggests that he failed conspicuously to interest the musical public in his new music of the 1580s and '90s.

In the same years in which his more recent books were being ignored, his pre-1580s books continued to be reprinted—in the 1580s and even the 1590s. A closer look at the publication history of Monte's books, and the two principal printers of those books, seems in order.

The First Book for Five Voices (1554) is Monte's only madrigal book whose first edition did not appear in Venice, but in Rome. In 1562, the First Book for Four Voices was printed in Venice by Antonio Gardano. The lost first edition of the First Book for Six Voices probably appeared between 1563 and 1569, when it was reprinted (see the evidence given below, p. 126). In 1567, Gardano published the Second Book for Five Voices. On the basis of Gardano's apparent policy towards reprinting Monte's madrigal books (see p. 27), it appears that Gardano also published the first edition of the six-voice book.

After his appointment in Vienna (1568) Monte initially favored Scotto with his works: the four books which appeared between 1569 and 1571 were all published by Scotto. A brief lull followed in Monte's madrigalian activity; no books appeared in 1572 or 1573.[67] No doubt he was hard at work preparing the three books of five-voice motets which appeared in these years—all issued by Scotto:[68]

1572 *Sacrarum cantionum cum quinque vocibus quae vulgo motetta nuncupantur, liber primus*. Venice, Girolamo Scotto, 1572.

1573 *Sacrarum cantionum cum quinque vocibus quae vulgo motetta nuncupantur, liber secundus*. Venice, Girolamo Scotto, 1573.

1574 *Sacrarum cantionum cum quinque vocibus quae vulgo motetta nuncupantur, liber tertius*. Venice, gli erede di Girolamo Scotto, 1574.

Thus, from 1569 until sometime in 1574, all of Monte's works, sacred and secular alike, were printed in Venice by Scotto, and his heirs.

In 1574, Monte's publications reverted to the Gardano firm, which printed his next four madrigal books, as well as a sacred one:

The Fifth Book for Five Voices	1574
The Sixth Book for Five Voices	1575
Libro quarto de motetti... a cinque voci	1575
The Third Book for Six Voices	1576
The Seventh Book for Five Voices	1578

From 1579 to 1581, Monte's work issued without any recognizable pattern from both the Gardano and Scotto presses. 1581, however, marks the final year in which Scotto printed a new publication of Monte's. After this year, all his new madrigal books (sacred and secular) and all his motet books were printed in Venice by Angelo Gardano, right up to the composer's death in 1603.[69]

Antonio Gardano had died in 1569, yet there is apparently no connection between his death and Monte's switch to Scotto in the same year. It seems likely, though, that a personal connection between Gardano's son Angelo and Monte accounts for Monte's renewed association with the Gardano firm in 1574, and with Gardano's monopoly in publishing Monte's works after 1582. Some time around 1582, Angelo Gardano commissioned Monte to write a book of three-voice madrigals, and Gardano's comments in the dedication reveal his esteem and affection for the composer.[70]

Nevertheless, the firm of Gardano generally took little interest in reprinting Monte's books; this activity was undertaken in the 1560s and 1570s almost exclusively by Scotto. It was Scotto's policy to reprint Monte's books regardless of which firm had printed the first edition.[71] Gardano's practice, at least in the case of Monte's publications, was quite different; this firm reissued Monte's books only if it had produced the first edition. Gardano began to reprint Monte's books in 1583, that is, only after the firm had secured its apparent monopoly on his music. Only six Gardano reprints survive; five of these reprint books which Gardano had first issued. In the sixth case—the 1592 reprint of the First Book for Six Voices—the first edition is lost, as we have seen. To judge from the situation with the other five, the first edition of this book, too, must have been published in Venice by Gardano. This is even more likely since the book probably appeared between 1563 and 1569, a period in which Gardano published Monte's other music.

The evidence also shows that whenever either Scotto or Gardano decided to reprint something of Monte's, they would reissue several books at a time.[72] Furthermore, Scotto's reprinting of the five-voice books reflects a continuing commitment to keep Monte's books before the public eye: in the 1570s and early 1580s there were reprints at regular intervals (all Scotto's work) of the First, Second, Third, and Fourth Books for Five Voices.

With the four-voice books, the picture is quite different. The *New Vogel* lists only one reprint each for these four books, all from the 1580s. A single partbook, now in the Berkeley Library,[73] is evidence for a hitherto unknown reprinting of Monte's Second Book for Four Voices (1569), but even with this newly discovered reprint of 1607 (see Plate 1), it is clear that the four-voice books did not enjoy the popularity of either the five-voice or the six-voice ones. As a genre, the four-voice madrigal declined in popularity in the final decades of the sixteenth century, though Monte's books seem to have failed more dismally than most. (Marenzio's only book of four-voice madrigals, for example, went through many more reprints than Monte's.) It is somewhat ironic, then, that this 1607 reprint of Monte's Second Book should be the last known reprint of any of his books, the only posthumous one, and the only one

BASSO

DI FILIPPO DI MONTE

MAESTRO DI CAPELLA

DELLA S. C. MAESTA' DELL'IMPERATORE

RODOLPHO SECONDO

Il secondo Libro de Madrigali, a quattro voci.

NOVAMENTE RISTAMPATI.

IN VENETIA, Appresso l'Herede di Girolamo Scotto.

MDCVII.

dating from the seventeenth century. In 1607, four years after Monte's death, Scotto turned not to any of Monte's recent works but to a nearly forty-year-old book. A more pointed example of Monte's failure to arouse interest in his new music could hardly be adduced.

To judge from the five reprints each of both the First Book for Six Voices and the Second Book for Five Voices, these seem to have been Monte's two most popular books. Yet these numbers pale in comparison with the reprint history of Lasso's first two books for five voices, published in 1555 and 1559. Lasso's First Book for Five Voices was reprinted ten times, and the Second Book for Five Voices eleven times, both as late as 1586. Yet Lasso's later works were apparently received with the same kind of indifference which greeted Monte's. Lasso's Fifth Book for Five Voices, his last work in this series, appeared in 1587 and was never reprinted. The reprint history of Giaches Wert's madrigal books tells a similar story.

The stylistic differences which separate the later works of these three great *oltremontani* are enormous. Yet all three of these figures failed, though perhaps in varying degrees, to maintain their early popularity with the madrigal's later followers of the 1580s and 1590s. Monte's failure is not as unique, then, as Einstein's comments, quoted in the Preface, suggest.

Finally, the scope of Monte's output as a whole has suggested another avenue of investigation. The question is this: what can we deduce, based on the extent to which all the printed editions of Monte's madrigals survive in modern libraries, about the relative numbers in which those editions were originally printed? In the absence of any hard archival evidence, we cannot know the actual number of copies printed of a particular book. It is still possible, though, to witness the rise and fall of Monte's popularity in the eyes of his contemporaries by marshalling this evidence. Table 1.2 gives a list in chronological order of Monte's secular madrigal prints, both first editions and reprints. For each publication, the number of modern libraries presently holding partbooks is given. (The numbers have been determined by collating the sources listed in footnote 59.)

This information is quite illuminating. The four books which Monte published prior to his Imperial appointment must each have come out in fairly modest numbers: the first edition of the First Book for Six Voices is lost, as we have already seen, and the first editions of both the First and Second Books for Five Voices survive incomplete. This strongly implies that Monte's first published efforts (like those, surely, of other composers) were issued in limited numbers, perhaps to test the public's response.

The first indication of a change in this pattern comes with the Second Book for Six Voices (1569), one of the two books which appeared in the year following his move to Vienna. The partbooks of this first edition survive in eleven libraries, indicating that this book was probably printed in an appreciably greater volume than his four earlier books. Apparently his

Table 1.2 The Present Distribution in Modern Institutions of Partbooks for Monte's Secular Publications.

RISM:A SIGLA	ABBREVIATED TITLES OF PUBLICATIONS		PRINTER	NUMBER OF INSTITUTIONS HOLDING PARTBOOKS	NUMBER OF COMPLETE INDEFECTIVE SETS OF PARTBOOKS
	First Editions	Reprints			
1. 1554	I.5		Dorico (Rome)	2	0
2. 1560		I.5	Girolamo Scotto	4	0
3. 1562	I.4		Antonio Gardano	1	1
4. 1567	II.5		Antonio Gardano	1	0
5. 1569a		I.6	Claudio da Correggio	3	1
6. 1569b	II.6		Girolamo Scotto	12	6
7. 1569c	II.4		Girolamo Scotto	2	0

Table 1.2 (cont.)

RISM:A SIGLA	ABBREVIATED TITLES OF PUBLICATIONS		PRINTER	NUMBER OF INSTITUTIONS HOLDING PARTBOOKS	NUMBER OF COMPLETE INDEFECTIVE SETS OF PARTBOOKS
	First Editions	Reprints			
8. 1570a	III.5		Girolamo Scotto	8	2
9. 1570b		I.5	Girolamo Scotto	4	0
10. 1570c		II.5	Girolamo Scotto	6	1
11. 1570d		I.6	Girolamo Scotto	3	1
12. 1571a	IV.5		Girolamo Scotto	7	2
13. 1571b		II.6	Girolamo Scotto	3	0
14. 1573		III.5	l'herede di G. Scotto	4	0
15. 1574a	V.5		li figliuoli di Antonio Gardano	10	6

Table 1.2 (cont.)

RISM:A SIGLA	ABBREVIATED TITLES OF PUBLICATIONS		PRINTER	NUMBER OF INSTITUTIONS HOLDING PARTBOOKS	NUMBER OF COMPLETE INDEFECTIVE SETS OF PARTBOOKS
	First Editions	Reprints			
16. 1574b		I.6	l'herede di G. Scotto	7	1
17. 1575a	VI.5		Angelo Gardano	4	2
18. 1576a	III.6		Angelo Gardano	7	3
19. 1576b		I.5	l'herede di G. Scotto	4	1
20. 1576c		II.5	l'herede di G. Scotto	2	1
21. 1576d		II.6	l'herede di G. Scotto	6	0*

*All of the partbooks of this edition survive, but not in a single institution.

Table 1.2 (cont.)

RISM:A SIGLA	ABBREVIATED TITLES OF PUBLICATIONS		PRINTER	NUMBER OF INSTITUTIONS HOLDING PARTBOOKS	NUMBER OF COMPLETE INDEFECTIVE SETS OF PARTBOOKS
	First Editions	Reprints			
22. 1576e		IV.5	l'herede di G. Scotto	4	2
23. 1578a	VII.5		Angelo Gardano	3	2
24. 1578b		III.5	l'herede di G. Scotto	4	1
25. 1580a	IV.6		Angelo Gardano	10	3
26. 1580b	VIII.5		l'herede di G. Scotto	13	7
27. 1580c	IX.5		l'herede di G. Scotto	12	7
28. 1580d		I.5	l'herede di G. Scotto	10	4

Table 1.2 (cont.)

RISM:A SIGLA	ABBREVIATED TITLES OF PUBLICATIONS		PRINTER	NUMBER OF INSTITUTIONS HOLDING PARTBOOKS	NUMBER OF COMPLETE INDEFECTIVE SETS OF PARTBOOKS
	First Editions	Reprints			
29. 1580e		II.5	l'herede di G. Scotto	12	4
30. 1580f		III.5	l'herede di G. Scotto	2	0
31. 1581a	X.5		l'herede di G. Scotto	15	9
32. 1581b	IV.4		Angelo Gardano	6	3
33. 1581c		III.5	l'herede di G. Scotto	16	5
34. 1581d		IV.5	l'herede di G. Scotto	17	5
35. 1582a	I.3		Angelo Gardano	3	3

Table 1.2 (cont.)

RISM:A SIGLA	ABBREVIATED TITLES OF PUBLICATIONS		PRINTER	NUMBER OF INSTITUTIONS HOLDING PARTBOOKS	NUMBER OF COMPLETE INDEFECTIVE SETS OF PARTBOOKS
	First Editions	Reprints			
36. 1582b		I.6	l'herede di G. Scotto	21	5
37. 1582c		II.6	l'herede di G. Scotto	16	4
38. 1583		VII.5	Angelo Gardano	8	2
39. 1584	V.6		Angelo Gardano	3	1
40. 1585a		III.4	l'herede di G. Scotto	8	2
41. 1585b		II.4	l'herede di G. Scotto	6	2
42. 1585c		III.6	Angelo Gardano	4	2

Table 1.2 (cont.)

RISM:A SIGLA	ABBREVIATED TITLES OF PUBLICATIONS		PRINTER	NUMBER OF INSTITUTIONS HOLDING PARTBOOKS	NUMBER OF COMPLETE INDEFECTIVE SETS OF PARTBOOKS
	First Editions	Reprints			
43. 1586a	XI.5		Angelo Gardano	3	2
44. 1586b		I.4	l'herede di G. Scotto	5	1
45. 1586d		VIII.5	l'herede di G. Scotto	4	1
46. 1587	XII.5		Angelo Gardano	5	2
47. 1588a	XIII.5		Angelo Gardano	7	4
48. 1588b		VI.5	Angelo Gardano	3	2
49. 1588c		IV.4	Angelo Gardano	4	2

Table 1.2 (cont.)

| RISM:A SIGLA | ABBREVIATED TITLES OF PUBLICATIONS | | PRINTER | NUMBER OF INSTITUTIONS HOLDING PARTBOOKS | NUMBER OF COMPLETE INDEFECTIVE SETS OF PARTBOOKS |
	First Editions	Reprints			
50. 1590	XIV.5		Angelo Gardano	5	1
51. 1591	VI.6		Angelo Gardano	1	0
52. 1591	VII.6		Angelo Gardano		
53. 1592a	XV.5		Angelo Gardano	6	2
54. 1592b		I.6	Angelo Gardano	1	0
55. 1592c		V.5	Angelo Gardano	2	0
56. 1592d		IV.6	Angelo Gardano	2	0*
57. 1593	XVI.5		Angelo Gardano	4	2

*All of the partbooks of this edition survive, but not in a single institution.

Table 1.2 (cont.)

RISM:A SIGLA	ABBREVIATED TITLES OF PUBLICATIONS		PRINTER	NUMBER OF INSTITUTIONS HOLDING PARTBOOKS	NUMBER OF COMPLETE INDEFECTIVE SETS OF PARTBOOKS
	First Editions	Reprints			
58. 1594	VIII.6		Angelo Gardano	2	0
59. 1595	XVII.5		Augelo Gardano	4	2
60. 1597	XVIII.5		Angelo Gardano	1	0
61. 1598a	XIX.5		Angelo Gardano	2	0
62. 1598b		II.5	l'herede di G. Scotto	1	0
63. 1599	La Fiammetta (I.7)		Angelo Gardano	6	0*
64. 1600	Musica sopra il Pastor Fido (II.7)		Angelo Gardano	3	1

*All of the partbooks of this edition survive, but not in a single institution.

Table 1.2 (cont.)

RISM:A SIGLA	ABBREVIATED TITLES OF PUBLICATIONS		PRINTER	NUMBER OF INSTITUTIONS HOLDING PARTBOOKS	NUMBER OF COMPLETE INDEFECTIVE SETS OF PARTBOOKS
	First Editions	Reprints			
65. 1603	IX.6		Angelo Gardano		
66. 1607		II.4	l'herede di G. Scotto	1	0

enhanced prestige—the result of his new position—had affected his publisher's attitude towards his music.

This change coincides with a change in publisher, as we have seen. Scotto, in taking up Monte's music for the first time, evidently began the collaboration auspiciously with a large edition, perhaps even larger than the immediately following ones. When Gardano once again secured the "rights" to Monte's music in 1574, that firm too seems to have published the first fruits of this renewed contract in large numbers, comparable with that of Scotto's edition five years earlier of the Second Book for Six Voices. Once again, the volume seems to drop after the first book in the renewed contract.

Monte's works printed around 1580 survive in the greatest quantity, evidence that in these years his music was printed in greater volume than at any other time in his career. It can hardly be a coincidence, for instance, that the Tenth Book for Five Voices (1580) survives in more libraries (fifteen) than any other single *editio princeps*. Furthermore, the evidence shows that reprints from these years of earlier books were also published in considerable volume. This would account for the widespread survival of the 1582 reprint of the First Book for Six Voices: there are partbooks in twenty libraries, the largest present dissemination of any of Monte's books.

The decline in Monte's popularity which occurred in the course of the 1580s and 1590s appears to have gradually affected the numbers of copies printed of his new works, as well as reprints of his older ones. In contrast with the large numbers of copies of the Tenth Book for Five Voices which survive, only three libraries now possess partbooks for his Eleventh Book, of 1586. All the evidence suggests that Gardano printed fewer and fewer copies of Monte's five- and six-voice music of the 1590s. Thus, neither of the two six-voice books published in 1591 survives complete. The final stage in this process comes with those books which have disappeared altogether (the Ninth Book for Six Voices, and possibly a third book for seven voices).

An exception to this pattern can be seen in Monte's two unusual publications from this period: *La Fiammetta* (1599), and *Musica sopra il Pastor Fido* (1600). Undoubtedly these titles were an editorial invention, designed to increase sales—it seems unlikely that Monte himself would have changed a lifelong pattern of giving his books a simple title according to the number of voice parts. Even the standard format of Monte's music was set aside for these two books, which are printed in regular quarto format, rather than the oblong quarto format of the preceding ones.[74] Perhaps this change was intended to lull his rapidly diminishing audience from its presumably jaundiced reaction to yet another Gardano print of Monte madrigals. The fact that these two books survive in somewhat larger numbers than both the preceding and subsequent ones suggests that they may have been printed in slightly greater volume.

The foregoing reflections have been speculative, but perhaps not overly so. Monte's output is so considerable in size that these conclusions are based on a statistically large body of data, and do not place undue significance on a single partbook in this or that library.

Yet the wealth of detail presented here should not distract us from the central conclusion to be drawn. The publication history of Monte's madrigal books presents a paradoxical picture of a man deeply committed to the art of madrigal composition, whose music was slowly but unequivocally abandoned by the public in the years of his greatest activity. It was Monte's lack of success, even as he essayed a *rapprochement* with the newer style, that partly prompted Einstein to characterize the situation as "little short of tragi-comic."[75] This critical perception is central to Einstein's interpretation of Monte's last years. The image is an attractive one: poor Monte, accommodating himself expediently to a new and decadent taste—all in vain! In later chapters, these views will be examined again alongside the music, in the hope of achieving a less fanciful picture of Monte's final period.

The Madrigals in Anthologies

To be complete, this survey of Monte's output as a madrigalist must include a few words about his madrigals in anthologies. Monte's madrigals appeared in over thirty anthologies during his lifetime, yet these contributions do not comprise a significant part of his entire *œuvre*. For the most part, the madrigals in anthologies had either already appeared in one of his own madrigal books, or (more rarely) turned up in one of his own books after appearing in an anthology. As a result, the number of pieces with no other source is fairly small.

Table 1.3 lists all the Monte madrigals which appeared in sixteenth and early seventeenth century anthologies, together with the principal source for these pieces in other contemporary publications, when one exists. It also includes the few pieces which appeared in publications mainly devoted to another composer's work.

Prior to 1580, madrigals by Monte appeared in ten anthologies, most of which appeared in Italy. It was in this period in his career that Monte most regularly contributed previously unpublished pieces to the anthologies. Often, these pieces are exceptional stylistically in one way or another, as we shall see in chapters 2 and 3.

In 1583, two large anthologies, *Musica divina* and *Harmonia celeste,* appeared in Antwerp. Few (if any) new compositions appeared in these large collections; rather, they reflect the somewhat conservative and retrospective tastes of the madrigal's admirers in the Lowlands. Both books were extremely popular: *Musica divina* was reprinted six times, the last time in 1634; *Harmonia celeste* was reprinted five times, the last in 1628.

Table 1.3 Monte Madrigals in Contemporary Anthologies*

ANTHOLOGY TITLE	*RISM:B* NUMBER	VOGEL-EINSTEIN NUMBER	TITLE OF PIECE; NUMBER OF VOICES WHEN UNCLEAR	OTHER PUBLICATIONS IN WHICH THE SAME PIECE APPEARS
1. *Secondo libro delle muse, a quattro voci.* . . Roma, A. Barré, 1558.	1558[13]	1558[1]	*Dolorosi martir*	
2. *Il terzo libro delle Muse a quattro voci.* Roma, A. Barré, 1562.	1562[7]	1562[3a]	*Se per un sguardo* *Voi mi ponesti in foco*	
3. *Di Cipriano et Annibale madrigali a quatro voci insieme altri eccelenti autori.* . . . Venezia, A. Gardano, 1561.	1561[15]	Vogel, see Rore 50a	*Aure che i dolci* *Puri lucenti 2p*	
4. *Il secondo libro de madrigali de diversi autori a notte negre.* . . . Venezia, G. Scotto, 1567.	1567[15]	1567[3]	*Si dolcemente è amor* *Donna da bei* *vostr'occhi* (both à 4)	

RISM:B in column 2 refers to *International Inventory of Musical Sources: Receuils Imprimés, XVIe–XVIIe siècles* (Munich, 1960).

Table 1.3 (cont.)

	ANTHOLOGY TITLE	RISM:B NUMBER	VOGEL-EINSTEIN NUMBER	TITLE OF PIECE: NUMBER OF VOICES WHEN UNCLEAR	OTHER PUBLICATIONS IN WHICH THE SAME PIECE APPEARS
5.	*Il terzo libro delle fiamme madrigali a cinque voci. . . .* Venezia, G. Scotto, 1568.	1568[12]	1568[2]	*Hor che ritorn'il sol* *Dolor lagrime* *Deh dov'è l'alma 2p* *Ahime cor mio 3p* *Deh fuss'almen 4p* *Piangi mi dice 5p* *Ma sia chi vol 6p*	
6.	*Gli amorosi concenti . . . a quattro voci.* Venezia, G. Scotto, 1568.	1568[13]	1568[3]	*La dolce vista* *Ohime deh 2p* *Io t'ho veduto 3p* *Quando per gentil 4p* *Amor la mia ventura 5p*	II.4 (1569).
7.	*Second livre des chansons a quatre et cinque parties, composés par Orlando di Lassus, Cuprian de Rore, & Philippe de Mons. . . .* Louvain, P. Phalèse, 1570.	1570[6]	Vogel, see Lasso 63	*Per divina bellezza* (à 4)	*Per divina bellezza* appeared in 1583[14] and *Musica transalpina* (*RISM* 1588[29]) with the text *In vayne he seekes.*

Table 1.3 (cont.)

	ANTHOLOGY TITLE	RISM:B NUMBER	VOGEL-EINSTEIN NUMBER	TITLE OF PIECE; NUMBER OF VOICES WHEN UNCLEAR	OTHER PUBLICATIONS IN WHICH THE SAME PIECE APPEARS
8.	Il primo libro di madrigali a quatro voci di Lancilotto Fidelis flamengo. . . . Venezia, figliuoli di A. Gardano, 1570.	1570[25]	Vogel, see Fidelis	Amor fortuna Ne spero i 2p (à 5)	
9.	Livre de Meslanges . . . a quatre parties. . . . Louvain, P. Phalèse, Antwerpen, J. Bellère, 1575.	1575[4]	1575[3]	Pianger l'aria e la terra	
10.	Musica di XIII. autori illustri a cinque voci. . . . Venezia, A. Gardano, 1575.	1576[5]	1576[1]	Gia verde e forte Nel fin 2p Perch'al viso d'Amor	VIII.5(1580).
11.	Il primo fiore della ghirlanda musicale a cinque voci. . . . Venezia, herede di G. Scotto, 1577.	1577[7]	1577[1]	Caro pegno del cielo Amor m'accende	VIII.5(1580).

Table 1.3 (cont.)

ANTHOLOGY TITLE	RISM:B NUMBER	VOGEL-EINSTEIN NUMBER	TITLE OF PIECE; NUMBER OF VOICES WHEN UNCLEAR	OTHER PUBLICATIONS IN WHICH THE SAME PIECE APPEARS
12. Trionfo di musica di diversi. A sei voci. . . . Venezia, erede di G. Scotto, 1579.	1579[3]	1579[2]	L'Arno illustre E la scorge 2p	
13. Harmonia celeste di diversi eccelentissimi musici a IIII. V. VI. VII. et VIII voci. . . . Antwerpen, P. Phalèse & J. Bellère, 1583.	1583[14]	1583[1]	Io son sì vago (à 4)	Possibly not by Monte.
			Per divina bellezza (à 4)	RISM:B 1570[6]; Vogel, Lasso 69: (Second livre des chansons a quatre et cinq parties . . .).
			Che fai, alma Tal'hor tace 2p (à 5)	II.5(1567).
			Veramente in amore (à 5)	V.5(1574).
			Correte fiumi Cosa non vada 2p (à 6)	II.6(1569).

Table 1.3 (cont.)

ANTHOLOGY TITLE	RISM:B NUMBER	VOGEL-EINSTEIN NUMBER	TITLE OF PIECE; NUMBER OF VOICES WHEN UNCLEAR	OTHER PUBLICATIONS IN WHICH THE SAME PIECE APPEARS
			I begli'occhi Questi son 2p	II.6(1569).
14. *Musica divina di XIX. autori illustri, a IIII. V. VI. et VII voci. . . . Antwerpen, P. Phalèse et J. Bellère, 1583.*	1583[2]	1583[15]	*Da bei rami scendea* (à 4)	Not by Monte, but by Arcadelt. See Charles Van den Borren, "Arcadelt ou Monte?", *Revue Belge de Musicologie* 6 (1952):159-160.
			Alma ben nata (à 4)	Possibly not by Monte.
			Quando dagl'occhi (à 4)	Not by Monte, but by Sessa d'Aranda, from his I.4(1571).
			Ahi chi mi rompe Di ch'ella mosse 2p (à 5)	III.5(1570).

Table 1.3 (cont.)

ANTHOLOGY TITLE	RISM:B NUMBER	VOGEL-EINSTEIN NUMBER	TITLE OF PIECE; NUMBER OF VOICES WHEN UNCLEAR	OTHER PUBLICATIONS IN WHICH THE SAME PIECE APPEARS
			Poi che'l mio largo pianto (à 6)	I.6(1569).
			Leggiadre ninfe *Il dolc'e desiato 2p* (à 6)	
			Amorosi pensieri (à 6)	III.6(1576).
			La dolce vista (à 6)	I.6(1569).
			Tempr'omai l'ira (à 7)	IV.6(1580).
			Anima dove vai (à 7)	III.5(1570).
15. *Il lauro verde, madrigali a sei voci de diversi autori. . . .* Ferrara, V. Baldini, 1583.	1583[3]	1583[10]	*Verde lauro è'l mio core* (à 6)	XI.5(1586). Here the piece is for five voices.

Table 1.3 (cont.)

	ANTHOLOGY TITLE	RISM:B NUMBER	VOGEL-EINSTEIN NUMBER	TITLE OF PIECE; NUMBER OF VOICES WHEN UNCLEAR	OTHER PUBLICATIONS IN WHICH THE SAME PIECE APPEARS
16.	*Musica de diversi auttori illustri per cantar e sonar in concerti a sette, otto, nove, dieci, undeci, et duodeci voci*. . . . Venezia, G. Vincenti et R. Amadino, 1584.	1584[4]	1584[1]	*Crudel aspro dolore* (à 8)	
17.	*Spoglia amorosa madrigali a cinque voci di diversi*. . . . Venezia, herede de G. Scotto, 1585.	1584[18]	1585[1a]	*Cari scogli* *O solitari 2p* *Che fai alma* *Tal'hor tace 2p* *Ahi chi mi rompe* *Di ch'ella mossa 2p* *Volsi hor non voglio* *Gratia e bellezza 2p*	II.5(1567). III.5(1570). Also in 1583[15]. IV.5(1571).

Table 1.3 (cont.)

ANTHOLOGY TITLE	RISM:B NUMBER	VOGEL-EINSTEIN NUMBER	TITLE OF PIECE; NUMBER OF VOICES WHEN UNCLEAR	OTHER PUBLICATIONS IN WHICH THE SAME PIECE APPEARS
18. *Symphonia angelica di diversi . . . a IIII. V. et VI. voci. . . .* Antwerpen, P. Phalèse & J. Bellère, 1585.	1585[19]	1585[1]	*Occhi vagh'amorosi Occhi leggiadri 2p* (à 5)	X.5 (1581).
19. *Sdegnosi ardori. Musica di diversi autori, sopra un istesso soggetto di parole. . . .* München, A. Berg, 1585.	1585[17]	1585[5]	*Ardo si, ma non t'amo* (à 5)	XI.5 (1586).
20. *Armonia di scelti authori a sei voci. . . .* Venezia, herede di G. Scotto, 1586.	1586[7]	1586[1]	*Poi che le tue ragioni E se gia 2p*	V.6 (1584).
21. *Corona di dodici sonetti di Gio. Battista Zuccarini. . . .* Venezia, A. Gardano, 1586.	1586[11]	1586[4]	*Tutte le gratie Non chiome d'or 2p* (à 5)	

Table 1.3 (cont.)

ANTHOLOGY TITLE	RISM:B NUMBER	VOGEL-EINSTEIN NUMBER	TITLE OF PIECE; NUMBER OF VOICES WHEN UNCLEAR	OTHER PUBLICATIONS IN WHICH THE SAME PIECE APPEARS
22. Musica transalpina. . . London, T. East, 1588.	1588[29]	1588[1]	Per divina bellezza (à 4)	Two earlier sources: RISM 1570[6], and 1583[14]. 1583[14], Harmonia celeste, is the most likely source for this piece.
			In qual parte del ciel / Per divina bellezza 2p (à 5)	IV.5(1571).
23. Giardinetto de madrigali et canzonette a tre voci. . . . Venezia, R. Amadino, 1588.	1588[19]	1588[6]	Caro dolce mio	This piece is not from 1582a, Il primo libro de madrigali a tre voci.
24. Liber secundus Gemmai. . . . Nürnberg, C. Gerlach, 1589.	1589	1589	Tirsi morir volea (à 5)	XI.5(1586).

Table 1.3 (cont.)

ANTHOLOGY TITLE	RISM:B NUMBER	VOGEL-EINSTEIN NUMBER	TITLE OF PIECE; NUMBER OF VOICES WHEN UNCLEAR	OTHER PUBLICATIONS IN WHICH THE SAME PIECE APPEARS
25. *Musicale esercitio di Ludovico Balbi. . . .* Venezia, A. Gardano, 1589.	1589[12]	*Vogel*, see Balbi 2	*Nov'Angeletta* (à 5)	I.4(1562), Canto only. (See *Vogel*, under Balbi 2 for a description of the *esercitio* involved here.)
26. *Dialoghi musicali de diversi . . . a sette, otto, nove, dieci, undeci, et dodeci voci. . . .* Venezia, A. Gardano, 1590.	1590[11]	1590[1]	*Bella Clori Cosi il pastor 2p* (à 7) *Stolto mio core* (à 7) *Era nell'imbrunir* (à 10) *Deh perch'amor* (à 10)	III.6(1576). Vogel-Einstein says that this piece is à 8; this is a mistake.
27. *Tertius Gemmae musicalis liber. . . .* Nürnberg, C. Gerlach, 1590.	1590[20]	1590[3]	*Sogliono i chiari spirti* (à 6)	V.6(1584).

Table 1.3 (cont.)

ANTHOLOGY TITLE	RISM:B NUMBER	VOGEL-EINSTEIN NUMBER	TITLE OF PIECE; NUMBER OF VOICES WHEN UNCLEAR	OTHER PUBLICATIONS IN WHICH THE SAME PIECE APPEARS
28. *Di Stefano Felis. . . . Il sesto libro de madrigali à cinque voci. . . . Venezia, herede di G. Scotto, 1591.*	1591[18]	*Vogel, see Felis 6*	*Al discoglier d'un gruppo*	
29. *La ruzina canzone di Filippo de Monte. . . . Venezia, Ang. Gardano, 1591.*	1591[23]	1591[2]	*Ecco ch'io veggio Inviolabil forme 2p Le labra timidette 3p Quando l'anima bella 4p La spirital virtù 5p All'hor gli spirti 6p Il gran Fattor 7p*	
30. *Il trionfo di dori, descritto da diversi, et posto in musica à sei voci. . . . Venezia, Ang. Gardano, 1592.*	1592[11]	1592[2]	*Lungo le chiare linfe (à 6)*	

Table 1.3 (cont.)

ANTHOLOGY TITLE	RISM:B NUMBER	VOGEL-EINSTEIN NUMBER	TITLE OF PIECE; NUMBER OF VOICES WHEN UNCLEAR	OTHER PUBLICATIONS IN WHICH THE SAME PIECE APPEARS
31. *Florindo, e Armilla canzon pastorale, ornata di musica da diversi.* . . . Venezia, R. Amadino, 1593.	1593[3]	1593[3]	*Poi che più volte* (à 5)	
32. *Nuova spoglia amorosa.* . . . Venezia, G. Vincenti, 1593.	1593[5]	1593[4]	*Io son si vago* (à 4) *Occhi vaghi amorosi Occhi leggiadri 2p* (à 5)	*RISM:B* 1583[14], *Harmonia celeste.* Two previous sources: XI.5(1581) and *RISM:B* 1585[19], *Symphonia angelica.* The latter is the more probable source.
33. *Madrigali a otto voci. De diversi.* Antwerpen, P. Phalèse, 1596.	1596[10]	1596[1]	*Crudel aspro dolore*	*RISM* 1584[4], *Musica de diversi autori.* . . .

Table 1.3 (cont.)

ANTHOLOGY TITLE	RISM:B NUMBER	VOGEL–EINSTEIN NUMBER	TITLE OF PIECE; NUMBER OF VOICES WHEN UNCLEAR	OTHER PUBLICATIONS IN WHICH THE SAME PIECE APPEARS
34. *Paradiso musicale di madrigali et canzoni a cinque voci, di diversi. . . .* Antwerpen, P. Phalèse, 1596.	1596^{10}	1596^3	*Tu mi piaghasti a morte*	X.5(1581).
35. *Fiori del giardino di diversi. . . .* Nürnberg, P. Kaufmann, 1597.	1597^{13}	1597^2	*Crudel aspro dolore* (à 8)	Two previous sources: RISM:B 1584^4 and 1596^{10}.
36. *Ghirlanda di madrigali a sei voci, di diversi. . . .* Antwerpen, P. Phalèse, 1601.	1601^5	1601^1	*S'io ti seguo* *Sì mi dicesti*	VIII.6(1594).
37. *I diporti della villa in ogni stagione. . . .* Venezia, Ang. Gardano, 1601.	1601^7	1601^3	*[Il Verno] Ma non di minor freggio Altri con maggior rischio 2p Alcun nel maggior freddo 3p*	The entire anthology is published in modern edition: (*I Diporti . . . Trascrizione in notazione moderna di Siro Cisilino*. Milan, n.d.).

Table 1.3 (cont.)

ANTHOLOGY TITLE	RISM:B NUMBER	VOGEL-EINSTEIN NUMBER	TITLE OF PIECE; NUMBER OF VOICES WHEN UNCLEAR	OTHER PUBLICATIONS IN WHICH THE SAME PIECE APPEARS
			Ma di fera più bella 4p / *Ceda ogn'altra stagion 5p* (à 5)	
38. *Scielta di madrigali à cinque voci de diversi . . . accommodati in motetti. . . .* Milano, herede di S. Tini et F. Lomazzo, 1604.	1604^{11}	1604^{3}	*Che fai alma* (*Tu es gloria mea*) / *Tal'hor tace* (*Deus judex justus*)	II.5(1567). This piece also appeared in 1583^{14} and 1583^{18}.
39. *Nervi d'Orfeo . . . a cinque et sei voci. . . .* Leiden, H. L. de Haestens, 1605.	1605^{9}	1605^{2}	*Tu mi piaghasti a morte* (à 5)	X.5(1581). This piece also appeared in 1596^{10}.
			Amorosi pensieri (à 6)	III.6(1576). This piece also appeared in 1583^{15}.
			La dolce vista (à 6)	I.6(1569). This piece also appeared in 1583^{15}.

Table 1.3 (cont.)

	ANTHOLOGY TITLE	RISM:B NUMBER	VOGEL-EINSTEIN NUMBER	TITLE OF PIECE; NUMBER OF VOICES WHEN UNCLEAR	OTHER PUBLICATIONS IN WHICH THE SAME PIECE APPEARS
				Poi che'l mio largo pianto	I.6(1569) and 1583[15].
				Verde lauro e'l mio core (à 6)	*RISM:B* 1583[10].
40.	*Fatiche spirituali di Simone Molinaro maestro di Capella del Duomo di Genova. Libro primo a sei.* Venezia, R. Amadino, 1610.	1610[2]	1610[2]	*Se giamai tempo o loco* (*O beate Laurenti*)	I.6(1569).
41.	*Fatiche spirituali di Simone Molinaro maestro di Capella del Duomo di Genova. Libro secondo a sei voci.* Venezia, R. Amadino, 1610.	1610[3]	1610[3]	*Leggiadre ninfe* (*Se scires fili*)	I.6(1569).
				Il dolce e desiato frutto (*Cum ergo tuo*)	Also in *RISM:B* 1583[15].

Table 1.3 (cont.)

ANTHOLOGY TITLE	RISM:B NUMBER	VOGEL-EINSTEIN NUMBER	TITLE OF PIECE; NUMBER OF VOICES WHEN UNCLEAR	OTHER PUBLICATIONS IN WHICH THE SAME PIECE APPEARS
			Se per far la mia vita (O peccator attende) Ma se volgete 2p (Sed quod non per-cipis)	IV.6(1580).
42. Musicalische Streitkranz-lein: . . . A. Wagen-Mann, 1612.	1612[13]	1612[1]	Lungo le chiare linfe (Justitiam dispar-- Jungfrawlein eurent)	1592[11]. (This anthology is a German reworking of Il trionfo di dori.)
43. Florilegium musicum . . . ac latino ecclesiastico textu donatorum. . . . Bambergai, . . . 1631.			Quanto di me (Ecce sacerdos)	IV.4(1581).
			Voi volete (Isti sunt viri sancti)	I.4(1562).
			Ohime lasso (Veni, Domine)	III.4(1585). In this print, this madrigal is not attributed to Monte, but to Gio. Battista de la Gostena.

These two anthologies offer more evidence that by 1583 the contemporary estimation of and affection for Monte's madrigals centered largely upon his achievements of the 1560s and 70s, rather than upon his most recent works of the early 80s. In *Musica divina,* Monte is represented with more compositions than any of the anthology's eighteen other composers, and his preeminence here (and in *Harmonia celeste* also) is not difficult to explain. As he was from Malines, which lies close to Antwerp, his works were bound to be particularly admired by the editors, proud of the accomplishments of a native son.[76]

The most recent Monte madrigals to appear in *Musica divina* come from 1576 and 1580, and the choice of pieces in *Harmonia celeste* is more retrospective yet; no piece of his published later than 1574 appears. At the same time, the madrigals of Luca Marenzio begin to appear in these anthologies, with pieces drawn from three of his books of the early 1580s.[77] Clearly, the editors of these anthologies were aware of the new and lighter kind of madrigal which these pieces exemplify; it is equally clear that they did not associate that style with Filippo di Monte.

After the prominence given to Monte's work in *Harmonia celeste* and *Musica divina,* the slighting of his music in the later volumes in this series of anthologies is all the more pointed. In *Symphonia angelica* (1585[19]), only one Monte madrigal appears; significantly, *Occhi vaghi amorosi* is the most up-to-date piece in his Tenth Book for Five Voices of 1581. *Melodia olympica* (1591[10]), the last of this series of big anthologies from Antwerp, ignores Monte's music altogether.[78]

In the 1580s and early 1590s, Monte continued to contribute madrigals occasionally to anthologies of new music, among them *Il lauro verde* (1583[10]) and *Il trionfo di Dori* (1592[11]). His last contribution to an anthology comes in 1601, with *I diporti della villa in ogni stagione* (1601[7]).

In the years following his death in 1603, a handful of older pieces appeared in a few retrospective anthologies. In addition, reprints of earlier anthologies continued to keep at least some of his music before the public. In the end, tiny fragments of his huge secular legacy were embalmed as spiritual *contrafacta* in a few motet collections, the first of which appeared in Italy.

Finally, two four-voice madrigals were spiritualized in a German publication of 1631, the *Florilegium musicum.* Here Monte's music suffers the posthumous indignity of being confused with the work of another: one of these pieces, taken from his Third Book for Four Voices, is actually the only madrigal in that book *not* by Monte, but by Giovanni Battista della Gostena, as the original print indicates.[79] By 1631, Monte's music had come to serve only a narrow, archaizing role in the music of the day.

The Poetry of the Madrigal Books

Monte's Poetic Choices

The unusual length of Monte's career as a madrigalist offers us the opportunity to observe the changes in literary taste and style in the Italian madrigal during the second half of the sixteenth century, as these manifest themselves in his thirty-five publications. Though Monte's changing texts do not reflect every important trend among madrigalists, his poetic tastes generally develop along contemporary lines. He was, on the whole, a follower rather than a trend-setter, in literary as well as in musical matters.

Monte's choice of poetry evidences two important changes from the early books of the 1550s and 60s to those of the 80s and 90s. The first development is external and formal: the strict poetic forms—sonnet, sestina, canzone, and ottava—gradually diminish in number until they all but disappear. They are replaced by the free madrigal, typically a poem of one stanza with no predetermined structure.

This formal development is the outward manifestation of a profound inner change in the style and content of the poetry. Monte began his career as a serious Petrarchist, and ended it with the pastoral and amorous poetry of Tasso, Guarini, and their lesser imitators. This gradual replacement of one poetic ideal by another is intimately tied to the considerable development in Monte's music over the years.

Petrarch's poetry abounds in Monte's first publications. The First Book for Five Voices (1554) is dominated by Petrarch's sonnets, the First Book for Four Voices (1562) by the sestinas. Only the First Book for Six Voices (1564?) is anomalous: Petrarch is entirely absent. Every other book Monte published up until 1580 contains the work of Petrarch, in varying measure; during these years, in fact, Monte set more of Petrarch's poetry than any other composer in the history of the madrigal. This early emphasis on Petrarch is consistent with the work of most other serious madrigalists at mid-century. The high point of Petrarch's popularity among composers was reached in the decades around 1550, as the publications of Rore, Lasso, Wert, and Willaert show.

Yet the underlying trend of the 1560s and 1570s was a gradual turning away from Petrarch, in favor of his contemporary imitators. Soon after he began to publish his madrigals, Monte discovered the works of Pietro Bembo and Jacopo Sannazaro; their poetry appears more frequently in Monte's books than that of any other single poet after Petrarch. (Monte set about fifteen poems by each of these authors.) Yet Monte turned more characteristically to a large number of lesser published poets, usually setting no more than one or two poems by each. The attention which Monte devoted to these *poeti minori,* taken as a group, is much greater than that he accorded to Bembo and Sannazaro.

The years around 1580 mark a significant turning point in Monte's poetic taste. In this year, he published three books, and Petrarch is entirely absent from two of these, as are Bembo and Sannazaro. After 1580, Petrarch's poetry makes only the rarest appearances, and these have a decidedly retrospective quality about them. From 1580 to 1584, Monte turned again and again to that large group of *poeti minori* mentioned above, whose works he culled from two large printed anthologies, to be considered later.

Finally, in 1586, Monte discovered the world of Tasso and Guarini. The Eleventh Book for Five Voices, published in this year, is emphatically devoted to their poetry: there are ten Guarini and five Tasso poems. This is the first time (with a single exception)[80] that Monte had set the words of either poet. (Marenzio and others had already begun to set Guarini and Tasso lyrics as early as 1580.) In the poetry of the eight madrigal books for five voices which follow, however, Tasso and Guarini do not dominate as they do in the Eleventh Book. Indeed, though Monte continued to explore Tasso's poetry for a short time after his initial discovery of 1586, he set no more Tasso after 1591.

In 1592, Monte turned briefly to the poetry of Livio Celiano, which first appears in the Fifteenth Book for Five Voices, of this year. He turned to Celiano again in the Sixteenth Book (1593), and only once more in a later five-voice book.

It was to Guarini's lyric poetry that Monte most consistently devoted himself in the final fifteen years of his life. He set thirty-five Guarini poems during these years, making Guarini Monte's most favored poet during this period. While Guarini's poems are concentrated in the Eleventh and the Fifteenth Books for Five Voices, they also appear in other volumes right up to 1600. Monte also devoted much attention to Guarini's highly fashionable *tragicommedia, Il Pastor Fido* (1589). His first encounter with the play comes in the Fourteenth Book for Five Voices (1590), where he sets a single passage, later to become a famous proving-ground of expressivity among madrigalists—*Cruda Amarilli.* Monte did not return to the play again until 1599, in *La Fiammetta,* where a number of the madrigals are drawn from the play. The publication opens with a cycle based on a poem in Giovanni Boccaccio's *Decameron;* after this unusual poetic choice, the book continues with a number of excerpts drawn from *Il Pastor Fido.* Finally, in 1600, Monte published an entire book devoted to Guarini's play, appropriately titled *Musica sopra Il Pastor Fido.* It is one of the few publications of the time devoted exclusively to texts drawn from Guarini's play. Monte's attitude towards *Il Pastor Fido* is typical of his lifelong habits; he is not one for half-measures, and when his interest in a poet's work is aroused (as his love for Petrarch had been aroused forty years earlier), he explores it thoroughly.

Guarini, Tasso and Celiano, then, are the favored poets of Monte's late years. Yet in his final work, the Ninth Book for Six Voices (1603), he abandons them all, turning to authors for the most part still unidentified. Only two poets have been discovered: Luigi Groto *("Il Cieco d'Adria")* and Ansaldo Cebà. Their poems here are brief and undistinguished.

More important a development than the occasional appearance of such poets as these is the growing prominence in Monte's late books of minor poetry whose authorship is not presently known. The Seventeenth Book for Five Voices (1595) can serve as an example: we know the poet of only one of its twenty-eight numbers. Significantly, the textual concordances with other composers' settings are few for this unidentified poetry; Monte does not seem to have drawn it from other composers' books. Again, the Seventeenth Book can serve as an example: only one poem among the unidentified ones was set by another composer.

Monte's Literary Sources

Throughout his career—though more so before 1585 than after—Monte turned often to printed sources for his texts. In setting the poetry of Petrarch, Bembo, and Sannazaro, he could have had access to any one of the dozens of editions of these poets' works. The situation is rather different, though, when we turn to the many lesser writers whose poetry Monte also set. Their poetry was most readily accessible in large printed anthologies, rather than in volumes devoted solely to their works.

On Monte's choice of poetry before 1580, Einstein makes the following observation:

> . . . One can see that Monte is working in exile—as it were, *in partibus infidelium.* There are exceptions; but in general he knows only the bipartite sonnet and the ottava, favors canzoni and sestine, and remains faithful to his favorite poets: Petrarch, Bembo (for whom he has an unfortunate predilection), and Sannazaro. A certain lyric anthology, edited by Lodovico Dolce, is his vade mecum.[81]

The lyric anthology to which Einstein alludes is in fact a two-volume set, both volumes of which first appeared in 1563. In view of these books' rarity, I give the title pages of each of these volumes, as they appear in the two copies now in the University of California Bancroft Library. The first book in the set has the following title page:

IL PRIMO VOLUME | DELLE RIME | SCELTE | DI DIVERSI AUTORI, | DI NUOVO CORRETTE E RISTAMPATE. | AGGIUNTEVI MOLTI SONETTI | nel Secondo Volume. | CON PRIVILEGIO. [emblem] *IN VENETIA, | APPRESSO I GIOLITI. | MDCLXXXVIII.*

This edition of 1588 is one of several reprints. The title page of the second volume reads:

> Secundo Volume | DELLE RIME | DA DIVERSI ECCELENTI | Autori, novamente mandato in luce. | AL NOBILISS. S. DAVID | IMPERIALE. | CON PRIVILEGIO | [emblem] IN VINEGIA APRESSO GABRIEL | GIOLITO DE' FERRARI | MDLXIII.

This volume, then, is the first edition of 1563.[82]

Such anthologies as these reflect a complex bibliographical situation. Most often, they took their poems from previously published anthologies, and this is certainly the case with these two volumes. Table 1.4 gives all the poetry which Monte drew from both volumes; it also shows that nearly all of the poetry from *Il Primo Volume* which Monte set had already appeared in an earlier anthology, the *Rime di diversi eccellenti autori, raccolte da i libri da noi altre volte impressi*, printed in Venice by Gabriel Giolito in 1553.[83] These *Rime* were, as the title page explicitly states, "gathered from books of ours printed at other times." (The books referred to were probably a combination of anthologies and books devoted solely to a single author's works.) Thus, the *Primo* and *Secondo Volume* represent a fairly late stage in a lengthy bibliographical unfolding.[84] From all this, one might conclude that Monte's exact source for any of these poems cannot be given with any certainty. Yet no other single anthology I have been able to examine contains so many poems set by Monte: over a twenty-year period he drew nearly fifty poems from this two-volume anthology. He turned to it most frequently in the years 1580-82.

Yet Monte had other anthologies to draw upon, and one of these—apparently known to Einstein though not mentioned by him—rivals the *Primo* and *Secondo Volume* in its importance as a source for Monte's texts. Once again, the publication in question is a two-volume anthology, devoted in this case exclusively to ottava stanzas. In the years before 1585, Monte set a considerable quantity of ottavas, many of which appear in these volumes. The title pages of these books, taken from the copies now in the University of California Bancroft Library, are given below. Here is the first volume:

> PRIMA PARTE | DELLE STANZE | DI DIVERSI | ILLUST. POETI. | RACCOLTE DA M. LODOVICO | DOLCE, à commodità, & utile de gli studiosi della Lingua Thoscana: | NUOVAMENTE RISTAMPATE, ET | con diligentia reviste & corrette. [emblem] IN VINEGIA, APPRESSO | i Gioliti MDLXXXI.

The first edition of the *Parte prima* appeared in 1553, and was titled simply as *Stanze di diversi...*, rather than the *Parte prima*.

Table 1.4 The Appearance in Three Lyric Anthologies of Poetry Set by Monte*

DATE; TITLE OF MADRIGAL BOOK	TITLE OF POEM	POET	RIME 1553	PRIMO VOLUME 1563	SECONDO VOLUME 1563
1564?: I.6	In me tanto ardore	Amaltheo	x	x	
	Quando muovo le luci / Di che l'anima 2p	Ariosto	x	x	
	Occhi, se voi pur sete / Cosi vengo di voi 2p	Amanio	x	x	
	Occhi sereni, occhi / Parlar soave 2p	Corfini		x	
	Tra bei rubini	Amaltheo		x	
1567: II.5	Con lagrime ch'ogn'hor / In me cresce 2p	Amaltheo	x	x	
	Presago del mio mal / E parmi in van 2p	Spira		x	
	Cosi havess'io	Amaltheo	x	x	

*See accompanying text for full citations.

Table 1.4 (cont.)

DATE; TITLE OF MADRIGAL BOOK	TITLE OF POEM	POET	RIME 1553	PRIMO VOLUME 1563	SECONDO VOLUME 1563
1569: II.6	Io son si stanco / Hora per far 2p	Guidiccioni	x	x	
	Aura soave, che si / Al tristo suon 2p	Mozzarello	x	x	
	Lunge è madonna	Gradenico		x	
1569: II.4	Al dolce vostro canto	Amaltheo	x	x	
	O desir de quest'occhi / O rose eterne 2p	Mozzarello	x	x	
1570: III.5	O messagi del cor / Sara che cessi 2p	Ariosto	x	x	
	Cara soave / Dolce mio duol 2p	Tansillo	x	x	
1574: V.5	Senno, gratia, valore	Bonfadio	x	x	

Table 1.4 (cont.)

DATE; TITLE OF MADRIGAL BOOK	TITLE OF POEM	POET	RIME 1553	PRIMO VOLUME 1563	SECONDO VOLUME 1563
1575: VI.5	Poiche, lasso Ch'io sent'ad hor 2p Come sole a cui'l 3p Ove le luci giro 4p Ella leggiadra 5p Verrà giamai 6p	Gradenico	x	x	
	Hor le tue forze	Amaltheo	x	x	
	Se non sete Nè varrà 2p	Di Constanzo	x	x	
	Mentre che l'aureo	B. Tasso	x	x	
	Già incomincià Non tornar 2p	B. Tasso			x
1576: III.6	Io giuro, amor Vist'ho faville 2p	Guidiccioni	x	x	
1580: VIII.5	Occhi, cagion Occhi, del viver 2p	Britonio			x
	Se le lunge fatiche	Lionardi			x

Table 1.4 (cont.)

DATE; TITLE OF MADRIGAL BOOK	TITLE OF POEM	POET	RIME 1553	PRIMO VOLUME 1563	SECONDO VOLUME 1563
	Hora che gl'animali Così sia l'una 2p	B. Tasso			x
	Come fido animal Così temendo 2p	B. Tasso			x
1580: IX.5	Questa fera gentil Fortunato 2p	Rinieri	x	x	
	Io son sì stanco Sì veloce 2p	B. Tasso			x
	Sì dolce è'l foco Dolce fiamma 2p	B. Tasso			x
	Stratiami pure Non fia mai 2p	G. B. Rinaldi			x
	Lagrime false Celar più 2p	Terminio			x
	Come esser può Se ciò non basta 2p	M. I. Politano			x

Table 1.4 (cont.)

DATE; TITLE OF MADRIGAL BOOK	TITLE OF POEM	POET	RIME 1553	PRIMO VOLUME 1563	SECONDO VOLUME 1563
1581: X.5	Amor m'impenna l'ale / Che s'altri 2p	Tansillo	x	x	
	Occhi vaghi, amorosi / Occhi leggiadri 2p	Mozzarello	x	x	x ascribed to M. I. Politano
	Dolci, amorose / parolette	Giraldi			x
	Nasci e venendo / Ella di neve 2p	Varchi	x	x	
1581: IV.4	Deh Flori, se pietà / Sola te cerco 2p	Montenero			x
	O fastiditi già / Tempo sarebbe 2p	Giraldi			x
	Quando Filli potrà / Poscia pien 2p	Varchi	x	x	
	Dolce mio caro / Qui trar del petto 2p	Veniero	x	x	
	Porta il buon villanel / Ma i pomi 2p	Coppetta/Beccuti			x

Table 1.4 (cont.)

DATE; TITLE OF MADRIGAL BOOK	TITLE OF POEM	POET	RIME 1553	PRIMO VOLUME 1563	SECONDO VOLUME 1563
	Se l'anime più belle	Fiorentino	x	x	
	Quanto di me	Fiorentino		x	
	Sotto quest'edra	Varchi	x	x	
1582: I.3	O mia lieta ventura Io so che non 2p	Piccolomini		x	
	Non vedete voi, donna	Barignano	x	x	
	Volontier canterei	Barignano	x	x	
	Ove lontan Così d'un olmo 2p	Fiorentino			x
	Ardo, sospiro e piango E son del mio 2p	Fiorentino			x

The second volume in this Berkeley set has lost its original title page, and one has been supplied by hand, in an attempt to give the appearance of a print. It reads:

STANZE | DI DIVERSI AUTORI | [printed emblem] *| PARTE SECONDA | VINEGIA MDLXIII. | PRESSO GIOLITO.*

This two-volume set contains over three thousand ottavas, and the work of more than thirty poets, as well as many poems *"d'incerto autore."* Throughout, the ottavas are arranged in narrative sequences of varying length. Such poems were sometimes called *canzone* in contemporary madrigal prints; no such titles appear in this anthology.

Monte turned to these books often, relying on them most heavily in his First Book for Three Voices (1582). Table 1.5 gives all the poems which Monte drew from these volumes, and cites the page numbers on which the poems appear in the Bancroft Library copies. Monte typically viewed this anthology as a sourcebook for individual stanzas; he was seldom interested in the merits of an entire poem. His attitude towards the integrity of these ottava sequences is casual and pragmatic; time and time again, he simply extracts single stanzas from their surroundings because they offer self-contained, lyrical moments. [85]

Einstein's perception that Monte's choice of poetry and his reliance on a large anthology reflects his growing isolation in Vienna merits close consideration. In fact, the evidence suggests that both his changes of taste and his reliance on large printed anthologies run parallel with other composers' text choices. Lasso and Wert, for example, also turned away from Petrarch to the same neo-Petrarchan poets we find in Monte: Sannazaro, Bembo, della Casa, Tansillo, and others. Even the *poeti minori* whose works Monte culled so frequently from his favored anthologies were known to other madrigalists as well. [86]

It is only in the early 1580s that Monte seems out of touch with contemporary developments in poetic taste. In the same years in which Marenzio and others began to set the lyrics of Tasso and Guarini, Monte continued to rely more and more on his two anthologies. Indeed, in both the Fourth Book for Four Voices (1581) and the First Book for Three Voices (1582), almost all of the poetry can be found in these two anthologies.

By 1586, when Monte first set Tasso's poetry, there were already a large number of editions of his *rime* in print. Thanks to Angelo Solerti's efforts, [87] we have a clear picture of these editions and their contents; Solerti's work makes it clear that no single edition of Tasso's lyric poetry printed before 1586 contains all the poems which Monte eventually set. If Monte set Tasso's lyrics from the printed page, he must have had several books at his disposal.

Guarini's lyrics present a similar problem. Since his poetry has not been subjected to the bibliographical scrutiny that Solerti devoted to Tasso, no

Table 1.5   The Ottava Stanzas Set by Monte Which Appeared in the
Stanze Di Diverse Autori

DATE; TITLE OF MADRIGAL BOOK	TITLE OF POEM	POET	VOLUME; PAGE NUMBER
1569: II.4	*O quant'è dolce*	*d'incerto autore*	P.p., p. 18*
	Danzava con maniera *Son presa 2p* *Io donna 3p* *Voi sciolta 4p*	Pompeo Pace	P.p., pp. 426ff.
1580: IX.5	*Lasso me*	Gandolfo Porrino	S.p., p. 191
	Dunque è pur ver *Crudel hor 2p* *Perfido ove mi lasci 3p*	Bernardino Martirano	S.p., pp. 12ff.
1581: IV.4	*Deh fate homai*	Gandolfo Porrino	S.p., p. 192
	Fa ch'io riveggia	Gandolfo Porrino	S.p., p. 194
	Mentre piena d'orgoglio *Vedrai mutata 2p* *Se dunque è ver 3p*	Gandolfo Porrino	S.p., p. 192
	Deh s'io potessi	Gandolfo Porrino	S.p., pp. 193-4

*Abbreviations: *Prima parte* = P.p.; *Seconda parte* = S.p.

Table 1.5 (cont.)

DATE; TITLE OF MADRIGAL BOOK	TITLE OF POEM	POET	VOLUME; PAGE NUMBER
1582: I.3	Amor che sol	d'incerto autore	P.p., p. 416
	O beata colei	Lodovico Martelli	P.p., p. 291
	Ohime dovè'l mio ben	Bernardo Tasso	P.p., p. 255
	Chi non sa	Cavalier Vendramini	S.p., p. 178
	Vostro fui vostro son	Bernardo Tasso	P.p., p. 257
	Non pur si duro	Luigi Alamanni	P.p., p. 207
	Mentre ameranno	Luigi Alamanni	P.p., p. 209
	Vago monte fiorite	Cavalier Gandolfo	S.p., p. 190
	O chi potrà mai ben	Cavalier Gandolfo	S.p., p. 189
	S'io odo alcun felice	Angelo Costanzo	S.p., p. 162
	Vissimi un tempo	Vincenzo Quirino	P.p., p. 437
	Dolce mia vita	Molza	P.p., p. 144
	La bocca onde	Hercole Bentivoglio	P.p., p. 262
	Poi c'hor è dolce	Hercole Bentivoglio	P.p., p. 260
	Spesso a consiglio	Angelo di Costanzo	S.p., p. 154
	Ahi dove lasso	d'incerto autore	P.p., p. 416
	Qual più scontento	Vincenzo Quirino	P.p., p. 436

Table 1.5 (cont.)

DATE; TITLE OF MADRIGAL BOOK	TITLE OF POEM	POET	VOLUME; PAGE NUMBER
	Quel desir c'hebbi	Angelo di Constanzo	S.p., p. 156
	Piango ch'Amor	d'incerto autore	P.p., p. 412
	Satiati Amor	d'incerto autore	P.p., p. 413
1584: V.6	*Mi havete Amor*	Pompeo Pace	P.p., p. 429
	Vita de la mia vita	Bernardo Tasso	P.p., p. 255
	Ahi dispietato amor	Bernardo Tasso	P.p., p. 256

single source of the 1580s can be proposed as Monte's most likely source for his selection of Guarini lyrics. We can, however, note that Monte's versions of Guarini's poetry frequently differ from those in early printed editions. This is true both of the lyric poetry, and of Monte's excerpts from the *Pastor Fido.* In both cases, Monte's readings may stem from early printed versions, or may point to Monte's access to corrupt or variant manuscript versions of the poetry. This issue will be taken up again in chapter 5.

Only in the case of Livo Celiano is it possible to point to the poetic anthology which Monte must have relied upon. Monte set sixteen madrigals by Celiano from 1592-97, and all of these appeared in the *Rime di diversi celebri poeti dell'età nostra...*, printed in Bergamo in 1587 by Comino Venturi, and edited by Luciano. This appears to be the only contemporary printed source for Celiano's poetry; Monte's readings follow this edition closely. It seems safe enough to point to it as Monte's source.

It is possible that further research will uncover other anthologies of the 1580s and 1590s, making possible the identification of many more of Monte's poets for these years. It is also possible that manuscripts of Italian poetry, still in Vienna or Prague, might hold a clue to some of Monte's poetic choices. This work is still in the future.

2

The Madrigal Books of the Italian Years

The First Book for Five Voices, 1554

Monte's First Book was printed in Rome, and was dedicated by Giovan
Battista Bruno to Honofrio Vigili, a Roman nobleman. As Monte later
declared, it appeared without his knowledge, or (apparently) his permission.[1]
Stylistically, these madrigals are conservative for the 1550s; some or all of them
might have been composed in the late 1540s. The book's conservative aspects
have been overlooked by previous writers, and will best be understood if the
book is compared with the first essays in the madrigal by Orlando di Lasso and
Giaches Wert, which appeared around the same time. Before proceeding to the
comparison, an account of the stylistic features in Monte's First Book must be
given.

The book contains sixteen pieces, of twenty-six sections (see Table 2.1).
Petrarch's poetry dominates; eight of the book's nine sonnets are his. There are
four ottava stanzas as well, one of which *(Credut' havria che fosse statua finta)*
is drawn from the *Orlando Furioso;* strangely, it is the only ottava from this
epic which Monte ever set. *Colonna di smeraldo,* one of the two madrigals in
this book, was interpreted by Einstein[2] as a dedicatory madrigal addressed to a
member of the prominent Colonna family of Rome. Though this seems
plausible, the poem does not refer to a particular person or occasion.

We can form an idea of the style of the whole publication by examining the
opening piece, a setting of Petrarch's *Zefiro torna*. This sonnet, which contrasts
the beauty and peace of nature with the poet's inner struggles (a *topos* in the

Table 2.1 The Poetic Contents of the First Book of Madrigals for Five Voices (1554)

	TITLE	POETIC FORM	AUTHOR
1.	*Zefiro torna* *Ma per me lasso 2p*	sonnet	Petrarch (310)
2.	*Non vegg'i ove scampar* *E l'imagini lor 2p*	sonnet	Petrarch (107)
3.	*Colonna di smeraldo* *In ferm-alta colonna 2p*	madrigal	?
4.	*Credut'havria che fosse statua*	ottava stanza	Ariosto, *Orlando furioso:* 10, 96.
5.	*Ogni mio ben crudel morte*	ottava stanza	?
6.	*Se tropp'alto desir*	ottava stanza	?
7.	*Lasso ch'io ardo* *Quest'arder 2p*	sonnet	Petrarch (203)
8.	*Ohime che belle lagrime* *Stavasi amor 2p*	sonnet	Lorenzo de' Medici Monte's version of the poem differs slightly from the one printed in the modern edition of his works: Lorenzo de' Medici, *Opere, a cura di Attilio Simioni.* 2 vols. (Bari, 1939); vol. 1, p. 221.

Table 2.1 (cont.)

	TITLE	POETIC FORM	AUTHOR
9.	*Di dì in dì* *Non spero del mio affan' 2p*	sonnet	Petrarch (195)
10.	*Uno nova Siren'*	irregular ottava stanza	?
11.	*I' mi vivea di mia sorte* *O Natura pietosa 2p*	sonnet	Petrarch (131)
12.	*Ove ch'i posi gl'occhi* *Amor e'l ver fur meco 2p*	sonnet	Petrarch (158)
13.	*Quel rosignuol, che sí soave* *O che liev'è ingannar*	sonnet	Petrarch (311)
14.	*Amor mi manda quel dolce* *In questo passa 2p*	sonnet	Petrarch (168)
15.	*I' vidi in terra*	sonnet quatrains	Petrarch (156)
16.	*So voi per me sentesti*	madrigal	?

Canzoniere particularly suited for musical realization) is given below, with a translation which appeared in the English anthology *Musica transalpina* (1588).

Zefiro torna e'l bel tempo rimena
E i fiori et l'erbe, sua dolce famiglia,
E garrir Progne et pianger Filomena,
Et Primavera candida et vermiglia;

Ridono i prati e'l ciel si rasserena,
Giove s'allegra di mirar sua figlia,
L'aria et l'acqua et la terra è d'amor piena,
Ogni animal d'amar si riconsiglia.

Ma per me, lasso, tornano i più gravi
Sospiri che del cor profondo tragge
Quella ch'al Ciel se ne porto le chiavi;

Et cantar augelletti, et fiorir piagge,
E'n belle donne oneste atti soavi
Sono un deserto et fere aspre et selvagge.

(Zephirus brings the time that sweetly senteth
With flowres and herbs and winters frost exileth,
Progne now chirpeth, and Philomele lamenteth,
Flora the garlands white and red compileth,

Fields doe rejoyce, the frowning skye relenteth,
Jove to behold his dearest daughter smyleth,
Th'ayre the water the earth to Joy consenteth,
Each creature now to love, him reconcileth.

But with mee wretch the storms of woe persever,
& heavy sighes, which from my hart she straineth,
That tooke the kay thereof to heaven for ever

So that singing of byrds & spring time flowryng
& ladies love that mens affection faineth
Are like a desert, & cruell beastes devouring.)[3]

The most striking feature in Monte's setting is its melodic charm and melismatic richness (see example 1). With elegant and skillfully crafted lines, Monte evokes the verdant landscape so vividly painted in Petrarch's quatrains. The melodic lines throughout have a plastic shape and a fluid rhythm which continually propel individual phrases beyond normal expectations. The opening Canto line, for example, seems to move towards a cadence on d" on the first beat of m. 6; that cadence is delayed by an elegant downward motion to a', before the line moves upwards again to d" (m. 7). The rhythmic fluidity is

Example 1. Monte: The First Book for Five Voices (1554)
Zefiro torna (complete) mm. 1-6

Ex. 1 (cont.) mm. 7-12

Ex. 1 (cont.) mm. 13-18

Ex. 1 (cont.) mm. 19-24

Ex. 1 (cont.) mm. 31-36

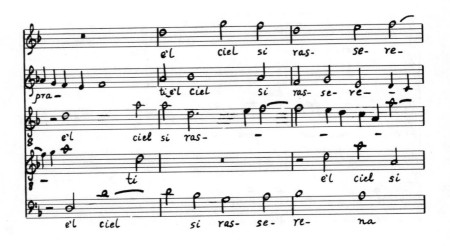

Ex. 1 (cont.) mm. 37-42

Ex. 1 (cont.) mm. 43-48

Ex. 1 (cont.) mm. 49-54

Ex. 1 (cont.) mm. 55-59

Ex. 1 (cont.) mm. 60-65

Ex. 1 (cont.) mm. 66-71

Ex. 1 (cont.) mm. 72-77

Ex. 1 (cont.) mm. 78-83

Ex. 1 (cont.) mm. 84-89

Ex. 1 (cont.) mm. 90-95

Ex. 1 (cont.) mm. 96-101

achieved by a liberal use of syncopation; as a result, the melodic lines are in a continual yet delicately balanced opposition to the prevailing *tactus*. Both the rhythmic placement of a line's melodic highpoints, and the syllabic stresses of its words combine to weaken the sense of pulse. This kind of fluid shape and rhythm is so prevalent that the imitative subjects themselves are not strongly etched, either rhythmically or intervallically, as the opening point demonstrates with particular clarity.

Because of this melismatic style, a more casual relationship exists between word and tone than one is apt to encounter in the madrigals of Monte's more scrupulous contemporaries. While Zarlinian principles of text underlay are never blatantly violated, Monte seems not to have given much thought to the refinements of declamation. Syllables are attached to portions of melismas with little attention to their relative stress in the word (see, for example, *tempo* in the Alto, mm. 3-4, and *e'l* in the Tenore, mm. 7-8). As a result of such passages as these, the text is not forcefully projected. Monte's contemporaries, particularly Rore, Willaert, and Wert, tend to devote more attention to proper declamation.

The melodic shapes in *Zefiro torna* are modally consistent to a remarkable degree. Extramodal excursions are rare, and melodic formulas which unambiguously establish and typify its G Dorian mode predominate.[4] The stereotypical quality of the opening Canto line is immediately evident if seen in the context of other pieces in the same mode. Example 2 gives the opening Canto phrases of two other contemporary madrigals. In each of these excerpts, the melody initially exposes the *re-la* fifth, follows with an expansion of the line upwards to f", and ends with a cadential formula on d". (Bernhardt Meier has shown this to be a typical gesture for this mode.)[5]

Modal consistency in the individual lines results in a harmonic language restricted to the principal triads of the mode. Striking harmonic effects and unusual chordal juxtapositions are entirely absent. There is no chromaticism, and the few cross-relations which appear do not carry expressive weight.

Dissonance treatment is equally unadventurous, and seldom text-expressive. Occasionally, however, the melismatic richness of individual lines creates incidental passing dissonances which are treated quite freely (see, for example, m. 57, in which the Tenore and Quinto clash on beat 2).

The harmonic plan expresses vertically the horizontal consistency in the individual voices already noted. Contemporary theorists stressed the idea that in each polyphonic mode only a few degrees were appropriate for cadences.[6] From their writings, it is apparent that the modal identity of any piece of polyphony is established by its cadences, internal as well as final. The cadence plan in *Zefiro torna* is quite orthodox for its mode, cadences occurring on only three degrees: G, B♭, and D.

Example 2.   Three G Dorian *Exordia*

a.   Rore: The First Book for Five Voices (1542)
      Cantai, mentre ch'i arsi mm. 1-5

b.   Monte: The First Book for Five Voice (1554)
      Zefiro torna mm. 1-7

c.   Annibale Padoano: The First Book for Five Voices (1564)
      Cantai un tempo mm. 1-5

Despite a regular pattern of cadences at the end of each poetic line, Monte carefully avoids emphatic cadences throughout the madrigal, so that the music may flow continuously from the cadence at the end of one poetic line into the music for the next. This kind of continuity had become a universal *desideratum* for most composers by 1550, and is discussed both by Vicentino in his treatise *L'antica musica ridotta alla moderna prattica*[7] (1550), and Zarlino in his *Istitutioni Harmoniche*[8] (1558). Zarlino discusses the *cadenza fuggita* (as it was called) at some length, and particularly notes that it is "useful when, in the midst of a beautiful passage, a composer feels the need for a cadence but cannot write one because the period of the text does not allow it, and it would not be honest to insert one."[9] The enjambments in the first tercet of *Zefiro torna* present just such a situation, and compel Monte to avoid strong cadences at the ends of lines 9 and 10 (see the *seconda parte*, m. 68 and mm. 73-74). The rhythmic and harmonic fluidity in Monte's setting of these lines admirably matches the subtle flow of Petrarch's verse. This passage gives early evidence of the care with which Monte treats this poetic device throughout his career.

Elsewhere in *Zefiro torna*, the continual application of the *cadenza fuggita* leads to a more bland effect. Monte seems so intent upon maintaining an uninterrupted polyphonic flow that his cadences tend towards a uniformity of gesture and weight. Monte's only method of giving greater weight to a cadence is to preface it with another cadence (see, for example, mm. 12-14). Indeed, he has studied more how to avoid cadences than how to make them, which points up the emphasis placed upon sophistication and refinement of means in the mid-century madrigal.

Zefiro torna, like all the other pieces in this book, is notated in C. Monte uses this, the more traditional mensuration, to set his music in a spacious and gently unfolding tempo. The text is declaimed mostly in minims, and the harmony moves at the same pace, by and large. *Zefiro torna* is entirely without the startling tempo contrasts of the *note nere* madrigal (typically notated in C). Such contrasts do, however, occur in a few other madrigals from the First Book; example 3 is taken from the setting of Lorenzo de' Medici's *Ohime, che belle lagrime*. Here we find two passages with declamation in semiminims.

Fluidity and continuity of harmony, rhythm, texture, and melodic language—these are the characteristic traits of *Zefiro torna*. On the whole, it impresses one as a gently unfolding polyphonic conception, with few striking moments. Text-expression is restrained; the meaning of single words, whether for affective or pictorial purposes, is seldom underscored. While Monte's purely melodic gifts are already highly developed in this book, a sense of variety and contrast is not so strongly evident. In *Zefiro torna*, this is a serious handicap: Monte's setting does not capture the violent contrast between the quatrains and the tercets, the sonnet's salient feature. The *prima* and *seconda parte* are expressive enough, but too similar in style to mark out the bold division in the poem.

Example 3.   Monte: The First Book for Five Voices (1554)

a.   *Ohime, che belle lagrime* mm. 19-22

b.   Ibid. mm. 59-61

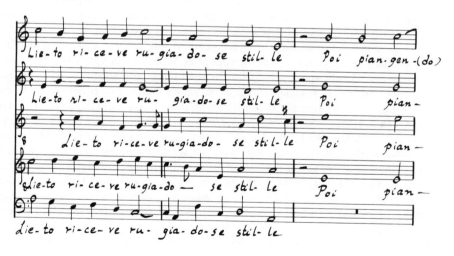

"Monte begins with great animation, freely and colorfully; Naples and Rome seem to have made him articulate."[10] So does Einstein characterize this first book. The reference to Rome and Naples is rather vague, however. He implies that these centers have influenced Monte's madrigalian style, but nowhere does he propose a specific composer in either city who might have directly influenced that style. The question is still an open one, as Othmar Wessely's comments in his preface to the new edition of this book reveal: "Suspected influences from Cipriano de Rore and Roman or Neapolitan masters on De Monte's early madrigals (till about 1570) still have to be proved."[11] Both these scholars' unwillingness to place the book in a more precise stylistic milieu reflects a real problem: these madrigals do not speak for any obvious stylistic allegiances, at least from the sphere of the Italian madrigal. The music is elegant and controlled enough to suggest that Monte has struck a note independent of the most obvious influences. What previous writers have not stressed sufficiently, however, is that the style set forth in the First Book is on the whole conservative for 1554, rather than modern. All the elements in *Zefiro torna*—the full and continuous texture, the absence of colorful harmonies and affective dissonance, the ¢ mensuration, and the lack of tempo contrasts—are retrospective ones for the mid-1550s. A comparison of this book with two books Orlando di Lasso and Giaches Wert published in the same decade will make evident the remarkable contrast between their more progressive styles and Monte's less adventurous one.

Orlando di Lasso, more than ten years Monte's junior, published his First Book for Five Voices in 1555, the year after Monte's.[12] Stylistically, these two books are worlds apart, which can be seen if we enumerate the outstanding features of Lasso's style. First, it is much more declamatory, and less melismatic, than Monte's. Second, though all of Lasso's madrigals are notated in ¢ (as are Monte's), there is a greater variety of tempo in Lasso's pieces, as example 4A shows. Third, Lasso relies to a greater degree than Monte on harmonically conceived writing, some of it quite colorful (see example 4B). Fourth, Lasso makes some use of linear chromatic writing (example 4C). Lastly, in his urge to express the text as vividly as possible, Lasso uses other "modern" techniques: unusual dissonance treatment (example 4D) and unusual melodic shapes (example 4E). All these features are absent from Monte's book, or present only in muted forms.

Three years later, in 1558, Wert published his First Book for Five Voices.[13] It contrasts strikingly both with Monte's and with Lasso's. The impression here is even more homophonic than in Lasso. Wert's most characteristic style can be seen in the five-part *canzone, Qual di notte talor chiara facella*,[14] to say nothing of the *dialogo a otto, Ch'io scriva di costei*.[15] In page after page, the music is overwhelmingly homophonic, with only brief melismas in the uppermost voice to give the music some variety. Already in this first book, Wert reveals a

Example 4.   Lasso: The First Book for Five Voices (1555)

a.   *Con lei fuss'io* mm. 1-3

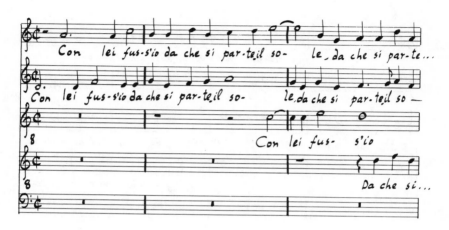

b.   *Cantai, hor piango* mm. 1-6

Ex. 4 (cont.)

c. *S'io talhor muovo gli occhi* mm. 1-4

d. *Fiera stella* mm. 1-3   e. *Solo e pensoso* mm. 1-4

tendency (which becomes more pronounced in later ones) to capture the accents of his texts with remarkable fidelity. As with Lasso's first book, Wert's reliance on homophony brings with it a greater awareness than Monte shows of purely harmonic possibilities. Wert's setting of della Casa's *O Sonno* (composed in emulation of Rore's setting) explores both expressive extramodal harmonies[16] and unusual dissonance treatment.[17]

These two books of Lasso and Wert are among those publications of the 1550s which proclaim in various ways a stylistic indebtedness to Willaert and Rore. To judge from Monte's First Book, he was either unaware of Rore's accomplishments, or chose resolutely to ignore them. The former supposition seems much more likely, particularly if these pieces were composed earlier than 1554, as they may well have been. In any case, the early evidence of a conservative tendency, which the First Book demonstrates, is typical of Monte's approach to his art throughout a lengthy career. Though his music will follow a unique path of growth and change over a nearly fifty-year period, an innate conservatism will always be present, channelling his expression into forms which avoid the daring and the controversial.

The First Book for Four Voices, 1562

Monte dedicated his next book to Colantonio Caracciolo, a Neapolitan nobleman (ca. 1538-1577) and the son of a famous heretic, about whose connections with music or with Monte we know as yet nothing. The book shows a decisive change in style. "All at once," Einstein writes, "... Monte becomes very modern.... He has studied the two books of four-voiced madrigals by Cipriano Rore."[18] The difference between this volume and its predecessor is indeed striking.

The two books of four-voice madrigals by Rore to which Einstein refers appeared in 1550 and 1557.[19] These two publications, and particularly the second one, represent a significant change in Rore's style, away from the relentlessly contrapuntal and often quite melismatic style of the 1540s. In their place comes a declamatory homophony and harmonic color. In such pieces as *O Sonno, Mia benigna fortuna,* and *Crudele acerba,* Rore writes in a style largely stripped of melismatic foliage and imbued with a new rhetorical urgency and harmonic richness.[20]

Monte's First Book is evidently indebted to Rore's four-voice music of the preceding decade, though Monte does not go so far as to quote directly from Rore's music. Indeed, there are no instances in any of Monte's madrigals, from this period or any other, in which he reworks material drawn from another composer's madrigal. Monte's apparent refusal to participate in the stylish game of imitating famous models indicates his independence as an artist, as well as his indifference to the more esoteric aspects of the madrigal tradition.

The high esteem in which Monte evidently held Rore's works expressed itself only indirectly: he composed three parody masses based on Rore's compositions.

The First Book is almost exclusively devoted to Petrarch, and particularly to the sestinas; Monte sets two in their entirety. Rore, too, had turned to the sestinas in his four-voice music, setting the first two stanzas of *Mia benigna fortuna* and all of *A la dolce ombra.*[21] Monte may have turned to Petrarch's sestinas in emulation of Rore's accomplishments.

On a broader level, though, the composition of large-scale madrigal cycles had become the high point of secular vocal music by the 1550s and 1560s. Rore gave considerable prestige to the genre in a publication of 1548, containing his setting of Petrarch's *canzone* to the Virgin.[22] Palestrina lavished his attention on the cyclic madrigal in his remarkable setting of a Petrarchan cento, the *canzon sopra Pace non trovo,* a cycle of fourteen sections. Lasso, Wert, Giovan Nasco, and many others devoted themselves to the cyclic madrigal in these years;[23] Monte's efforts in his First Book should be seen in this context.

The order of the pieces in the first edition was thoroughly jumbled by the printers, and not corrected in the 1586 reprint (see Table 2.2, which retains the order in the original print).[24] A number of irregularities appear. In the middle of *Mia benigna fortuna,* an extraneous setting of Petrarch's sonnet *Mie venture al venir* intrudes. Its placement here is mysterious, though it may reflect the fact that its mode is the same as the surrounding pieces. Similarly, the other sestina *(L'aer gravato)* is also interrupted by an extraneous text, again a Petrarch sonnet. There is no discernible reason for the sonnet's placement here; it is not in the same mode as the sestina cycle, nor does it even use the same combination of clefs. Furthermore, the order of the sestina's stanzas is jumbled, and this disorder can only be put down to editorial incompetence. Clearly, Monte was not present to oversee the printing.

The poetry here is entirely the work of Petrarch, with only two exceptions. An anonymous poem entitled *A le dolenti note* scored *a voci pari,* has the following text:

> A le dolenti note per le valli
> Ecco risponde, e non fu mai di verno
> Arbor di frondi a la stagion più fera
> Spogliato sì, che questa acerba vita
> Non sia men verde, e d'herbe incanti o d'acque;
> Opra non val per adolcirne l'hore;
> Fuggiran presto l'hore e questa vita
> Quasi acque d'alti mont'in basse valli,
> Il verno e seco anchor mia doglia fera.

> (To my sorrowful notes in the valleys, [only] an
> Echo responds, and there was never in winter a

tree so stripped of its leaves in the fiercest
season as this bitter life of mind is stripped of
its youth, and the enchantments of grass and water.
There is nothing that can sweeten its hours. The
hours and [with them] this life will quickly flee,
like water from high mountains to deep valleys;
winter, and with it still my fierce anguish [will flee].)

The appearance in the last three lines of the words *hore, vita, acque, valli, verno* and *fera*—the end words of the preceding six lines—make it clear that these nine lines form the conclusion of a sestina.

The real textual anomaly in this volume, though, is the following madrigal, which appears without attribution in Girolamo Parabosco's *I Diporti:*[25]

Voi volete ch'io moia,
E mi date dolor si crudo e forte,
Che mi conduce a morte;
Ma per vederne voi cosi contenta
Mentr'io moio, il morir vita diventa
Di che vedend'ohime, dolente voi,
Da questa vita poi
Mi vien tanto martire,
Ch'io pur giung'al morire;
E così mille volte il giorno
Per voi moro, e morend'in vita torno.

(You want me to die, and you give me such cruel
and severe suffering, that I am led to my death.
But to see you so pleased by it, as I die, my
death becomes life. Whence, seeing (alas) that
you are grieved by my revival, there comes to me
such suffering, that I again arrive at my death.
And thus a thousand times a day I die for you,
and dying, return to life.)

The poem was popular with madrigalists, and was set often after mid-century by such figures as Taglia (1555), Rufilo (1561), Lasso (1577), Wert (1581), and Giovanelli (1593). Its appearance here, in the context of Petrarch's exalted poetry, is rather jarring.

Nearly every aspect of musical style in this book has been significantly affected by what must have been Monte's widened musical contacts. Extravagant word-painting, unusual dissonance treatment, splashes of harmonic color, and contrasts of tempo are among his newly acquired techniques. He now distinguishes between madrigals in C *(note nere* madrigals) and those in ₵; this development merits particular attention.

Table 2.2   The Poetic Contents of the First Book of Madrigals for Four
Voices (1562)*

TITLE	POETIC FORM	AUTHOR
1. *Mia benigna*	sestina stanza 1	Petrarch (332)
2. *Crudel acerba*	2	
3. *Ov'è condotto*	3	
4. *Gia mi fu*	4	
5. *Chiaro segno amor*	5	
6. *Fuggito è'l sonno*	6	
7. *Nessun visse*	7	
8. *Morte m'ha morto*	8	
9. *Hor havess'io*	9	
10. *Amor io ho molti*	10	
11. *Mie venturo*	sonnet (first quatrain)	Petrarch (57)
12. *Lasso le neve 2p*	(remaining lines)	
13. *Se sì also pon gir*	sestina stanza 11	Petrarch (332)
14. *O voi che*	sestina stanza 12 and	
sospirate	concluding tercet	
15. *Vive faville*	sonnet (quatrains)	Petrarch (258)
16. *L'alma nudrita 2p*	(tercets)	
17. *Amor che'ncende*	sonnet (quatrains)	Petrarch (182)
18. *Di queste pene 2p*	(tercets)	
19. *Nova angeletta*	Petrarchan madrigal	Petrarch (106)
20. *A le dolente note*	final stanza and	?
	concluding tercets	
	of a sestina	
21. *Quando mi vene*	sonnet (quatrains)	Petrarch (175)
22. *Quel sol che 2p*	(tercets)	

---

*The numbering in this table is dictated by the errors in the
original print.

Table 2.2 (cont.)

TITLE	POETIC FORM	AUTHOR
23. *Voi volete ch'io moia*	madrigal	appears without attribution in Girolamo Parabosco, *I Diporti*, also Parabosco, *Rime diverse*. The *New Vogel* erroneously ascribes it to Guarini.
24. *L'aere gravato*	sestina stanza 1	Petrarch (66)
25. *Più volta gia dal bel*	sonnet (quatrains)	Petrarch (170)
26. *Ond'io non poti 2p*	(tercets)	
27. *Ma lasso a me*	sestina stanza 4	Petrarch (66)
28. *Et io nel cor*	sestina stanza 2	
29. *In picciol tempo*	sestina stanza 3	
30. *Mentre ch'al mar*	sestina stanza 5	
31. *Ben debb'io perdonar*	final stanza and concluding tercet	

The preceding decades of the 1540s and 1550s had seen a sudden flurry of interest in the *note nere* madrigal. On a superficial level, this kind of madrigal was a mere notational and stylistic fad: by the 1560s, the term had largely dropped out of fashion. On a deeper level, though, the practice of writing pieces which consistently use the widest range of note values available and which favor text declamation on the minim, semiminim, and even fusa level, was revolutionary and lasting in its effect.

James Haar has characterized the style of some of the earliest examples of the *note nere* madrigal in the following way:

> *Nasce bella sovente, Troppo scharsa madonna*, and *Quando son più lontano* [three madrigals by Yvo in *Il Primo Libro di Madrigali . . . a Misura di Breve; RISM* 1542[17]] are settings of serious madrigalistic verse. . . . Note values range from occasionally breves, even longs, to chains of *crome* and pairs of *semicrome* . . . the musical atmosphere is one of nervous haste and instability. Even if the tempo for these pieces is not particularly fast, . . . the air of nervousness is still pervasive.[26]

Cipriano da Rore's First Book for Five Voices (1542) embodies the first fully artistic adaptation of the new expressive possibilities of the *note nere* madrigal. The many ways in which Rore's madrigals in this publication differ from *note nere* madrigals of the kind discussed by Haar have been summed up admirably in an article by Don Harrán.[27] Significantly, that "air of nervousness" which Haar finds in the music of Yvo and others is absent in Rore. Extreme juxtapositions of tempo are rare; the text is seldom declaimed in fusas. Yet a piece like *Cantai, mentre ch'i arsi*, the book's opening madrigal, is greatly enriched by the melismatic writing and tempo contrasts typical of the *note nere* manner.[28]

Rore's two influential books of four-voice madrigals (1550 and 1557) are mostly notated in $\mathbb{C}$. Yet they too embody a rapprochement between the two initially opposed mensurations: pieces written in $\mathbb{C}$ favor declamation on the minim level, but also incorporate the changes of tempo associated with the *note nere* madrigal (see, for example, the opening bars of *Mia benigna fortuna* from the Second Book).

It is this more refined version of the *note nere* madrigal that Monte seems to emulate in his First Book. The majority of the pieces here are notated in C, and for the first time in Monte's integral publications we encounter madrigals which continually juxtapose faster and slower tempos. Though Monte's use of C permits him to explore this freer approach to tempo and to text setting, he shows a characteristic restraint as well. Extreme juxtapositions of tempo are rare in the book, and entirely absent from the Petrarch settings, where greater rhythmic activity always coincides with melismatic rather than syllabic text setting. In only one moment in one piece *(A le dolente note)*, does Monte avail himself of the extreme contrasts of tempo possible in the *note nere* madrigal. At the words *fuggiran presto l'hore e questa vita*, the text is suddenly set in fusas, for obvious text-expressive purposes (see example 5).

Example 5.   Monte: The First Book for Four Voices (1562)
    A le dolenti note mm. 18-24

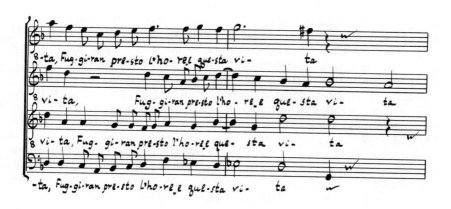

The few pieces notated in $\mathrm{C}\!\!\!\!/$ reveal contradictory traits. *Mie venture al venir* is in a rhythmic style which very nearly duplicates that of the C pieces (see example 6). In this sense, it is a counterpart of Rore's four-voice pieces in $\mathrm{C}\!\!\!\!/$, which display the same variety of tempo. In contrast, Monte's setting of *Et io nel cor* (stanza 2 of *L'aer gravato*) is clearly distinguished in its rhythmic style from the other stanzas, all of which are notated in C. Here, Monte seems to have chosen $\mathrm{C}\!\!\!\!/$ as a means of reflecting the stanza's dominant poetic image: the closing lines refer to stagnant rivers *(stagnanti fiumi)* and slowly falling rain *(Quando cadde dal ciel più lenta pioggia).* Example 7 gives the opening bars of this stanza, whose spacious rhythms are maintained throughout the remainder of the piece.

It did not take Monte until 1562 to effect the remarkable change in rhythmic style which these pieces display. After his return to Italy some time after 1555, he was active in Rome, where a single madrigal, *Dolorosi martir,* appeared in the *Secondo libro delle muse,* an anthology of 1558 (see example 8). (It is the first known Monte madrigal to appear in an anthology.) Its text is an ottava stanza attributed to Luigi Tansillo; Monte's is the first known setting of a poem which became a favorite among composers of the next generation, among them Striggio (1577), Ingegneri (1580), Marenzio (1580), Nanino (1581 and 1586), and Luzzaschi (1594).[29] Here Monte uses for the first time that extreme manner of *note nere* writing already observed in *A le dolente note.* The rhythmic vivacity, startling contrasts of tempo, and the even more characteristic use of syncopated rhythms in all the parts give the music a tense and unstable quality well suited to its extravagant text. Monte's setting may well be the *fons et origo* for this striking set of emulative settings; already in 1558, Monte creates a highly charged atmosphere for this poem. It appears that Striggio, nearly twenty years later, still had Monte's treatment of the words *empi lacci* in mind when he set them, for we find the same nervous syncopations. (Unfortunately, the print containing Striggio's piece does not survive complete.) Striggio's *Dolorosi martir* evidently brought the poem to the attention of the younger generation, leading (eventually) to the extravagances of Marenzio, Nanino, and Luzzaschi.

Mia benigna fortuna, Petrarch's only double sestina, occupies pride of place in this book and deserves special consideration. Monte is the only composer to have set all of this poem; most madrigalists were content to extract one or more of its twelve stanzas and concluding tercet.

Monte's setting does not present a clear picture of modal organization: though the same vocal scoring, mensuration sign, and "key signature" (no flat) occur in all twelve sections, the cycle does not end in the same mode in which it begins. The first half appears to be either in the Aeolian or Phrygian mode, a tonal area abandoned in the second half in favor of the Dorian. A look at the cadences which come at the end of each section shows that a shift away from the A-E center begins in stanza 8 (see example 9). Prior to this, $B\flat$ makes only a

Example 6. Monte: The First Book for Four Voices (1562)
Mie venture al venir (closing measures)

Example 7. Monte: The First Book for Four Voices (1562)
          Et io nel cor mm. 1-6

Example 8.   Monte: *Il secondo libro delle Muse* (1558)
             Dolorosi martir (complete) mm. 1-6

Ex. 8 (cont.) mm. 7-12

Ex. 8 (cont.) mm. 13-18

Ex. 8 (cont.) mm. 19-24

Ex. 8 (cont.) mm. 25-30

Ex. 8 (cont.) mm. 31-36

Example 9.   Monte: The First Book for Four Voices (1562)
            The cadences which conclude the twelve sections of
            Mia benigna fortuna

Stanza 1

Stanza 2

Stanza 3

Stanza 4

Stanza 5

Stanza 6

Stanza 7

Stanza 8

Stanza 9

Stanza 10

Stanza 11

Stanza 12

superficial appearance in a few of the preceding stanzas. Suddenly at the beginning of stanza 8, that note is thrust into the expressive limelight for the words *Morte m'ha morto*. B♭ continues to appear in this stanza, and as example 9 shows, figures prominently in the final cadence. After this stanza, B♭ and even E♭ appear regularly in the remaining stanzas. The sestina ends firmly in the Dorian mode.

It is tempting to ponder what a contemporary theorist like Zarlino or Vicentino would have made of such a tonal plan. Would they have considered its wandering as evidence of a lack of cyclic unity or intent? Or would such an issue have been of interest to the *cinquecento* theorist? Whatever the answer, modern scholarship seems to show that other composers were normally more scrupulous in their approach to sestinas and other multi-stanza poems than Monte is here. Patricia Myers, in her remarks on sestina settings from Roman composers, states:

> Scoring, clef combinations, vocal ranges, mensuration signs, key signatures and modes were usually the same for each movement. The predominance of one mode throughout the cycle is very important, since the choice of mode determined the character of the melodic material as well as the pitches upon which major cadences would fall.[30]

An exception to this comes only in the work of a master like Rore. In his *Vergine* cycle, he begins and ends in the same mode, but achieves variety by writing some of the internal movements in contrasting modes. Evidently such a solution did not occur to Monte, and his setting of the entire poem (an ambitious enterprise) is marred by its lack of large-scale tonal (that is, modal) control.

Monte's growing expressive powers are most apparent in his harmony, which is both more focused within individual phrases and more colorful than anything in the First Book for Five Voices. Still, Monte reserves harmonic color for a special effect, and in the entire sestina there is only one fleeting moment of chromaticism (see example 10). Yet his use of harmonic color can be strikingly expressive: the setting of the words *ben riconoscerà il mutato stile* in stanza 11 (see example 11) moves swiftly through the triads of F, E♭ and B♭ major to a sudden half-cadence on E major. It is surely no coincidence that this passage, the most unusual one harmonically in the entire sestina, sets a text referring to a change in style *(il mutato stile)*. Monte evidently wishes to underline one of the ways in which he has changed his own style.

Monte's dissonance treatment shows a similar growth in freedom and imagination. In order to express his text more vividly, he now begins occasionally to violate the normal rules of dissonance treatment. Thus, in stanza 4, the words *agro stile* (bitter style) prompt Monte to write a striking passage (see example 12). The two-part suspension formula between Tenore and Canto (m. 8) is artfully camouflaged by the other voices, while the Canto's

Example 10. Monte: The First Book for Four Voices (1562)
      Nessun visse giamai mm. 17-22

Example 11. Monte: The First Book for Four Voices (1562)
         Se sì alto pon gir mm. 16-19

Example 12. Monte: The First Book for Four Voices (1562)
   Già mi fu co'l desir mm. 1-10

upward motion to d″ creates an unprepared dissonance with the Basso. The novelty of this passage lies in its combination of these various contrapuntal events to create an unusual and striking harmony, marked in example 12 with an asterisk. Monte's predilection for this kind of sonority (here a 6-4-2 chord) remains with him until the late 1580s, when his style undergoes a significant change.

The variety of tempo in the First Book for Four Voices is achieved by a melodic style itself much richer in invention and variety than we found in the First Book for Five Voices. Melismas, both in semiminims and fusas, enliven the now normally syllabic and declamatory style. In the First Book for Five Voices, the melodic shapes tended to be elegant yet diffuse; now they are less elegant, less diffuse, more unpredictable in direction, and occasionally even angular. This latter quality is evident in the opening imitative point in stanza 4 (example 12), where the e′-d″ seventh is prominent. The Canto line in mm. 8-10 is hardly less striking. This passage and the one cited in example 10 reveal Monte's new and bolder melodic style.

This sestina displays an equally adventurous attitude towards word-painting. We have already seen Monte attempting to convey the sense of such phrases as *agro stile* and *mutato stile* by using an unusual dissonance, or a particularly expressive series of harmonies. Word-painting of a more conventional kind appears elsewhere in the book, as can be seen in the opening bars of *Mentre ch'al mar descenderanno i fiumi,* where Monte paints both the descent of the rivers to the sea, as well as the swelling waters themselves (see example 13).

We find the same fluidity and subtlety of texture here as in the First Book for Five Voices, except that the greater reliance on homophonic declamation in the four-voice book carries with it a tendency towards simpler and more effective contrasts between the homophonic and contrapuntal sections. An innovation of some importance here is Monte's use of silence, used for a punctuative, or rhetorical effect.

In sum, this cycle reveals Monte's awareness of a new range of musical and expressive devices: harmonic color, chromaticism (albeit one brief moment), tempo contrasts, word painting, and unusual dissonance treatment. Monte's sudden acquisition of these techniques is a striking phenomenon in his career; just as striking is the restraint with which he employs them.

In view of Einstein's statement that, with this book, "all at once, Monte becomes very modern,"[31] it is odd that he divided Monte's madrigalian output in the way that he did: "The first [period] extends from his beginnings to his summons to Vienna."[32] Monte's First Book for Five Voices is so strikingly different from this four-voice one that the earlier, conservative one seems to deserve a special category of its own. In any case, we will see that Monte's subsequent madrigals of the 1560s and 1570s are much more attuned to the

Example 13. Monte: The First Book for Four Voices (1562)
   Mentre ch'al mar mm. 1-6

vigorous and rhetorical style of this four-voice book than to that of its predecessor. The seriousness of this book—proclaimed initially by its overwhelming emphasis upon Petrarch's most elevated poetry, and borne out by its insistence upon a vivid yet restrained expression of the text—shows Monte aware of the accomplishments of his finest contemporaries, and fashioning his own unique response.

The First Book for Six Voices

The first edition of the First Book for Six Voices is lost, as we remarked in chapter 1. The reprint of 1569 affords at least a clear *terminus ante quem;* a *terminus post quem* is not so obvious. One of the madrigals in this book, *Il più forte di Roma,* celebrates the ill-fated marriage of Duke Paolo Orsini da Bracciano and Isabella de' Medici, which took place in Rome in 1558. Presumably, Monte wrote this madrigal for the wedding itself. (Einstein hypothesized on the basis of this piece that Monte dedicated the book to Orsini; he later dedicated his Sixth Book for Five Voices of 1575 to Isabella.) This piece, then, and perhaps some others were written in the late 1550s. Five texts from this book[33] appeared in the *Primo Volume delle rime scelte* of 1563; in chapter 1 this anthology (and its second volume, which appeared in the following year) was established as an important poetic source for Monte. On this basis, it seems highly likely that the *terminus post quem* for the composition of these five poems, and thus for the publication of the whole book, is 1563. The lost first edition, then, must have appeared in the years from 1563 to 1569. Einstein's suggestion that the book appeared "around 1564"[34] may have been based on his knowledge of this anthology, though his *Notes* suggest that the date was merely a guess.

    Einstein characterized the book as Roman in content, citing both the presence of madrigals on Roman subjects, as well as Roman musical traits. Besides *Il più forte di Roma,* only one other text has a Roman allusion—the sonnet which follows *Il più forte di Roma.* Here is the full text:

Orni un più bel smiraldo la riviera
Al Tebro altiero; e con il crine adorno
Ballino le sue Ninfe e d'ogni intorno;
Cantino gli augelletti a schiera a schiera;

Goda d'amor la bella madre altiera;
Più lieto Apollo a noi faccia ritorno
E ne rimeni con felice giorno,
La desiata e dolce primavera.

Creschino a gara in sin al Ciel le piante;
E ne' campi di rose e di viole
Scherzino insieme i pargoletti amori;

Hora che'l mio lucente e vivo sole,
Dopo si lunghi affanni e gran dolore,
Mi fa felice sopra ogn'altro amante.

(May a more lovely emerald green adorn the banks of
the proud Tiber; and with their tresses adorned,
may his nymphs dance all around; may the birds sing,
flock upon flock; may the beautiful and proud mother
rejoice with love; may a happier Apollo make his
return to us, and bring with him on that happy day,
the sweet and longed-for springtime. May the plants
grow, as in competition, up to the heavens; and in
the fields of roses and violets, may the cupids
frolic together—now that my shining and living sun,
after such long sufferings and great sorrow, makes
me the happiest of all lovers.)

The mythological reference (line 6), the dancing nymphs and playful cupids (lines 3 and 11), and the picture of man and nature in harmonious accord are all themes which strike a pastoral and hedonistic note which we encounter here for the first time in Monte's publications. It seems likely that this poem celebrates a noble betrothal or marriage.

Petrarch's poetry is entirely absent from this book, and as a result, the verse here has a more worldly, less exalted tone than either of Monte's previous publications (see Table 2.3). In the place of Petrarch come Ariosto, Bembo, and Sannazaro, yet each of these poets is represented with only a single sonnet. Although there are eight sonnets in the book, it is perhaps indicative that the opening number is a madrigal, *In me tanto l'ardore,* by Giovanni Battista Amaltheo. As a result of such choices as these, the literary quality of the poetry here is not as high as in the preceding books. Monte sets, for the example, the following tidbit of *poesia per musica* (the translation is drawn from Thomas Morley's Madrigals to Four Voices of 1594):[35]

Poi che'l mio largo pianto,
Amor, ti piace tanto;
Asciuti mai quest'occhi non vedrai,
Fin che non venga fore
Ohime, per gl'occhi il core.

(Since my tears and lamenting,
False love, breed thy contenting,
Still thus to weep for ever,
These fountains shall persever;
Till my heart grief brimfilled,
Out, alas! be distilled.)

Despite its banality, the poem was extremely popular among madrigalists throughout the century.[36] Monte's musical instincts were far better than his

Table 2.3   The Poetic Contents of the First Book of Madrigals for Six Voices

	TITLE	POETIC FORM	AUTHOR
1.	*In me tanto l'ardore*	madrigal	G. B. Amaltheo
2.	*Dolce vista* *Tu vedi 2p*	sonnet	?
3.	*Poi che'l mio largo* *pianto*	madrigal	?
4.	*Come havrà vita*	madrigal	Luigi Cassola
5.	*Alma se stata* *Altro non si potea 2p*	sonnet	Bembo
6.	*Credendomi di gir*	ottava stanza	?
7.	*Se giamai tempo o loco*	madrigal	?
8.	*Quando muovo le luci* *Di che l'anima 2p*	sonnet	Ariosto
9.	*Se per farmi lasciar* *Dunque quanto 2p*	sonnet	Sannazaro
10.	*Il più forte di Roma*	madrigal celebrating the marriage of Paolo Orsini and Isabella de' Medici, 1558	?
11.	*Orni un più bel* *smiraldo* *Creschino a gara 2p*	sonnet	?
12.	*Se scior si vede*	madrigal	?
13.	*Occhi, se voi* *Così vengo 2p*	sonnet	Amanio
14.	*Occhi sereni* *Parlar soavi 2p*	sonnet	Corfini
15.	*Tra bei Rubini*	madrigal	Amaltheo
16.	*Leggiadre Ninfe* *Il dolce e desiato 2p*	sonnet	?
17.	*La dolce vista*	ottava stanza	?

poetic ones; the text's emptiness merely provoked a contrary response: his music is unexpectedly serious and expressive, as we shall see shortly.

The First Book for Six Voices offers the first glimpse of a quite different side of Monte's musical personality. Here he reveals a lighter touch, expressed by a deftly handled contrapuntal virtuosity, and a new sensitivity to vocal color. As Einstein remarked in his *Notes,* we find *"ein Stil von wunderbarer Fleissigkeit und Freiheit."* An entire book devoted to six-voice madrigals was still rather unusual at this time; prior to around 1560, six-voice madrigals tended to appear at the ends of books mostly devoted to four-voice or five-voice pieces. (Willaert's *Musica nova* exemplifies this kind of arrangement.) In 1560 (or perhaps shortly before), Alessandro Striggio published his First Book for Six Voices, one of the earliest books devoted exclusively to the six-voice genre. Like Monte's, Striggio's was a popular work, and was often reprinted. (Indeed, Gardano brought it out for the last time in 1592—a year he also reprinted Monte's First Book.)

For the first time, Monte explores the textural and coloristic possibilities inherent in the six-voice medium. The one extra voice appears to have been sufficient to incline Monte towards a much more vertical approach to composition. On this matter, Einstein had the following to say:

> Also 'Roman' in this work is the use of the technique of choral division that we note and admire in Palestrina's *Missa Papae Marcelli* and to which we have given the name 'alternazione.' By 'alternazione' we mean the alternating and combining of three-, four-, and five-part half-choirs within the general framework of the six-part texture, a much finer technique than the cruder, echo-like writing for two and more choruses, which is simply more obvious to the eye and ear. After Willaert and Rore, Monte is among the first to make use of this style, and he does so without yielding anything of the artistry and inner animation of his voice-leading.[37]

Taking a closer look at the technical innovations to which Einstein alludes, we observe that the resources of the six-voice madrigal frequently induce Monte to conceive his music in discrete blocks of sound, which can then be rescored, transposed or perhaps more significantly altered. A passage from *La dolce vista* (a madrigal which Monte later used as the basis for a parody Mass)[38] reveals the most straightforward vertical treatment of his material (see example 14). For the words *morendo mille volte il dì* (dying a thousand times a day), Monte devises a brief homophonic setting for four voices; he then repeats that setting at the same tonal level, scored for a higher combination of voices. Finally, he transposes the passage down a fourth, returning to the original four-voice scoring. Though the vertical layout of the chords changes in each restatement, the melodic material (and the chords themselves) remains intact in all the individual lines. One further point: this passage moves at a swifter and more colorful harmonic rhythm than anything yet observed in Monte's music.

Example 14. Monte: The First Book for Six Voices (before 1569)
      La dolce vista mm. 30-35

A freer use of these techniques can be seen in the opening of the *seconda parte* of *Leggiadre ninfe* (see example 15). Here Monte composes a four-voice setting of the words *Il dolce e desiato frutt'ho colto,* and immediately repeats the passage, transposing it down a fourth. What distinguishes this procedure from the one described above is the fact that both the harmonic and melodic content of the first statement are significantly modified in the repetition. The Quinto line (mm. 1-3) is literally transposed down a fourth (see the Basso, mm. 4-6), but the melodic shapes above these two "bass lines" are quite different in each statement. Despite the similarity in shape between the Sesto (mm. 1-4) and the Alto (mm. 4-7), the harmonies are different in two instances (compare m. 3 and m. 6).

Moments later in the *seconda parte,* we observe Monte treating an imitative passage, not a chordal one, as a discrete block, to be reworked and rescored (see example 16). Though the points of imitation are quite fluid in outline, the passage is clearly composed of two sections (mm. 11-13, and mm. 13-15), the first of which begins on F and cadences there, the second of which begins on F and cadences on C. Once again, the lowest voice in each statement reveals the sectional nature of this imitative passage. The changes are many, and most likely designed to camouflage the repetitive nature of the passage.

Finally, the opening of *Poi che'l mio largo pianto* exemplifies the freest treatment of recomposed material (see example 17). As we already noted, Monte's approach to this brief poem is unexpectedly serious, and the music of the opening two lines remarkably drawn out: line 1 is set three times, line 2 twice. In the first two statements of line 1, there is little shared material; the closest similarity can be seen in the Canto line, the end of which ascends from c" to e" in both settings. After setting line 2, Monte returns to line 1, recomposing it for a second time. He now refers to the opening music more closely, though the material is transposed down a fourth, and wanders off in a new harmonic direction. The two settings of line 2 are clearly related, though once again Monte seems intent on blurring the relationship between them. Both phrases move to a cadence on F; the transposition in the Basso (mm. 14-15) of the Tenore phrase (mm. 8-10) merely clouds the fact that the same harmonic goal is achieved in both instances. Out of these contrasting yet interrelated textual and musical repetitions, Monte fashions an unusually long opening section centered around F, and gives the poem an unexpected and almost unwarranted dignity of tone.

All the pieces in this book are written in ₵. This mensuration no longer implies the rhythmic restraint associated with it in the First Book for Five Voices. Rather, its use here corresponds with those pieces in the First Book for Four Voices in which variety of tempo and textual declamation approach at times the *note nere* madrigal. "Monte knows only the *misura comune* but within its limits he often pushes the animation to the point of great vivacity."[39] Einstein goes on to give an example of that great vivacity, drawn from *Leggiadre ninfe.*

Example 15. Monte: The First Book for Six Voices (before 1569)
Leggiadre ninfe: Seconda parte mm. 1-7

Example 16. Monte: The First Book for Six Voices (before 1569)
        Leggiadre ninfe: Seconda parte mm. 11-15

Example 17. Monte: The First Book for Six Voices (before 1569)
Poi che'l mio largo pianto mm. 1-8

Ex. 17 (cont.) mm. 9-16

Indeed, this marvelous piece can serve as an example of all the more uninhibited features which distinguish this book from its two predecessors. (The entire piece is in the *Opera Omnia,* vol. 25.) For the first time, Monte uses a brightly colored Ionian on F mode to portray the exuberant and pastoral tone of the poem (see example 18). In the opening bars a rich contrapuntal fabric enlivens a quite simple and regular harmonic pattern of alternating tonic and dominant chords. The imitative point is fashioned from a light scalar figure filling out a fifth, and is imitated at the unison and octave. Both of these are traits which later became associated with the light, pastoral madrigal of the 1570s and 1580s which Gabrieli initiated and Marenzio brought to perfection.

Finally, *Orni un più bel smeraldo* exemplifies yet another of this book's progressive traits: its gay and uninhibited text gives rise to the first appearance of triple time in any of Monte's published music. The reference to playful cupids evokes a stylized triple-meter dance pattern, which ends with a hemiola (see example 19). With later composers, Marenzio among them, any reference to cupids immediately produces this triple-meter dance, with its requisite cadential hemiola. Monte's first use of triple meter is worth noting, if only because it is rare in his madrigals, and entirely absent from a great many of his books.

Not surprisingly, this publication proved to be more popular than either of its two predecessors. Though the First Book for Five Voices was reprinted at least four times, none of its pieces ever appeared in contemporary anthologies. The First Book for Four Voices was reprinted only once; while two of its pieces were put to rather unusual use in two anthologies,[40] none appeared in its original guise in a madrigal anthology. In marked contrast, the First Book for Six Voices was reprinted as late as 1594, and several of its pieces appeared in a variety of places throughout the remainder of the century, and even into the early 1600s. Eight pieces were copied into the Tarasconi Codex,[41] making this book the best represented of the several Monte publications anthologized there. *Poi che'l mio largo pianto* appeared in the Flemish anthology *Nervi d'Orfeo* (1605); *Leggiadre ninfe* and *Se giamai tempo o loco* were among the spiritual contrafacta in Simone Molinaro's *Fatiche spirituali* of 1610. Finally, *Poi che'l mio largo pianto,* rather like *Dolorosi martir* before it, stands at the head of a long list of settings of this poem; its uncommon excellence and wide dissemination may account at least in part for this typical process.

The popularity which these madrigals achieved reflects their mastery of a lighter, yet technically highly accomplished species of madrigal. Whether that style is actually Roman, as Einstein proposes, could only be determined by a more thorough investigation of Roman music of the period than has yet been undertaken. In any case, a madrigal like *Leggiadre ninfe,* with its deft combination of contrapuntal virtuosity and bright harmonic colors, reveals Monte as an early master of a kind of madrigal which Marenzio elaborated with even greater success and stylishness in his six-voice books of the early 1580s.

Example 18. Monte: The First Book for Six Voices (before 1569)
Leggiadre ninfe mm. 1-6

Example 19. Monte: The First Book for Six Voices (1567)
Orni un piu bel smeraldo: Seconda parte mm. 10-18

Ex. 19 (cont.)

The Second Book for Five Voices

Monte dedicates this book, his last to appear prior to his appointment in Vienna, to Lorenzo Celso da Nepe, of whom nothing is known. In it, Monte consolidates the many technical and expressive discoveries of his first three books. There are no surprising new features, only an increasing mastery of musical rhetoric, and a pleasing variety of style and figure.

The poetic contents show a continuing reliance on the poetry of Petrarch; there are five of his sonnets (see Table 2.4). At the same time, the work of several neo-Petrarchans is given equal prominence: there are two Sannazaro sonnets, and one each by G.B. Amalteo, Bembo, and Fortunio Spira. Only the book's closing sonnet (an anonymous one) strays from the standard Petrarchan themes and images: *Carlo, che'n tenerella acerb'etade* is an elegy on the death of a young child, presumably written for some particular occasion.

Of the six madrigals, one is worth special comment. *Porta sì lieti giorni,* a *partenza* which laments the departure from Rome of an unidentified person, gives evidence of Monte's continuing Roman connection in these years. Einstein construed the poem (which he quotes in its entirety)[43] as "the lament of a Roman or of Rome herself on the departure of a lady, presumably Isabella Medici-Orsini at the time of her separation from her husband."[44] In the absence of any specific reference to Isabella, Einstein's idea remains hypothetical.

Che fai, alma, che pensi, the opening piece, is perhaps the most impressive in the entire book. One of the several pieces from the book included in later anthologies,[45] it was even fitted out with English words by Byrd's patron, Edward Paston.[46] The style here is more thoroughly homophonic than in any previously published madrigal (see example 20). Monte uses this textural clarity to capture the rhetorical immediacy of this Petrarch sonnet (150), in which the poet converses energetically with his own soul:

> Che fai, alma? che pensi? avrem mai pace?
> avrem mai tregua? od avrem guerra eterna?...
>
> (What are you doing, soul? What do you think?
> Shall we ever have peace? Shall we ever have a
> truce? Or shall we have eternal war?)

The poem's urgent tone leads Monte to use this declamatory homophonic style; points of imitation occur rarely, and are used to intensify the expression.

The opening bars, which admirably convey the poet's restlessness, have a purely harmonic *élan* which is new in Monte's work; his use of harmonic color in the First Book for Four Voices, is, in contrast, fleeting, almost timorous. In five bars, the harmony moves from an A-major to a Bb-major triad, through the circle of fifths. Yet the motion through the circle of fifths is not the obvious one

Table 2.4   The Poetic Contents of the Second Book of Madrigals for Five
Voices (1567)

TITLE	POETIC FORM	AUTHOR
1. *Che fai alma* *Tal'hor tace la lingua 2p*	sonnet	Petrarch (150)
2. *Lasso ben so* *So come i dì 2p*	sonnet	Petrarch (101)
3. *Cari scogli* *O solitari colli 2p*	sonnet	Sannazaro
4. *Solingo augello* *Privo in tutto 2p*	sonnet	Bembo
5. *Con lagrime* *In me cresce l'ardor 2p*	sonnet	G. B. Amaltheo
6. *Donna l'ardente fiamma* *Signor la vostra fiamma*	2-stanza canzone	?
7. *Vaga bella soave*	madrigal	?
8. *Perche non cangi*	madrigal	?
9. *Ite rime dolenti* *Sol di lei ragionando 2p*	sonnet	Petrarch (333)
10. *Porta si lieti giorni* *L'istro di tanta gioia 2p*	madrigal	?
11. *Lasso quante fiate* *L'aura soave 2p*	sonnet	Petrarch (109)
12. *Presago del mio male* *E parmi in van 2p*	sonnet	Fortunio Spira
13. *Ite pensier miei vaghi* *Ritornate a me 2p*	sonnet	Sannazaro
14. *Qual'hor la vaga luce*	madrigal	?
15. *Amor natura e la bell'alma* *Così lo spirto 2p*	sonnet	Petrarch (184)
16. *Così havess'io*	madrigal	G. B. Amaltheo
17. *Al partir lagrimoso*	madrigal	?
18. *Carlo che'n tenerella* *Tu in tanto 2p*	sonnet	?

Example 20. Monte: The Second Book for Five Voices (1567)
Che fai, alma, che pensi mm. 1-6

Ex. 20 (cont.) mm. 7-12

of continual root movement by fifth; rather, three times in this opening section, the harmony moves from one major triad to another one a whole step lower. Madrigalists throughout the century called upon this harmonic device to evoke a diversity of images; Monte's use of it here, in a prominent context, is another example of his growing consciousness of harmonic color.

Che fai is in the Dorian mode, and its two parts cadence respectively on A (a half cadence) and D. *Zefiro torna* (from the First Book for Five Voices) and the concluding three stanzas from *Mia benigna fortuna* (from the First Book for Four Voices) are also in this mode, yet a simple comparison of the number of signed accidentals in the original partbooks for these pieces helps show the striking changes in harmonic language which have taken place in Monte's music over these years. *Zefiro torna* (a piece of 101 breves) has 30 signed accidentals, and is filled with many passages of untainted modal writing. The last three stanzas of *Mia benigna fortuna* (97 breves) have 100 signed accidentals, while *Che fai* (70 breves) has 92 signed accidentals. Though statistically close, the latter pieces do not operate harmonically in the same way: set beside *Che fai,* the harmonic color in *Mia benigna fortuna* seems experimental, almost tentative, as though set within a too active and volatile framework to speak effectively. In contrast, the harmonic color of *Che fai* is allowed to resonate more effectively within a simplified, homophonic style.

Che fai gives evidence of an important development in Monte's art: the abandonment of a more traditional linear conception of modality in favor of a more harmonically based modality. A piece like *Zefiro torna* revealed a close adherence to its (transposed Dorian) mode. Its melodies, as we saw, had the standard shapes for this mode, and its cadence plan, seamless counterpoint, and harmonic austerity all combined to achieve its characteristic modal sound. *Che fai,* also in the Dorian mode, is in a style far removed from *Zefiro torna:* its harmonic clarity, expressed by the homophonic treatment, gives to nearly every phrase a focus and direction quite absent in *Zefiro torna.* Rather than perpetually avoiding cadences (as does *Zefiro torna*), *Che fai* cadences regularly, and makes the cadences emphatic by textural, rhythmic, and harmonic means (the third in the chord of resolution is almost invariably raised).

While composers apparently continued to view their music in modal terms, their methods in the second half of the sixteenth century underwent a drastic change. The opening of *Che fai* displays one of these changes: its harmonic exuberance establishes no modal (or tonal) center. Only the cadence at the end of line 2 (m. 7) touches upon D. After this, the mode is regularly confirmed, not by the linear writing typical of *Zefiro torna,* but by a new harmonic focus. Phrase after phrase cadences clearly on a D major triad, or on the other permissible cadence degrees of the mode, F and A.

On the one hand, then, harmonic color can serve to undermine the modal identity of a composition. On the other, it can bring that modal identity into sharp focus in an entirely new way by ignoring the more traditional demand for linear modal consistency, but continuing to touch upon the proper cadential degrees of the mode, asserting it by purely harmonic means.

The Second Book thus embodies a (perhaps only subconscious) reformulation of Monte's modal practice. For the remainder of his career, he is loyal to this more harmonically conceived modality, which hovers between the extremes of tonal clarity and tonal obscurity.

The closing piece in this book, *Carlo, che'n tenerella,*[47] allows us to return to the difficult question of stylistic influence. In an attempt to give a precise example of Monte's indebtedness to Rore, Einstein wrote:

> Yet in this very book he again betrays his direct dependence upon Rore. At the end of the print there is a dirge on the death of a certain Carlo, evidently the little son of a patron.... It is modelled on one of Rore's madrigals, *Tu piangi e quella:* it shows precisely the same poetic motif, the same use of dark low voices, and the same unusual combination of clefs—two altos, tenor, and two basses.[48]

Yet this example of Monte's dependence upon Rore is not as clear as Einstein suggests. It may be instructive to compare the two texts (both are anonymous):

Carlo, ch'en tenerella acerb'etade
Lassand'in terra il fral corporeo velo
Candido spirto sei volato al cielo
Ove godi l'eterna alta bontade

Prega il gran padre in ciel c'habbi pietade
Di noi che sian rimasi al caldo e gielo
Acciò di sant'amor pieni e di zelo
Trovian di gire ove tu sei le strade

Tu intanto nel celeste almo soggiorno
Puro angeletto mira il gran motore
Le stelle erranti e l'uno e l'altro polo

Lieto, felice, aventuroso giorno
Fù alhora il tuo, o pargoletto amore
Quando con l'ali al ciel t'alzasti a volo.

(Carlo, you who at a tender [yet] bitter age,
leaving your frail bodily form on earth, flew as
a pure spirit to heaven, where you enjoy the
eternal, high benevolence, ask the Great Father
in heaven to have pity on us who have remained in
the heat and the cold, so that filled with holy
love and with zeal, we might find a way to where
you are. You, pure angel, meanwhile, in you
heavenly and beloved resting place, regard the
celestial motions, the wandering stars, and the

one and the other Pole. A happy and joyful day
it was then for you, Cupid of Love, when you
raised yourself heavenward in flight.)

Rore's text:

Tu piangi, e quella per chi fai tal pianto
Ne ride, e ride'l ciel che l'ha raccolta
Fra l'alme elette libera e disciolta
Dal fral caduco e corruptibil manto

Lei tutta intenta al lume divo e santo
Dolc'harmonia per ogni parte ascolta
Poi volgendosi a se si dice: "O stolta,
Perchè se'in terra dimorata tanto?"

E quando gli occhi suoi qua giù declina
Vedendo la pregion d'ond'è partita
Si duol di tua misera e trista sorte

E'l viver nostr'è un fior colta da spina
Però piange la tua, non la sua morte
Che morte è quella che si chiama vita.

(You cry, and the one for whom you are crying
smiles. And the heavens smile, who have taken
her to them, free amongst the chosen souls and
released from her frail, ephemeral, and cor-
ruptible mantle. She, entirely intent upon the
divine and holy light, listens to sweet harmony
on all sides, then turns to herself, and says:
"Thou fool! Why did you stay so long on earth?"
And when she looks down here, seeing the prison
she has left, she laments your miserable and sad
fate. Our life is a flower plucked from the
branch; weep, therefore, for your death, not for
hers, for what is called life is but death.)

Both are laments of a kind, and therefore share a certain similarity in tone and diction. Yet there are no firm correspondences in poetic imagery. More importantly, the musical correspondences are purely conventional: both pieces are in the Phrygian mode; both have a low scoring. The Phrygian mode had long been associated with mournful texts and with a lower tessitura; there is little justification for offering Rore's *Tu piangi* as the inspiration for Monte's choice of mode and scoring here. In fact, the two pieces are quite different: Rore's, written in C, is for the most part contrapuntal, while Monte's, written in ₵, is homophonic. There is no common thematic material, and in a self-conscious age in which an artist like Monte could have subtly rendered homage to Rore had he wished, this is persuasive evidence of his independence from Rore in this instance.

We can end by considering a broader question. Why was Monte chosen for the post in Vienna, one of the most prestigious positions in all of Europe? There is no evidence that he served in any church in Italy or elsewhere as *maestro di capella*. And prior to 1568, we know of only one sacred publication, a single contribution to a motet collection of 1564, published in the North.[49] (Nor are there apparently any lost sacred publications before 1568; the first book of motets, and the first book of masses are still in the future.) In this context, it is not difficult to see why Palestrina was first considered for the position: in 1568, he had already been *maestro di capella* in two Roman churches, and as early as 1554 had published a book of masses.

Perhaps Maximilian's agents in Rome turned to Monte in part for his fine personal qualities; in a post-Tridentine atmosphere of reform these may have counted for a great deal. Monte's connections in Rome with powerful patrons, among them Cardinal Flavio Orsini, would have helped as well. Taking these factors into account, we must still conclude that Monte was chosen not for any prior accomplishments in sacred music, but for the mastery he displayed in his first four secular works, which laid the foundation for his European-wide prestige. That Monte in Vienna lived up to what was expected of him is evident from his sudden burst of creative energy following his appointment. His sacred output increased enormously, and so did his secular work.

3

Monte in Vienna: The First Ten Years

Che nella mia fanciullezza mio padre b. m. mi mandò alla scola di musica, et osservai ch'erano in uso le composizioni dell' Archadelt, di Orlando Lassus, dello Striggio, Cipriano de Rores, e di Filippo di Monte, stimate per le migliori di quei tempi, como in effetto erano...

Vincenzo Giustiniani, in his *Discorso sopra la musica* (1628?)

Introduction

In the years following Monte's appointment at the Imperial Court, his creative energies greatly increased, as he proudly noted in his letter of 1574 to Emperor Maximilian: "... in six years, I have written twenty masses, an infinite number of motets, madrigals, and French chansons."[1] After ten years in Vienna, he could look back on the following madrigal publications:

The Second Book for Four Voices	1569
The Second Book for Six Voices	1569
The Third Book for Five Voices	1570
The Fourth Book for Five Voices	1571
The Fifth Book for Five Voices	1574
The Sixth Book for Five Voices	1575
The Third Book for Six Voices	1576
The Third Book for Four Voices	after 1569, before 1576
The Seventh Book for Five Voices	1578

These books make no stylistic break with his Italian past; rather, they continue to intensify and elaborate the serious idiom he had cultivated in his first four books. Gradually, however, his style evolves into a quite personal one, which fully arrives with the Seventh Book for Five Voices. In achieving this personal style, Monte turns away to some extent from the manner of his Italian years: his harmony becomes less, rather than more, colorful, his textures more contrapuntal, his melodic lines increasingly intricate. The Seventh Book, dedicated to Emperor Rudolf, embodies all these trends. Its prevailing tone, too, is melancholy, and this mood dominates much of Monte's best music of the late 1570s and early 1580s.

Because of its intrinsic interest and its importance in Monte's development, the Seventh Book and its quite unusual poetry will be discussed in some detail at the end of this chapter. Before turning to this book, we will consider Monte's music from earlier in the decade under two headings, the first devised to give an idea of his earliest essays in the lighter canzonetta-madrigal, the second a consideration of his masterful settings from these years of Petrarch's verse.

The Lighter Style

We begin with a piece which occupies a special category. In his Second Book for Four Voices (1569), Monte included *La dolce vista,* a madrigal cycle which had first appeared in *Gli amorosi concenti,* an anthology of the preceding year. It is doubtless a product of his Italian years. Though not so designated, it is one of Monte's few essays in the *madrigale arioso,* a genre which became popular in the 1550s.[2] Stefano Rossetti contributed to the form in his First Book for Four Voices (1560), in which several pieces are specifically called *madrigali ariosi.*[3] Giaches Wert's First Book for Four Voices of the following year contains a number of pieces for which the term is appropriate.[4] The salient features of the genre are a consistently transparent homophonic texture, bright harmonic colors, and a melodic style focused on a tuneful Canto. Monte's cycle exhibits all these features, and is the most colorful piece from moment to moment that he ever wrote (see example 21, which gives the first two stanzas).

This example reveals a skillful blend of serious and light elements. There are at least three features drawn from the lighter forms: the sprightly declamatory rhythms, set out in clear homophonic blocks (mm. 1-5); the brief, single-note up-beat figure[5] (here used to launch an imitative passage, mm. 22ff.); and, most characteristically, the triple-time patterns embedded in the prevailing duple meter (mm. 36ff.). As a counterbalance to these elements, Monte turns to the serious tradition for other resources: extraordinary harmonic color; chromatic inflections (Canto, m. 5; Alto, mm. 34-35; Tenore, m. 41); and affective dissonance (m. 10; m. 16). The combination of these elements, drawn from a stylistic spectrum extending from the villanella to the serious madrigal, gives this piece an unusual expressive cast. Neither flippant nor deeply expressive, it delicately hovers between thse extremes, with a result now ironic, now engaged.

La dolce vista is unique in Monte's output; it may have been composed especially in the *madrigale arioso* manner as the result of a specific commission (perhaps from the editor of *Gli amorosi concenti,* which also contains cycles by Rossetti and Gabrieli).

Example 21.   Monte: The Second Book for Four Voices (1569)
   La dolce vista (Stanza prima and *stanza seconda)* mm.
   1-6

Ex. 21 (cont.) mm. 7-12

Ex. 21 (cont.) mm. 13-18

-gia-drie ga-i Cha-ver so-lea d'a-mo- re Por- to de-sii nel

-gia-drie ga-i Cha-ver so-lea d'a-mo- re Por- to de-sii nel

-gia-drie ga-i Cha-ver so-lea d'a-mo- re Por- to de- sii nel

-gia-drie ga-i C'ha-ver so-lea d'a-mo- re Por- to de- sii nel

co- re Che son na- ti di mor- te

co- re Che son na- ti di mor- te

co- re Che son na- ti di mor- te Per la par-

co- re Che son na- ti di mor- te Per

Ex. 21 (cont.) mm. 19-24

Ex. 21 (cont.) mm. 25-29

Stanza seconda

Ex. 21 (cont.) mm. 30-35

Non mi fe-ri- sti si ch'io fus-si mor- to, ch'io

Non mi fe-ri- sti si ch'io fus- si mor- to, ch'io

Non mi fe-ri- sti si ch'io fus-si mor- - to ch'io

mi fe-ri- sti si ch'io fus- si mor- to ch'io

fus- si mor- to Per-che non di-par-ti-sti da me las-

fus- si mor- to Per-che non di-par-ti- sti da me las-

fus-si mor- to Per-che non di-par-ti-sti da me las-

fus- si mor- to Per-che non di-par-ti-sti da me las-

Ex. 21 (cont.) mm. 36-41

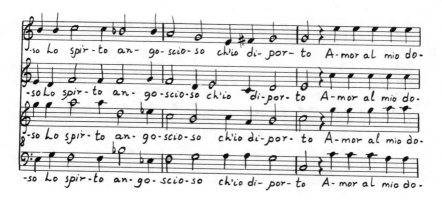

-so Lo spir-to an- go-scio-so ch'io di-por- to A-mor al mio do-

-so Lo spir-to an- go-scio-so ch'io di-por- to A-mor al mio do-

-so Lo spir-to an- go-scio-so ch'io di-por- to A-mor al mio do-

-so Lo spir-to an-go-scio-so ch'io di- por- to A-mor al mio do-

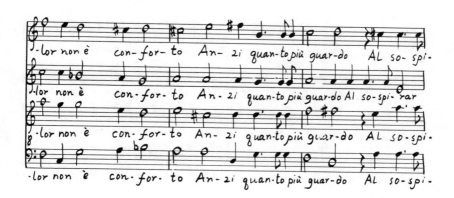

-lor non è con-for- to An- zi quan-to più guar-do AL so-spi-

-lor non è con-for- to An- zi quan-to più guar-do AL so-spi- rar

-lor non è con-for- to An- zi quan-to più guar-do AL so-spi-

-lor non è con-for- to An-zi quan-to più guar-do AL so-spi-

Ex. 21 (cont.) mm. 42-47

Ex. 21 (cont.) mm. 48-49

Oddly, Monte abandoned this colorful style soon after his move to Vienna. Odd, because it is hard to explain why, once acquired, a rich harmonic language sould not remain with a composer for the remainder of his career, as one resource among many to turn to. Yet Monte's renunciation of colorful harmony is not without parallel in other composers' works. Lasso, for example, apparently never returned to the highly chromatic and colorful manner of some of the motets and madrigals he composed in Italy in the 1550s.

There is no evidence that *La dolce vista* was ever reprinted in a later anthology. The situation is quite different with *Veramente in amore,* the first piece in the Fifth Book for Five Voices (1574). Einstein called it "a lachrymose affair that is actually beneath his *niveau* . . . and is copied from older models," stating further that it achieved "a 'world success,' what we should call a 'hit'."[6] This claim is a bit extreme; *Veramente in amore* was no more popular than several other Monte madrigals, which like it were included in later anthologies and instrumental intabulations.[7] It is not clear why Einstein singled this one out; subsequent writers have followed him blindly, one of whom refers to *Veramente in amore* as Monte's "greatest success in his own day."[8]

The poem, ascribed to Bembo in the *New Vogel,* is a quite undistinguished epigrammatic madrigal:

Veramente in amore
Si prova ogni dolore;
Ma vie più ch'altr'avanza
Goder sol una volt'e perder poi
Tutti i diletti suoi,
E viver sempre mai fuor di speranza.

(Truly, in love one experiences every pain. But greater than any other is the pain of enjoying only once and then losing all of love's delights, and living ever after with no hope [of ever enjoying them again].)

Monte responds to it with one of the shortest madrigals he had yet composed, a mere twenty breves (see example 22). The music is almost entirely homophonic, and moves along rapidly in semiminims. (Indeed, Monte moves through the poem so quickly that he is constrained to repeat lines 3-5 (mm. 8-10 are transposed, rescored, and reworked in mm. 12-15) before setting the final one.

The madrigal is pleasant, if rather slight. Its significance lies in its forward-looking aspects: the high scoring, sprightly declamatory rhythms, and the frequent and clear-cut cadences are all elements to which Monte turned again in 1586, when he came to write a whole book given over almost entirely to the canzonetta-madrigal. To be sure, the products of 1586 are rather more subtle than *Veramente in amore.* Yet they derive ultimately from Monte's formulation of the canzonetta-madrigal first adumbrated here.

Example 22. Monte: The Fifth Book for Five Voices (1574)
   Veramente in amore (complete) mm. 1-6

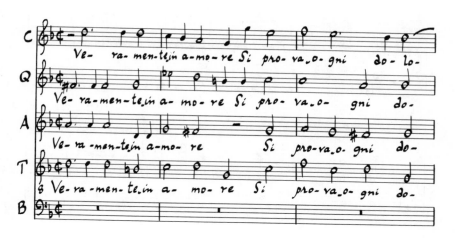

Ex. 22 (cont.) mm. 7-12

Ex. 22 (cont.) mm. 13-18

Ex. 22 (cont.) mm. 19-20

In 1577, Monte contributed two madrigals, *Caro pegno del cielo* and *Amor m'accende* to the Italian anthology *Il primo fiore della ghirlanda musicale.* Both are exercises in the canzonetta-madrigal, and use a variety of techniques culled from the lighter forms. Monte chose to include both pieces in his Eighth Book for Five Voices (1580).

Caro pegno del cielo sets an undistinguished poem in praise of a lady:

Caro pegno del cielo,
Donna del chiaro lambro, honore e gloria,
Ond'ha de cori invitti amor vittoria;
Il tuo sguardo sereno
Ch'al sol fa invidia e scorno
Apre sovente a mezza notte il giorno.
E nel candido tuo leggiadro seno,
Che spira Arabi odori,
Scherzan le gratie e i pargoletti amori.

(Dearest pledge from heaven: honor and glory to you, Lady from the clear Lambro, whence you have victory over the invincible choirs. Your serene glance, which brings envy and shame to the sun, often brings the day at midnight. And on your white and comely breast, which exhales Arabian odors, the graces and cupids frolic.)

The piece announces at the outset its hybrid style: the short, finely chiselled, triple-time motive for line 1 suggests the lighter style, while the imitative texture in which it is embedded conjures up a more madrigalian style (see example 23). Lines 1-6 are set quickly in this style (mm. 1-19); the remaining three lines are set more expansively in the following twenty-three measures (mm. 19-42), where the music is repeated once (mm. 28-37) and given a brief coda (mm. 37-41). For line 7, Monte turns to the syncopated homophony and clear Romanesca-like harmonies of the villanella and canzonetta.[9] The graces and cupids of line 9 call forth a triple-time dance with its obligatory cadential hemiola, now a mere cliché.[10] These undiluted references to the lighter forms are particularly noteworthy in view of their extreme rarity in Monte's music of this decade: there is not one other moment of (notated) triple meter in any of the five-voice books from these years, nor anything quite as blunt as the setting of line 7.

Amor m'accende reflects a similar attempt to master a lighter vein. The poem itself is a fashionable madrigal on a standard theme of love and its flames.

Amor m'accende et io d'ardir m'appago,
Poi che la donna mia
Si scalda al foco mio, si dolc'e pia.
Ella si dolc'e pia si scalda e'nfiamma,
Ch'io non pur mi contento
Di sfavillar per lei, ma dolmi ch'io

Non possa esca venir di magior fiamma,
Sì m'è dolc'il tormento
Arder vedendo lei d'egual desio.
Ma poi che'l foco mio
Sì mi giova, e non puot'esser maggiore
Prego che'l serbi amore
Tal ch'egli eterno sia;
Ne mai sdegno lo turbi o gelosia.

(Love, inflames me, and I am happy to burn, since my lady, so sweet and compassionate, is inflamed by my fire. She, so sweet and compassionate, is excited and inflamed, so that I am not content in sparkling for her, but I lament that I cannot become the spark of a greater flame, so sweet is the torment of seeing her burn with an equal desire. But since my fire is of such use to me, and cannot become greater, I pray that Love may keep it so that it may be eternal, and that disdain and jealousy may never disturb it.)

This poem, with its trivialized sexual imagery and poverty of invention, is (alas) a harbinger of a kind of poem which Monte and his contemporaries set with increasing frequency after 1580.

Amor m'accende shows Monte working with a technique which was to become an indispensable one for the madrigalist of the 1580s. It is a technique of canonic or pseudo-canonic imitation at the unison between the two highest voices (see example 24, which gives the first part). (Typically, these two voices have the same scoring and range.) In *Amor m'accende,* nearly every phrase is imitated at the unison in the two upper voices, a procedure which gives rise to a certain harmonic regularity in the lower voices, which tend to move in simple patterns as a support for the pseudo-canonic writing in the upper voices. Occasionally, the lower voices proffer their own mildly contrasting point of imitation, itself typically imitated at the unison or octave. The bright Mixolydian mode contributes greatly to the clarity and appeal of Monte's setting, as does his occasional use of homophony. Again, this piece is noteworthy because it is Monte's only piece published in the 1570s to use this pseudo-canonic technique so thoroughly, indeed singlemindedly.

Both *Caro pegno del cielo* and *Amor m'accende* are pleasing compositions which reflect Monte's continuing awareness and cultivation of a lighter style. Yet they cannot stand comparison with the canzonetta-madrigals of Giovanni Maria Nanino and Andrea Gabrieli published in these years,[11] not to say those of Luca Marenzio, soon to make his debut as a composer. Before 1580, Monte's most successful style remains the serious one, which he had cultivated so assiduously over the years. That style is dominated by Petrarch's lyric poems, and their contemporary imitations. We can now turn to Monte's achievements in this realm.

Example 23. Monte: *Il primo fiore della ghirlanda musicale* (1577)
            Caro pegno del cielo (complete) mm. 1-6

Ex. 23 (cont.) mm. 7-12

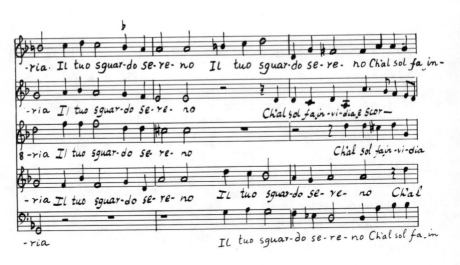

Ex. 23 (cont.) mm. 13-18

Ex. 23 (cont.) mm. 19-24

Ex. 23 (cont.) mm. 25-30

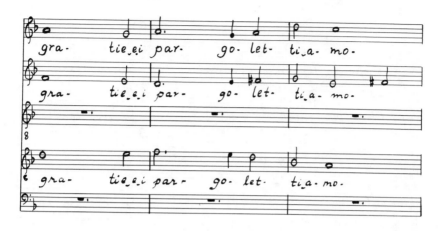

Ex. 23 (cont.) mm. 31-36

Ex. 23 (cont.) mm. 37-41

Example 24. Monte: *Il primo fiore della ghirlanda musicale* (1577)
                    Amor m'accende mm. 1-6

Ex. 24 (cont.) mm. 7-12

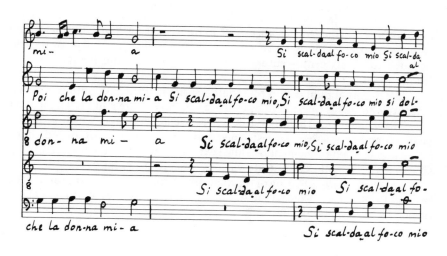

The Petrarchan Achievement

The years from 1569 to 1576 were Monte's most active ones as a composer of Petrarch's verse; indeed, his corpus of Petrarch settings outstrips that of any other composer. This is so, even though he gradually turned away from Petrarch to his sixteenth-century imitators, Sannazaro and Bembo foremost among them.

The eventual publication of Monte's entire madrigalian output may well reveal this to be his finest period, for here we find mature and masterful music allied with poetry of the highest order. He achieves a style which is at once vigorous and expressive, yet restrained and balanced—in short, one of almost classical poise and refinement. A single example each from the four-, five-, and six-voice books will demonstrate various aspects of his mastery.

Poi che'l camin, a setting of the quatrains from sonnet 130, appeared in the Second Book for Six Voices (1569). Its sombre text is typical of Monte's choice of poems for that book:

Poi che'l camin m'è chiuso di mercede,
Per disperata via son dilungato
Dagli occhi ov'era i non so per qual fato
Riposto il guidardon d'ogni mia fede.

Pasco il cor di sospir ch'altro non chiede
E di lagrime vivo, a pianger nato;
Ne di ciò duolmi, perchè in tale stato
È dolce il pianto più ch'altri non crede.

(Since the road to mercy is closed to me, on a despairing way I have come far from the eyes where had been placed (I know not by what fate) the guerdon of all my faithfulness. I feed my heart, which asks for nothing else, with sighs, and I live on tears, born to weep; nor do I suffer for that, for in such a state weeping is sweeter than anyone would believe.)

In its abundant use of homophony, clear textures, rhythmic simplicity, and subtle harmonic colors, Monte's setting reflects some of the techniques he had explored in his First Book for Six Voices, and further refined in his Second Book for Five Voices (see example 25). What is distinctive about this piece, though, is the way that it gradually moves from a fairly simple approach to a much more complex one. Thus, in the setting of line 1 (mm. 1-8), the neutral chanson rhythm, the static harmonic motion (the phrase begins and ends on the chord of E major), and the untransposed repetition of the phrase all combine to give an impression of numbness or alienation which Petrarch's first line expresses.

In the remainder of the piece, the music gradually escapes from this tone, becoming more and more overtly expressive with each successive line of poetry.

Example 25. Monte: The Second Book for Six Voices (1569)
  Poi che'l camin (complete) mm. 1-6

Ex. 25 (cont.) mm. 7-12

Ex. 25 (cont.) mm. 13-18

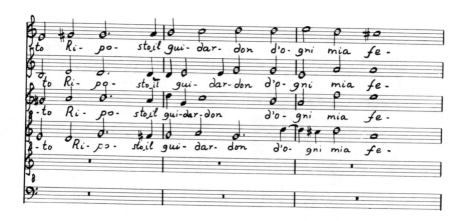

Ex. 25 (cont.) mm. 19-24

Ex. 25 (cont.) mm. 25-30

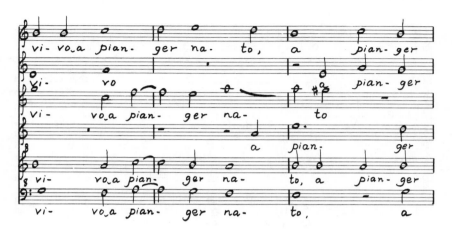

Ex. 25 (cont.) mm. 31-36

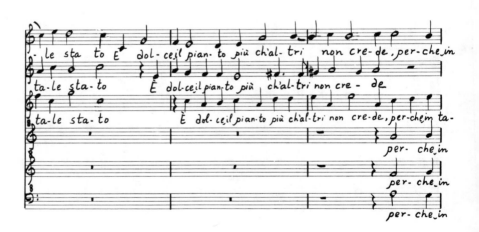

Ex. 25 (cont.) mm. 37-42

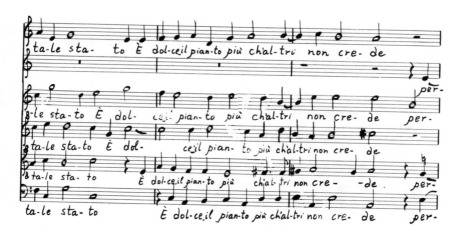

Ex. 25 (cont.) mm. 43-44

The sudden turn to a C major triad in an open (and "new") vocal scoring, followed immediately by a suspension between Canto and Bass (m. 9) give the first indication of this more expressive style. While the harmonic rhythm continues (for the most part) at the same steady pace, the harmonies themselves become steadily richer. Notice how the setting of line 5 (mm. 19-23), with its transposed repetition of *ch'altro non crede,* is followed in line 6 by harmonies which move quickly in a different direction. The Phrygian half-cadence on A major (m. 23), which might have implied a motion towards D in the next phrase, is succeeded instead by a progression in which the triads of E minor and B major are heard for the first time in the piece. Thus, by controlling and juxtaposing his harmonic material in unexpected ways, Monte enhances the expressivity of his chosen chords: the B major triad (m. 24) sounds particularly fresh and unusual. (It is not heard again.)

The second half of line 6 is set in the expressive style of line 2 (note an analogous 7-6 suspension in m. 26), yet cadences in a new harmonic area, G major. Monte now sets the first half of line 7 *(né di ciò duolmi)* to slow, expressive harmonies (as in line 2 and 6) but joins the second half *(perchè in tale stato)* with line 8, setting both in a quicker tempo and faster harmonic rhythm, which he has saved for the ending. Suddenly the music takes flight, abandoning the sombre rhythms which have dominated thus far. The melodic lines are now heavily syncopated, and dissonances appear on the semiminim level. The second setting of the final line (mm. 37-39) is particularly impressive: a string of suspensions and a change of harmony on every semiminim achieve an intensity of expression toward which the madrigal has slowly been building. Finally, in the concluding bars, that tension is released by a return to the slower-moving harmonic style of the opening.

In sum, the success of this piece lies in the ways in which it combines and reconciles a restrained style of writing, which prevails at the beginning, with a more aggressively expressive one, which gains in importance as the piece unfolds.

In the following year, Monte's Third Book for Five Voices appeared; its penultimate number is a setting of *I' piansi, hor canto* (sonnet 230):

> I' piansi, hor canto; che'l celeste lume
> Quel vivo sole a gl'occhi miei non cela,
> Nel qual honesto amor chiaro rivela
> Sua dolce forza, e suo santo costume;
>
> Ond'e suol trar di lagrime tal fiume,
> Per accorciar del mio viver la tela,
> Che non pur ponte, o guad'o remi o vela
> Ma scampar non potemi ale ne piume.
>
> Sì profond'era e di sì larga vena
> Il pianger mio, e si lungi la riva
> Ch'i v'aggiungeva col pensier a pena.

Non laur'o palma ma tranquill'oliva
Pietà mi manda, e'l tempo rasserena,
E'l piant'asciuga, e vol ancor ch'io viva.

(I wept, now I sing; for that living sun does not hide from my eyes her heavenly light, in which virtuous Love clearly reveals his sweet power and his holy ways. Thus he is wont to draw from me such a river of tears to shorten the thread of my life, that wings and feathers could not rescue me, let alone bridge or ford or oars or sail. So deep and from so full a source was my weeping and so distant the shore, that I could hardly reach it even in thought. Pity sends me not laurel, or a palm, but the tranquil olive, and clears the weather, and dries my tears, and wishes me still to live.)

I' piansi is unique to Monte's *œuvre:* it is his only madrigal in the Phrygian mode transposed to D, with a signature of two flats[12] (see example 26). Together with this choice of mode goes a harmonic style of unusual richness: on several occasions, Monte uses A♭, and in one striking passage, D♭.[13] In line 1, the harmony suddenly moves away from the modal center by means of a circle-of-fifths progression, until the triad of D♭ is reached (m. 6). The impulse here is textual: after painting the contrast between weeping and sighing, Monte ventures into the flat region in an attempt to paint the *celeste lume* of Laura's eyes.

I' piansi, though extraordinary in these ways, is not a tentative experiment, but a masterful piece which uses this harmonically enriched vocabulary as part of a serious and weighty style. In contrast with its harmonic exuberance, the piece is rhythmically quite restrained, with only muted contrasts of tempo. Word-painting is similarly restrained.[14] It is in its harmonic plan that Monte's masterful control of detail and love of variety are most evident. Table 3.1 gives the cadence plan for the whole piece, showing (in column 4) the cadential degrees at the end of each poetic line, and (in column 3) the kind of cadence involved. Essentially, Monte had four cadential formulas at his disposal: authentic; plagal; and two varieties of discant cadences, one Phrygian, in which the octave is approached by whole step in the upper voice and by half-step in the lower one, and the other, here called VII⁶-I, in which the octave is appraoached by half-step in the upper voice and by whole-step in the lower one.

A glance at this cadence plan shows that in the *prima parte* Monte is careful to end each poetic line on a different pitch, or to approach the same pitch in different ways. In the *seconda parte,* the only degree which is given more cadential weight than any other is B♭, which in Monte's transposed schema is a standard area of contrast explored in the second half of a Phrygian piece. In the final measures of the *seconda parte,* the cadences come much more frequently, in preparation for the final close.

Nearly every one of these cadences is announced by either a 4-3 suspension (in the authentic cadences) or a 7-6 suspension (in the discant ones). This

Example 26. Monte: The Third Book for Five Voices (1570)
    I' piansi (complete) mm. 1-6

Ex. 26 (cont.) mm. 7-12

Ex. 26 (cont.) mm. 13-18

Ex. 26 (cont.) mm. 19-24

Ex. 26 (cont.) mm. 25-30

Ex. 26 (cont.) mm. 31-36

Ex. 26 (cont.) mm. 37-42

Seconda parte

Ex. 26 (cont.) mm. 43-48

Ex. 26 (cont.) mm. 49-54

Ex. 26 (cont.) mm. 55-60

Ex. 26 (cont.) mm. 61-66

Ex. 26 (cont.) mm. 67-72

Ex. 26 (cont.) m. 73

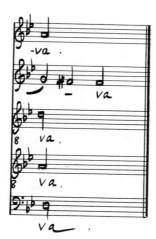

Table 3.1   Cadence Plan of *I' Piansi*

POETIC LINE	END WORD	MEASURE NUMBERS	CADENCE TYPE	BASS MOTION (OR LOWEST VOICE)
1	*lume*	6	Phrygian	Db - C
2	*cela*	11 - 12	Authentic	A - D
3	*rivela*	14 - 15	VII^6 - I	A - G
4	*costume*	20 - 21	Authentic	G - C
5	*fiume*	26 - 27	VII^6 - I; Plagal	F - Eb Eb - Bb
6	*tela*	29 - 30	Authentic	C - F
7	*vela*	34 - 35	VII^6 - I	C - Bb
8	*piume*	38 - 39	Plagal	C - G

Seconda parte

POETIC LINE	END WORD	MEASURE NUMBERS	CADENCE TYPE	BASS MOTION (OR LOWEST VOICE)
9	*vena*	44	Phrygian	Eb - D
10	*riva*	50 - 51	Authentic	F - Bb
11	*pena*	54 - 55	Authentic	F - Bb
12	*oliva*	58	Plagal	D - A
13	*rasserena*	64	Authentic	D - G
14	*viva*	69 70 - 71 72 - 73	Authentic; Authentic; Plagal	D - G D - G G - D

regular pattern of suspension-bearing cadences gives shape to an otherwise seamless polyphony, and keeps before us (in however fluid a fashion) the underlying structure of the poem.

Even as he makes these cadences, his overriding concern is for continuity, forward momentum. This he achieves by rhythmic, textural, and harmonic means. His harmonic means are particularly sophisticated: as soon as a cadence is reached, the music moves off quickly in another direction. For example, the firm cadence on D in m. 12 is followed immediately by a motion in the following phrase to B♭ (there is even a suspension formula which briefly confirms that note), before a further motion to G in m. 15. Over and over again, Monte moves deftly and quickly from one area of his tonal landscape to another, so as to maintain momentum across his cadences.

A few details will show Monte's ability to convey the text's images vividly, yet with restraint. The dissonance treatment, for example, is quite regular throughout, with a few notable exceptions: in m. 16 Monte deftly conjures up the image of *dolce forza* (sweet force) by a sudden increase in the dissonance level as Alto, Quinto and Basso descent in parallel $^6_3$ chords *(dolce)* against two held notes in the Canto and Tenore *(forza)*. A similar passage occurs at the words *di lagrime tal fiume* (of tears such a river) in mm. 23-26.

There is some evidence that the Third Book for Five Voices (from which *I' piansi* is drawn) was composed in Italy, prior to Monte's move to Vienna. The book's dedication was written not by Monte but by Leandro Mira, a minor composer, who dedicated the book to Antonio Molino, the Venetian poet, merchant, and composer.[16] In his dedication, Mira states that "... since these present madrigals by the most excellent musician *maestro* Filippo di Monte have fallen into my hands, and not being able to ignore the demands of many of my gentlemen friends to publish them, I have wished to dedicate them to you...."[17] These comments suggest that Mira may have acquired the music from Monte or some third party prior to Monte's journey northward. Whether composed in Italy or not, a piece like *I' piansi* is redolent of Monte's Italian experience, and its harmonic richness is an element which he gradually removes from his music after his move to Vienna. Yet while pulling back in harmonic areas, Monte's music pushes forward in other areas, as we shall see.

Monte's setting of *Lasso, amor* (sonnet 235) from his Third Book for Four Voices (first edition lost; 1569-1576) reveals other aspects of his serious style of the 1570s. Here is the complete poem:

Lasso, Amor mi trasporta ov'io non voglio,
E ben m'accorgo che'l dever si varca;
Ond'a chi nel mio cor siede monarca
Sono importuno assai più ch'io non soglio.

Ne mai saggio nocchier guardò da scoglio
Nave di merci preciose carca,

Quant'io sempre la debile mia varca
Da le percosse del suo duro orgoglio,

Ma lagrimosa pioggia e fieri venti
D'infiniti sospiri hor l'hanno spinta
Che nel mio mar horribil notte e verno

Ove altrui noie, a se doglie e tormenti
Porta e non altro già da l'onde vinta
Disarmata di vele e di governo.

(Alas, Love carries me off where I do not wish to go, and I see well that we are crossing
beyond what is permitted; thus to that one who is enthroned as queen in my heart I am more
importunate than it is my custom to be. Nor did ever a wise helmsman keep from the rocks a
ship laden with precious merchandise, as I always keep my weak boat from the blows of her
harsh pride, but a tearful rain and fierce winds of infinite sighs have driven it, for in my sea
now there is horrible night and winter, whence it brings annoyance to others and nothing but
pain and torment to itself, already beaten by the waves, bereft of sails and tiller.)

The vibrant imagery here evokes more vigorous word-painting, as well as
a more volatile rhythmic style, than we have observed in the previous Petrarch
settings (see example 27). The first example of word-painting is rather subtle:
Petrarch's image in line 1 of being carried off by Love "where I do not wish to
go" evokes melodic lines which are irregular in shape (see the Alto, mm. 2-7)
and a harmonic plan which cadences on B♭, not the most obvious degree for the
first cadence of a G Dorian composition (see m. 4 and m. 8).

The *prima parte* goes on to repeat its entire second quatrain, in an
interesting process: line 5 (mm. 16-19) is literally repeated (mm. 28-31); line 6
(mm. 19-22) is repeated almost literally (the full cadence of m. 22 is changed to a
half-cadence in m. 33); lines 7-8 are significantly recomposed and expanded
(compare mm. 22-28 with mm. 33-41). Such a procedure reveals Monte's
typical love of detail and contrapuntal elaboration. An expressive purpose is
served as well: the reworking of the material the second time adds considerably
to its expressivity, as can be seen in the piling up of dissonances and the use of
cross-relations in the closing measures (mm. 39-41).

The *seconda parte* presents the most vivid pictorialisms yet encountered in
Monte's music. The *fieri venti* (fierce winds) come before us with lightning-
quick melismas in eighth-notes (mm. 43-44); moments later, the breadth of the
sea is conjured up with equal ease (mm. 49-50). Monte's use of harmonic word-
painting is rather more subtle. The image in line 10 of being driven out to sea
(hor l'hanno spinta) is mirrored by a sudden turn to a different harmonic area:
after g minor is prepared (however fleetingly) in m. 46, the d minor which
follows (m. 47) is a jarring yet typically sensitive response to the poetic image.
Notice, too, that even as Monte indulges in the rather formulaic word painting
of *Che nel mio mar,* his dissonance treatment remains expressive (note the
crunching $^6_5$ in m. 49), thus maintaining the anxious tone of the whole.

Example 27. Monte: The Third Book for Four Voices (1569-1576)
       Lasso, Amor (complete) mm. 1-9

Ex. 27 (cont.) mm. 10-18

Ex. 27 (cont.) mm. 19-27

Ex. 27 (cont.) mm. 28-36

-glio Ne mai sag- gio noc- chier guar-dò da sco-
-glio Ne mai sag- gio noc- chier guar-dò da sco-
-glio Ne mai sag- gio noc- chier guar-dò da sco-
Ne mai sag- gio noc- chier guar-dò da sco-

-glio Na- ve di mer-ci pre-ci- o- se car- ca Quan-
-glio Na- ve di mer-ci pre-ci- o- se car- ca
-glio Na- ve di mer-ci pre-ci- o- se car- ca Quan-
-glio Na- ve di mer-ci pre-ci- o- se car- ca Quan-

-t'io sem- pre la de- bi- le mia var-ca Da
Quan- t'io sem- pre la de- bi- le mia var-ca Da le per-
-t'io sem- pre la de- bi- le mia var- ca Da le per-
-t'io sem- pre la de- bi- le mia var-ca Da le r-

Ex. 27 (cont.) mm. 37-41

Ex. 27 (cont.) mm. 42-50

Seconda parte

Ma la- gri-mo- sa piog- gia e fie-ri ven- - -

Ma la- gri-mo- sa piog- gia e fie- - ri ven-

Ma la- gri-mo- sa piog-gia e fie- - ri ven- ti

Ma la- gri-mo- sa piog- gia

ti D'in- fi- ni- ti so- spi- ri hor l'han-no spin- ta, hor l'han-no

ti D'in-fi-ni- ti so-spi- ri hor l'han-no spin-ta, hor l'han- no

D'in-fi- ni- ti so-spi- ri hor l'han-no spin-ta, hor l'han- no

D'in- fi- ni- ti so- spi- ri hor l'han- - no

spin-ta Che nel mio mar - - - - -

spin-ta Che nel mio mar - - hor- ri- - -

spin-ta Che nel mio mar - - hor-

spin-ta Che nel mio mar - - - hor-

Ex. 27 (cont.) mm. 51-59

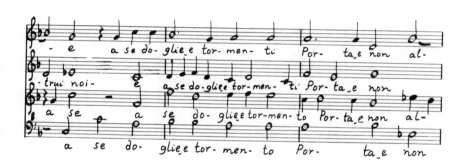

Ex. 27 (cont.) mm. 60-62

What most distinguishes this piece from the two previously considered Petrarch settings is its almost unsettling rhythmic vitality, epitomized in the *prima parte* in the treatment of lines 5-6, and in the *seconda parte* in the treatment of the first three words *(Ma lagrimosa pioggia)*. In the former example, the supple homophonic declamation and sure harmonic focus are striking. The latter passage (mm. 42-3), however brief, sums up *in nuce* Monte's new-found ability to focus a great deal of rhythmic and melodic energy in a small space: he begins by writing an accelerando into the music, as it were; the two outer voices move purposefully in contrary motion; and each successive harmony is a new and deftly chosen one.

These three settings are offered as exemplars of Monte's most serious and accomplished madrigals of these years—what I have called his Petrarchan achievement. In his early years in Vienna, Monte pushed his music forward in a remarkable way, achieving a cogent and forceful style, prompted largely by his prolonged encounter with Petrarch's verse. Yet, like many madrigalists of these same years, he felt the need to move away from Petrarch; his Third Book for Six Voices (1576) is the last book which Petrarch dominates. With the Seventh Book for Five Voices (1578), we enter a new poetic territory. As we shall see, though, Monte continues to build on the extraordinary musical achievements of his Petrarchan period.

The Seventh Book for Five Voices

This book, dedicated to Monte's new patron, the Emperor Rudolf, embodies the dominant musical trends of the decade. It is dark and serious, and its music explores the stylistic innovations already noted in his Petrarchan settings. Yet in its poetic choices, the Seventh Book emphatically signals the end of Monte's Petrarchan period: there is only one Petrarch sonnet here; Sannazaro and Bembo are absent as well.

The dedication to the Emperor Rudolf is an odd document. In his dedication of the Second Book for Six Voices (1569) to Maximilian, Monte had delivered something of a lecture on musical aesthetics.[18] He now unburdens himself of some rather recondite Classical learning. As in the earlier dedication, Monte eventually focuses his comments on the patron himself, in whom Monte discovers the virtures of sobriety and discretion in his appreciation of the arts. Here is the full text:

> PILADE [Oticilius Plotus], that most famous rhetorician of Augustan times, importuned by Hila his student to compete with him, spoke these words to that rash and ungrateful youth, wishing him to accompany them with a gesture: "THE GREAT ATREUS." He [Hila] raised himself up as much as he could with his person, and with his arm. "You have imitated his stature, not his greatness." And, Pilade, asked by the people (who were the judge of their controversy) if he might be content to accompany the same words with a suitable action,

uttered them with his hand upon his cheek, and struck a pensive pose. He was highly praised for it. The people understood him to mean that the greatness of kings consists in their occupying themselves with the thoughts and cares of the people brought together by divine providence under their rule.

But since all things that are done with labor have need of some amount of time between them, and need of something which gives comfort in a certain fashion to a dejected nature (since, without these intervals that nature would not endure), that kind of pleasure is sought which might be suitable for great princes with needs of this kind. We conclude this pleasure to be music, which as it is performed, besides giving pleasure, creates in human souls which are well attuned, those divine and marvellous effects and affects which are already so well known.

And although Philip of Macedon said to Alexander the Great [his son] that it was enough (and perhaps too much) that the Prince had the leisure to listen to others who sang, this happened because that wise king, zealous for his son's glory, and compelled by human tenderness, feared not that Alexander would apply himself to it [music] (which he would have praised), but that he might occupy and immerse himself in it too much. This cannot happen to Your Imperial Majesty, who takes advantage of all the pleasures, however virtuous, with such sobriety and discretion, that it is a marvel to hear and see.

For all these things, I shall not refrain from dedicating to you this trifling Italian music (which I have resolved to send to the printers), just as I already long ago dedicated to you my heart, and my whole being. If Your Majesty considers this, rather than the inadequacy of the gift (if the gift is what it should be), I hope that your humanity is such that it will be satisfied with the purity of my intention, and with my most ardent desire to see Your Serene Majesty always more glorious and more happy, as God may will it.

Vienna, 1 February 1578.

Your Serene Majesty's most
humble and devoted servant,

Filippo di Monte[19]

It would be difficult to point to a madrigal book dedication more obscure than this one. Though Monte evidently culled his anecdote concerning the Roman rhetorician Oticilius Plotus from some Classical author, his source remains unidentified.[20] Alexander the Great's love of music was a much more frequently invoked topic. Both anecdotes are intended to flatter his patron: from the first we are to infer that Rudolf, like "the great Atreus," occupies himself with the "thoughts and cares of his people." Monte then claims for music the power to refresh the Emperor's spirits, after he has diligently devoted himself to the affairs of state. In his second anecdote, Monte makes the parallel himself: like Alexander the Great, Rudolf's devotion to the arts is tempered with sobriety and discretion. There may be a double meaning here; Monte may be subtly regretting that Rudolf, unlike Alexander, did not seem tempted to immerse himself too much in music. In light of the Emperor's later near-disappearance into a private world of astrology and other arcane pursuits—which occupied him to the detriment of his Imperial duties[21]—Monte's comments also take on a certain irony. A further irony comes with the music itself: its pervasive melancholy seems hardly designed to offer the kind of "comfort" and "delight" which Monte claims for music in his dedication. (Yet this obsessive melancholy might have been intended as an agent of catharsis.) In any case, there is evidence, albeit indirect, that this music failed to please Rudolf and perhaps other influential patrons at the Imperial Court. That evidence comes only in 1580 and 1581, in the dedications of two five-voice books. These must wait until the following chapter; now we must consider the poetry and music of the Seventh Book.

For the first time in any of his madrigal books, Monte largely forsakes the sonnet: there are only two here, one of which (Beccuti's *Fui vicino al cader*) is placed at the head of the book. The other sonnet, Petrarch's *Io canterei d'amor* (131) is relegated to its closing pages. The great central portion of the book is taken up with ottava stanzas, eighteen in all. It is rare to find such a large number of ottavas set consecutively in a madrigal book of the 1570s, and even more rare that they should form, as they do here, a single narrative poem. In these stanzas, an unknown poet of mediocre gifts has written a confused story, filled with abrupt changes of mood and tone, and dominated by an obsessive melancholy. Since the original form of the poem is unknown, it may be that some of the confusion here is Monte's work: he may have omitted some stanzas, or changed the order of some, as well. In any case, the poem is not set as a cycle (as we shall see), and there are no such indications as *prima parte, seconda parte,* etc. Here is the complete poem:

1

O voi c'havete di pietade'l viso
Dipinto, e dal vezzoso vostro core
Non si vide giamai amor diviso:
Per gratia, udite il grave mio dolore,
Che m'ha fatt'obliar il cant'e'l riso,
U me ne vivo in sempitern'horrore,
E pascomi de tema, e di desire,
Ne viver voglio, ne vorrei morire.

(O you whose face is painted with pity, and from whose charming heart love is never divided: for mercy's sake hear my grave sorrow, which has made me forget song and laughter, whence I live in eternal horror, and feed upon fear and desire. I neither want to live, nor do I wish to die.)

2

Pietosi spirti, in libertate io vissi,
Senza timore d'amorose pene;
E tal felice stato al'hora scrissi—
In tronch'in carte, e'n le mie antiche arene.
Ma presago del mal futuro i dissi:
"Mia spem'a un debil filo si ritiene."

Hor ch'a l'angoscia cede la mia vita,
Scopre gli affanni suoi tutta smarrita.

(Piteous spirits, I lived in liberty, without fear of love's pains. And in that happy state I then wrote—on tree trunks, on paper, and upon my ancient sands. But in foreboding of my future pain, I said: "My hope is held by a weak thread." Now that my wholly bewildered life gives way to anguish, it disovers its own woes.)

3

Da gli aspri colpi di mia sorte ria,
Satio e roso posava tutto intento
A nuovi studi; quand'amor tra via
Ferimmi con lo stral pien di spavento.
"Dhe! Chi dal mio riposo mi desvia?"
Gridai, et egli sparve com'un vento.
L'alm'in due parti mi si fe'n un punto,
E fui da un freddo e da un calor compunto.

(Sated and worn down by the bitter blows of my wretched fate, I placed all my intentions in new studies, when Love, in my path, wounded me with an arrow full of terror. "Alas! Who leads me astray from my tranquillity?" I cried, and he [Love] disappeared like a wind. My heart was rent in two in an instant, and I was stung by cold and heat.)

4

Timido'n ghiacci'e'n foc'ardito, i provo
D'intender la cagion che sia, e quale;
Se buona—l'aspro, inusitato, e novo
Strale—perche si mostra si mortale?
Se ria, perch'a fuggir lento mi movo?
Ohime! Ch'adunqu'è questo: bene, o male?
Se ben, da lunge se ne vien pian piano.
Se mal, da presso vola a man'a mano.

(Timid in ice, and courageous in fire, I attempt to understand the reason that this may be [that Love has wounded me] and its nature. If [the reason is] good, why does the bitter, unusual and novel arrow reveal itself to be so deadly? If [the reason is] bad, why do I move to flee so slowly? Alas! What is it, therefore, good or evil? If [the arrow is] good, it comes very slowly from afar. If [the arrow is] bad, it flies gradually from near.)

5

Tra me così dicendo, ecco m'assalse
Una gran luce, chiara più che'l sole,
Che gli occhi m'abbaglio, e non li calse.
Di me quasi orb'e muto, che parole
Formar non seppi, e sogni et ombre false
Mi parean (come a molti avenir sole),
Io resto, et ella va tosto e non meno,
Come resta la nube e va'l baleno.

(Thus speaking to myself, behold, I was attacked by a great light, brighter than the sun, which dazzled my eyes and [yet] did not lower them. I remain, almost blind and mute, so that I knew not how to form words; and dreams and false shadows appeared before me (as customarily happens to many), and the light goes quickly, and no less [quickly] than [when] the flash of lightning goes, and the cloud remains.)

6

Il gran signor di Delo al'hor s'ascose
Calando in basso le sue rote aurate
Nel gremb'a Theti, u'l suo splendor depose.
Et io, con note gravi, e poco usate
A pianger cominciai, et a dir cose
Diverse, paventose'e sconsolate.
Con pena in seno, e con Amor al fianco,
Su'l letto mi gettai, stordito e stanco.

(The great lord of Delos then concealed himself, lowering his golden wheels upon Thetis' lap, where he lay down his splendor. And I, with grave and little used notes, began to weep, and to say diverse, terrifying, and disconsolate things. With pain in my breast, and with Love's arrow in my side, I threw myself upon my bed, bewildered and exhausted.)

7

S'arreser gli occhi a due gran luci chiare,
Ch'abbagliati restaro, onde fui preso
Da un duro sonno; e le mie cur'amare
Io diedi in pred'a lui, perche tal peso
Se gli convenne, & tosto i vidi rare
Meraviglie, che m'han per sempr'offeso.
Io restò da l'estremo chiar'oppresso,
E al l'altr'estrem'oscuro fui commesso.

(My eyes surrendered before two large and bright lights, and they remained dazzled, so that I was seized by a harsh sleep; and I gave my bitter cares wholly over to sleep, because such a burden suited it. And suddenly I saw rare marvels which have hurt me forever. I remained oppressed by that extreme brightness, and then I was committed to the other extreme [of] darkness.)

8

Tosto mi si scoperse una gentile,
Leggiadra, vaga, honesta e pellegrina
Donna, ch'en man'havea l'esc'e'l focile;
Ne gli occhi, amor; e gravita divinà
Nel viso, & era ne suoi gesti humile,
Tal che fece di me dolce rapina.
Da me partì l'antico odio e furore,
Lasciando'n vece lor pace et amore.

(Suddenly a gentle, pretty, charming, decent, and foreign lady showed herself to me; she had tinder and flint in her hand, and a divine gravity in her face. She had such humility in her manner that she sweetly ravished [my senses]. The old hate and fury left me, leaving peace and love in their place.)

9

Quest'era il più bel pegno che natura
Formar potesse a noi egri mortali;
Scelse tra l'altre idee per la più pura
Quest'Angioletta, e'l cielo spirti uguali
A santi diede a lei, e ugual figura;
E al suo celeste nome piume et ali.
Io col favor di si felice oggetto
Sgombrai di molto affanni dal mio petto.

(This lady was the most lovely pledge which nature could give to us feeble mortals. [Nature] chose this little angel from among the other forms as the purest, and heaven gave her spirits equal to the saints, and their same appearance, and to her heavenly name [gave] feathers and wings. [Blessed] with the favor of such a happy subject, I swept many of the woes from my heart.)

10

Incominciò a parlar, e si fermaro
I cieli con la lor dolce armonia;
Rasserenossi l'aria, ne turbaro
I venti il mar ne la procella ria;
I regni di Plutone s'allegraro,
Ripieni al'hor d'amore e cortesia,
Che ritornata fosse l'età d'oro,
Credei nel rimirar cotal thesoro.

(She began to speak, and [even] the heavens ceased their sweet harmony [to listen]; the air was cleared, nor did the winds stir up the sea into an evil storm. Pluto's kingdoms rejoiced, and were filled with love and courtesy. Beholding such a treasure, I believed that the Golden Age had returned.)

11

Come suonora tromba, una gran voce
Ribombò ne l'orecchio mio e disse:
"Il tempo fu s'ingordo e sì veloce,
Ch'ogni ben fuggitivo ci prefisse;
Lento e [è] ben al partir cio che ci noce;
Tal empia legg'al mondo sempre visse.
Mentre pero'l fatal giorno ti chiama,
Servirai questa Dea che'l mondo brama."

(Like the sound of a trumpet, a great voice reverberated in my ear and said: "Time was so greedy and swift in its passing, that every fleeting good thing has a prefixed end, and that which is harmful to us is slow in leaving. Yet until that destined day calls you, you will serve this goddess which the whole world desires.")

12

"Venere e Daphne, Palla, Arachne e Flora
Altiere van che'l lieto lor soggiorno
Fanno'n costei ch'ogni bel spirto adora;
E degn'è il suo gran merto che fia adorno
D'incenso, e d'Are a che giamai non mora.
Tu dunque adoreraila e notte e giorno;
Ella sarà beata in ogni parte:
Fattura e figlia e di natura et arte."

("Venus and Daphne, Pallas, Arachne, and Flora go proudly [forth], and make their happy sojourn with that one which every beautiful spirit adores. And her great merit is worthy of being adorned with incense and with temples, and of never dying. You, then, will adore her night and day; she will be blessed in every part, the creation and daughter of nature and art.")

13

Scosso dal sonno ratto corro al loco,
Che breve pace diede, e lunga guerra.
Vaga de la mia mort'e del mio foco,
Non scorgo chi m'ancide e chi m'atterra.
Si fortuna mi prese a scherz'e a gioco,
Che'l ciel mostrommi e mi caccio sotterra;
Pensai e Gnido e Pafo d'habitare,
Ma'n Scithia e'n Ponto mi convenne andare.

(Shaken from my sleep, I quickly run to that place which gave brief peace and long war. Desirous of death and of my flame, I do not see who slays me and throws me to the ground. If Fortune makes such jest and play of me, that it reveals heaven to me and chases me underground—I thought I was living in Cnidus and Paphos, but it was necessary to go into Scythia and Pontus.)

14

Non con sì stretti nodi Ellere o Acanti
Tener si vide mai arbori avinti;
Ne si sentir per doglia sì gran pianti,
Com'io tenni co i miei pensier non finti
La Dea, e come le piangei innanti,
Si che gli spirti miei restaro vinti.
Se di dolcezza piansi, che fia poi,
Quando privo sarò de gli occhi suoi?

(Ivy and acanthus have never been seen to hold the trees with such tight knots, nor for sorrow has such great lamenting been heard, as I held—with my not at all feigned thoughts—the Goddess, and as I wept before her, so that my spirits were overcome. If I wept from tenderness, what may happen when I am deprived of her eyes?)

15

Ella mi fece di sua gratia degno,
Non men honesta, che cortese sempre.

E per due lustri mai non m'hebb'a sdegno.
Il mio cor di soavi e dolce tempre
Nodriva, & lo facea di pene indegno.
"Son tua," dicea, "pur c'honestà ti tempre."
Così vivend'in tal felice stato,
Mai non credei morir, se non beato.

(She made me worthy of her mercy; she was no less honest than courteous, and for two lustra [ten years] she never disdained me. She nourished my heart with gentle, sweet qualities, and made it unworthy of any pains. "I am yours," she said, "as long as honesty moderates your nature." Thus living in such a happy state, I believed I would never die, unless[thus] blessed.)

16

Ma, lasso! presi voluntario bando
Dal mio bel sol, dal mio infinito bene.
Desio d'honor, anz'io me stess'odiando
Ne fui cagion, ond'hor non mi convenne
Dolor, se non di me, che lagrimando
Intenerisco i marmi in tante pene.
Ministro adunqu'io del mio inferno, il tergo
Rivolsi a quei piacer, ch'en carta aspergo.

(But, alas! I made a voluntary exile from my sweet sun, from my infinite happiness. Desirous of honor, indeed, hating myself, I was the cause of it [exile]; whence no grieving for me is proper, only my own. Thus weeping in so many woes, I move the marble stones to pity. Minister, then, of my own hell, I turned my back upon those pleasures with which I besprinkle my verse.)

17

Un adirato mar, pien di martiri
Solco, senza sperar salute o porto.
Che s'adivien che i languidi occhi giri?
Altro non veggo ch'un camino torto.
Tra sassi, sterpi, e dumi i miei sospiri
Spargendo vo, senza ver [haver] un conforto.
Gli alpestri monti e le caverne oscure,
Et echo odon le mie querele dure.

(An enraged sea full of suffering I sail, without hope of salutation or port. And what happens [what does it matter] if I should turn my languid eyes? I see nothing but a tortuous road. Between rocks, underbrush, and thornbushes, I go scattering my sighs, without having any comfort. The wild mountains, the dark caverns, and echoes hear my harsh laments.)

18

L'orecchie di pietà son chiuse homai,
Onde fra monte Barbaro et Averno
Con lagrimosi accenti gli miei guai
Faccio palese, e'l mio dolor interno.
Non resplendon per me di Febo i rai,

Ne si parte da me l'horrido verno.
Questo barbaro calle in parte forse
Condurrammi ove'l pianto mio già forse [fors'è].

(The ears of pity are closed henceforth, so that between Mount Barbarus and [Lake] Avernus, I make known my woes with tearful accents, and my internal suffering. Phoebus' rays do not shine for me, nor does horrid winter part from me. Perhaps this barbarous path will lead me to those parts where my weeping perhaps already is.)

Before considering the literary background of this poem, we should first attempt to unravel the tangled sequence of events it describes. In stanzas 1-2, the poet addresses the listener, begging for his pity, and expressing a habitual sadness which marks the poem as a whole. Though once a free and happy man, he is yet an easy prey for despair, anguish, and the "sorrows of love" *(amorose pene)* which Cupid's arrows inflict (stanzas 3-4).

Beginning with stanza 5, the poet recounts a series of visions or hallucinations; first he is struck by a great light, then beset by "dreams and false shadows." In stanza 6, night comes.[22] Stunned and exhausted by his visions, the poet throws himself upon his bed. The stanzas which follow constitute a vivid sequence of dreams, which are initially described in a manner similar to those visions which preceded the poet's "harsh sleep." Suddenly a *donna* appears in his dream, upon whose various perfections the poet expatiates for several stanzas. In stanza 11, a voice reverberates in his ear (though still during his dream); it commands him (in stanza 12) to serve this goddess, who has as her companions Venus, Daphne, Pallas Athena, Arachne and Flora.

After this point, I find some confusion in the order of stanzas as Monte transmits them and propose the following reordering, which brings some sequential coherence to an otherwise jumbled narrative. As it stands, stanza 13 is certainly out of place, and should come *after* stanzas 14 and 15. The sequence of events then becomes: a voice commands the poet to serve and adore his goddess (stanzas 11-12); he does so, still as part of his dream (stanzas 14-15); he is *then* shaken from his sleep (stanza 13). It further seems to me that stanzas 14 and 15 might be reversed so that *Ella mi fece,* a generalized paean to the beloved, is followed up in a more impassioned vein with *Non con sì stretti nodi,* a stanza which ends with the tremulous question: "What may happen when I am deprived of her eyes?" Placing this stanza after *Ella mi fece* makes the following one *(Scosso dal sonno)* answer that question most emphatically.

In stanza 13, the poet returns to his melancholy burden: Fortune has played cruelly with him, showing him heaven, but chasing him underground.[23] In the concluding three stanzas, the poet speaks of a voluntary exile from his beloved, and brings his work to a melancholy and lachrymose dénouement.

These stanzas, quite mediocre in style and diction, are heavily indebted to an elegiac strain of the pastoral tradition best represented by Sannazaro's *Arcadia.* Indeed, the tone of the poem, as well as certain aspects of its story, broadly recall the *Prosa duodecima* of the *Arcadia*.[24] The poet of these stanzas may have had the *Arcadia* in mind, or possibly some intervening imitation of it. In the *Prosa duodecima,* Sincero (Sannazaro) falls into a melancholy slumber, and is beset by a number of visions. Suddenly a nymph appears; here Sannazaro's description is closely echoed in stanza 8:

> ... in un punto mi si offerse avanti una giovene doncella ne l'aspetto bellissima et nei gesti et ne l'andare veramente divina.[25]

Compare this with these lines from stanza 8:

> Tosto mi si scoperse una gentile
> Leggiadra, vaga, honesta, e pellegrina
> Donna, ch'en man' havea l'esc'e'l focile
> Ne gli occhi amor, e gravità divina
> Nel viso, & era ne suoi gesti humile....

The nymph then acts as Sincero's guide on an extraordinary subterranean journey, at the end of which he confronts the river Sebeto. Abandoned by his companion, and at the end of his journey, he is once again overwhelmed by sadness:

> ... io mi trovai in tal punto si desideroso di morire.... Et essendo ad me medesimo venuto in odio, maladissi l'hora che da Arcadia partito mi era.[26]

The self-hatred and melancholy of stanza 16 recall these lines.[27]

Just as the poet of these stanzas relies on the pastoral tradition for his narrative details, so does he turn to Petrarch for words, phrases, and occasionally whole sentences. The most substantial borrowing comes from Petrarch's sonnet *S'amor non è* (132), which opens with these lines:

> S'amor non è, che dunque è quel ch'io sento?
> Ma s'egli è amor, per Dio, che cosa et quale?
> Se bona, ond'è l'effetto aspro mortale?
> Se ria, ond'è sì dolce ogni tormento?

> (If it is not love, what then is it that I feel? But if it is love, before God, what kind of thing is it? If it is good, whence comes this bitter mortal effect? If it is evil, why is each torment so sweet?

Compare the Petrarch with stanza 4:

> Timido'n ghiacci'e'n foc'ardito, i provo
> D'intender la cagion che sia, e quale;
> Se buona—l'aspro, inusitato, e novo

Strale—perchè si mostra si mortale?
Se ria, perch'a fuggir lento mi movo?

There are other Petrarchan echoes similar to these.

The poet of these eighteen stanzas knew his Ariosto as well. For his evocation of idyllic happiness in stanza 14, he borrowed freely from Ariosto's description of Ruggiero and Alcina in the seventh canto of the *Orlando Furioso:*

Non così strettamente edera preme
Pianta ove intorno abbarbicata s'abbia
Come si stringon li dui amanti insieme...[28]

Compare this with the opening of stanza 14:

Non con sì stretti nodi Ellere o Acanti
Tener si vide mai arbori avinti...

In sum, these stanzas reveal their mediocrity not only in their many inelegant phrases, but in their ill-digested quotations and echoes from the works of other masters.

It is impossible to say what might have impelled Monte to set these verses. They are so far below the level of Petrarch's poetry (to which Monte had been faithful for so long) that we may speculate that special circumstances may have caused him to set them. The stanzas might be the work of an amateur poet at the Imperial Court, and may encode an esoteric meaning which only a member of Rudolf's inner circle could penetrate.

Although these eighteen stanzas form a narrative poem (however jumbled or corrupt), they are not set as a musical cycle. Several features make this quite clear: the first and last stanzas are not in the same mode, and there are many intermediate changes of mode; there is a change roughly halfway through in key signature; and there are several changes of vocal scoring (see Table 3.2).

Rather than attempt a large-scale cycle, Monte was content to use musical means to link pairs of stanzas which belong together poetically, and he does this several times. Stanzas 1 and 2, which make up the initial rhetorical address, are modally linked (the cadence in stanza 1 can be heard as a half-cadence in a larger G Dorian unit), and identical in scoring and length (48 breves). Similarly, stanzas 3 and 4, linked poetically by their common reference to fire and ice, are identical in mode (Phrygian on A), scoring, and length (45 breves). Stanzas 9 and 10, which paint a picture of idyllic happiness, are also bound together by their common mode (F Ionian), scoring and length (35 breves). The closing three stanzas, in which the poet makes his melancholy exile, are similarly related.

Table 3.2   Original Clefs and Modal Endings of the Eighteen Stanzas

TITLE	CANTO	ALTO	TENOR	BASSO	QUINTO	SIGNA-TURE	TWO FINAL CHORDS OF EACH OTTAVA
1. O voi c'havete	c^1	c^3	c^4	F^4	c^4	♭	g – D
2. Pietosi spirti	c^1	c^3	c^4	F^4	c^4	♭	D – G
3. Da gli aspri	c^1	c^3	c^4	F^4	c^3	♭	A – D
4. Timido'n ghiaccio	c^1	c^3	c^4	F^4	c^3	♭	d – A
5. Tra me cosi	c^1	c^3	c^4	F^4	c^4	♭	D – G
6. Il gran signor	c^1	c^4	c^4	F^4	c^3	♭	A – D
7. S'arreser	c^1	c^4	c^4	F^4	c^3	♭	Penultimate chord: F#; C – G / A
8. Tosto mi si	c^1	c^3	c^4	F^4	c^4	♭	G – C
9. Quest'era il	c^1	c^3	c^4	F^4	c^4	♭	F – C
10. Incomincio	c^1	c^4	c^4	F^4	c^3	♭	C – F
11. Come suonara	c^1	c^4	c^4	F^4	c^3	-|	A – D

Table 3.2 (cont.)

TITLE	CANTO	ALTO	TENOR	BASSO	QUINTO	SIGNA-TURE	TWO FINAL CHORDS OF EACH OTTAVA
12. Venere e	c^1	c^3	c^4	F^4	c^4	—	E – A
13. Scosso dal	c^1	c^3	c^4	F^4	c^4	—	D – G
14. Non con si	c^1	c^3	c^4	F^4	c^4	—	E – A
15. Ella mi fece	c^1	c^3	c^4	F^4	c^4	—	A – D
16. Ma lasso	c^1	c^3	c^4	F^4	c^3	—	E – A
17. Un adirato	c^1	c^3	c^4	F^4	c^3	—	E – A
18. L'orrechie	c^1	c^2	c^4	F^4	c^3	—	a – E

The remaining stanzas are not linked to one another in any of these ways. In chapter 2, we observed a setting in twelve sections of Petrarch's *Mia benigna fortuna*. It displayed a similar modal confusion, though the confusion in this later case is much greater still. In spite of the consistently dark two-tenor scoring, and in spite of his efforts to fashion pairs of stanzas, we are left with a piece without any large-scale coherence. Rather, Monte's approach has been to work through the poem, reflecting its continual changes of mood with appropriate changes of mode and style—without attempting a larger design.

Da gli aspri colpi and *Non con sì stretti nodi* will demonstrate different aspects of Monte's style in these stanzas. The first exemplifies a more hyperactive style, which surfaces often here as Monte responds to the extravagant poetic imagery. The second is more restrained and lyrical.

Da gli aspri colpa (stanza 3; see example 28) is filled with vivid word-painting, in which nearly every image is matched by musical means. In some instances, Monte's methods are quite obvious. Line 7, for example (in which the poet's soul is "rent in two in an instant"), is set as a duet for Basso and Tenore (mm. 25-28). The setting of the preceding line is no less blunt: at the word *gridai* (I screamed), the Canto reaches up to its only high f″ in the piece, and in the remainder of the line ("and he disappeared like a wind") Monte writes a rapid chordal passage which dissolves into a momentary silence (mm. 23-25).

Other instances of word-painting are more subtle. In the setting of lines 1-2, the slow tempo, metrical ambiguity, flaccid rhythms, unfocused melodic lines and expressive suspensions all combine to convey the image of a man "sated and worn away by the bitter blows of a wretched fate." The metrical profile of mm. 1-14 is so fluid that these measures can be heard either as notated, or in hyper-measures of $\frac{3}{1}$. Yet this hidden meter is itself not forcefully projected until the cadence of mm. 12-13. Only these two measures are unmistakably in $\frac{3}{1}$ (note that the previous, analogous dissonance had occurred three semi-breves before). The sudden metrical, textural, and harmonic clarity of these measures sensitively underscores the poetic meaning here ("I placed all intentions in renewed study"), and also subtly conveys the music across the enjambments of lines 2-3.

Equally subtle is the word-painting for line 5 ("Alas! Who leads me astray from my tranquillity?"). The previous line has cadenced on a D major triad. For line 5, the harmonies move in downward-slipping triads from D major to B♭ major (mm. 18-19). The opposition of these tonal areas (D major and B♭ major) and the attendant cross-relation between the Canto's f♯ and the Tenore's f♮ aptly express the image of being led astray. The sudden shifts in tempo and tessitura contribute to the effect as well, and serve as a foil to the violent effect of *gridai,* already noted.

Example 28. Monte: The Seventh Book for Five Voices (1578)
  Da gli aspri colpi (complete) mm. 1-6

Ex. 28 (cont.) mm. 7-12

Ex. 28 (cont.) mm. 13-18

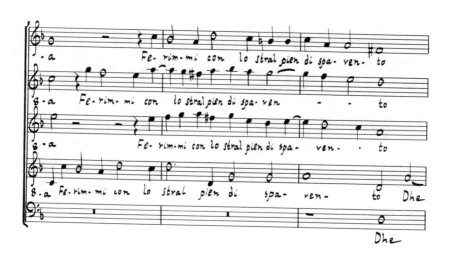

Ex. 28 (cont.) mm. 19-24

Ex. 28 (cont.) mm. 25-32

Indeed, the constant contrasts of tempo, texture, and melodic figure in *Da gli aspri colpi* threaten to disrupt the music and to dissolve it into a series of expressive yet discrete moments. As a counterbalance to these disturbing forces, Monte focuses his attention on a few musical ideas, which appear in a variety of guises. We hear, for example, a recurrent 2-3 suspension involving the dissonance of A and B♭, most often expressed as a $^6_5$-$^6_4$ over a D in the lowest voice (mm. 3, 9, 17, 22, 23, 28, and 29). At the same time, he also uses a descending tetrachord to generate much of his melodic material (see example 29).

The recurring use of both a single expressive dissonance and a descending tetrachord does not create any sense of a unified design for this madrigal. In general, madrigalists do not seem to cultivate that kind of motivic or thematic unity which one occasionally encounters in instrumental music of the period. The recurring patterns in *Da gli aspri colpi* serve rather to intensify the expression by focusing the musical material, which is so varied on the superficial level, on a few characteristic motives. The result is yet another reflection of the text, another madrigalism: the poet's obsessive melancholy is echoed by an obsessive motivic treatment.

Non con sì stretti nodi (stanza 14) reveals the gentler, more elegiac style which Monte also cultivates in these eighteen stanzas (see example 30). The restless discontinuity of texture and melodic figure which was so dominant a trait in *Da gli aspri colpi* appears here only in line 1 (mm. 1-4); after this, the music unfolds in a steady harmonic rhythm, with declamation mostly in breves and semibreves.

A close reading of this piece reveals some of the same kinds of subtle internal echoes which we noted in *Da gli aspri colpi*. For example, a 4-3 suspension over C recurs several times, with a similar expressive effect (mm. 6, 9 and 16). Similarly, the harmonic progression in mm. 11-13 is close to that in mm. 20-21. In both cases, an A-major chord cedes expressively to an a-minor chord, and is followed by F major. A more substantial kind of recurrence comes with the treatment of lines 6 and 8. Line 6 (mm. 25-28) is set to a lyrical trio which moves homophonically from d minor to a firm G major cadence (the only one in the piece). In line 8 (mm. 37-43), the Alto takes up its previous phrase, transforming it into a more pointed one, which is then tossed back and forth between semi-choirs, as the music gathers in momentum for the final cadence.

But the penultimate line is the most skillfully handled (mm. 28-37). An imitative point of typically fluid outline (the variations are, in fact, *inganni)* is arranged so as to imply a series of harmonic goals—F in mm. 29-30, C in m. 31, and B♭ in m. 32—none of which is achieved. The harmonic ambiguity of these measures is remarkable. In mm. 35-36 d minor is approached, but, typically, C♯ is withheld until the last possible moment, and the line ends not on a full

Example 29. The Descending Tetrachord in *Da gli aspri colpi*

Canto, mm. 1-2

Da gli a-spri col-pi

Canto, mm. 5-7

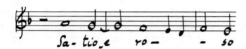

Sa-tio e ro- - so

Canto, mm. 20-23

Ohe chi dal mio ri-po-so mi de-svi- a

Canto, mm. 24-25

e- gli spar-ve co-miun ven-to

Canto, mm. 26-27

l'al- m' in due par-ti

Canto, mm. 28-29

E fui da un fred-do

Example 30. Monte: The Seventh Book for Five Voices (1578)
Non con sì stretti nodi (complete) mm. 1-6

Ex. 30 (cont.) mm. 13-18

Ex. 30 (cont.) mm. 19-24

Ex. 30 (cont.) mm. 25-30

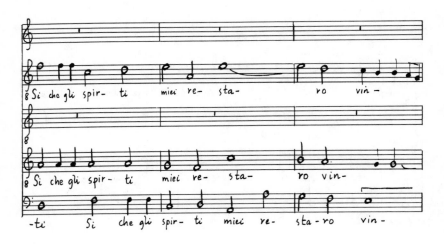

Si che gli spir- ti miei re- sta- ro vin-

Si che gli spir- ti miei re- sta- ro vin-

-ti Si che gli spir- ti miei re- sta-ro vin-

Se di dol- cez- za pian- si

- ti Se di

Se di dol- cez-

ti Se di dol- cez- ze pian- si

- ti Se

Ex. 30 (cont.) mm. 31-36

Ex. 30 (cont.) mm. 37-42

Ex. 30 (cont.) m. 43

cadence but a half-cadence, which then flows beautifully into the next phrase. Monte's skill in handling these contrapuntal, harmonic, and rhythmic details is considerable. Just as skillful is the way in which he manages to sustain the tone of gentle melancholy which marks this ottava setting more than any of the others. Monte evidently viewed this stanza as the high point of the poem, and so it is the longest (fifty-eight breves) and the most expressive by far.

The music in the Seventh Book shows Monte turning in an idiosyncratic direction, not only in his choice of poetry but in his music. The book makes an overwhelmingly serious impression; even its few lighter pieces (*Fuggend'amor, Vaga e pura Angioletta,* and *Saggia bella gentil*) are more madrigalian, less canzonetta-like than any of the lighter pieces discussed earlier in the chapter. While turning away from chromatic and even colorful harmony, Monte has formulated a style which is uniquely his, in which subtlety and volatility of texture, motive and rhythm are paramount features. Many of these can be seen in the music of his contemporaries, yet Monte's combination and deployment of them is personal and inimitable.

It is tempting to speculate on the critical reception of this book. The fact that it was reprinted only once (in 1583) and that none of its pieces ever appeared in a later anthology gives us a broad indication of the book's European reception. An indirect indication of its reception at Rudolf's court comes in the dedication of Monte's next book of madrigals for five voices, published in 1580 and once again dedicated to Rudolf. Monte's comments (which we will examine closely in the next chapter) reveal a personal sense of failure: his previous music has not pleased "those whose spirits are wearied by the necessities of political life." This might well be a reference to the music of the Seventh Book, and the reaction at Rudolf's court to it. It is not difficult, after all, to see how this music might have been a critical failure: its melancholy tone might have caused displeasure, and the style of even those more cheerful pieces might have been found too subtle or too timorous in their approach to the popular forms. In the following chapter, we will observe Monte attempting to change his style, and to give renewed pleasure to his patrons.

4

The Crisis in Style: 1580-1584

... Ho cercato, & cerco tuttavia col variar stile dar qualche contento a quelli à chi havessero poco piaciute l'altre mie compositioni....

Monte, in the dedication of his Tenth Book for Five Voices (1581)

Introduction

The years 1580-1584 represent the high point of Monte's productivity in the madrigal, and the high point of his international popularity as well. In these years, the following books were published, revealing a pattern of intense compositional energy at the beginning of the decade, tapering off slowly to mid-decade:

The Eighth Book for Five Voices	1580
The Ninth Book for Five Voices	1580
The Fourth Book for Six Voices	1580
The First Book of Spiritual Madrigals for Five Voices[1]	1581
The Tenth Book for Five Voices	1581
The Fourth Book for Four Voices	1581
The First Book for Three Voices	1582
The First Book of Spiritual Madrigals for Six Voices	1583
The Fifth Book for Six Voices	1584

In 1584, Monte also published a book of motets. In the following year, not a single madrigal book appeared.

In these years, Monte became increasingly aware of a new and lighter style of writing, cultivated principally by his younger Italian contemporaries. Acutely aware of the changes taking place in the world of the Italian madrigal, he began to change his style. Yet the process was a gradual one, and Monte's new style did not fully emerge until 1586, with the Eleventh Book for Five Voices. In 1580 and 1581, though, Monte's dilemma was (apparently) twofold: he was not only troubled by the vagaries of musical taste and style, but also dismayed by the failure at the Imperial Court of his most recent music. He addresses these issues in two dedicatory letters to his most exalted patron, Rudolf II. Before turning to the music, we must consider the dedications from these years.

The Dedications

Monte's dedication of the Eighth Book to Rudolf is one of the most important documents of his career. In contrast with the dedication of the Seventh Book of 1578, which was cast in obscure and impersonal terms, the dedication of the Eighth Book is direct and personal, and presents its message without the encumbrance of any recondite Classical allusions:

> To His Sacred Imperial Majesty, the Emperor Rudolf II, my Most Clement Lord:
>
> Imperial Majesty, when we see that until now every one is doing his best to lead music to greater perfection by means of a new style, it necessarily follows that music has not yet attained the perfection that it might. Since I am one of those whose profession is music, I have done all I could to find a way to give more pleasure to those who should and can form a judgment on it, but it is perhaps true that the more I try the less I succeed. Nevertheless, I do what I can, particularly to give pleasure to those for whom it is necessary in order to restore their spirits, wearied by the necessities of political life, and if I deserve no praise for what I have accomplished, I at least deserve no blame for my intention.
>
> Since each person must render thanks for his accomplishments and good intentions first to God and then to the instruments by which God grants his favors; and finding myself so richly rewarded by the generosity of Your Majesty and of your father of glorious memory that I am still able to devote myself most comfortably to this study [of music]; and having no other way to prove to Your Majesty and to the world how great is my obligation to you (having already dedicated my humble service to you for many years), I again dedicate to you the present works, which I hope you will deign to accept with your accustomed kindness, not considering the gift's shortcomings, but [both] the spirit in which it is proffered, and my devoted service.
>
> Prague, May 4, 1580

> Your most humble and devoted servant,

> Filippo di Monte[2]

Einstein characterized this dedication as a "painful and historically remarkable self-confession."[3] It is indeed rare for a composer of this period to underscore so vigorously in a dedicatory letter his feelings of failure and frustration. One phrase in particular holds a clue as to why these feeilings were so acute: when he refers to his attempts to give pleasure to those who are "wearied by the necessities of political life" he is quite clearly referring to his immediate circle of patrons in Rudolf's court (and perhaps to Rudolf himself), rather than to the amorphous international public to whom his madrigals would become commercially available. The image of the political figure wearied by the duties of state and in need of the comforts which music offers had already surfaced in the dedication of the Seventh Book, in Monte's anecdote concerning King Atreus. Now, Monte seems to be doubly vexed: since he apparently felt that one of his duties at the court was to refresh his wearied patrons with his music, his failure to do so was all the more painful to him.

The two other dedicatory letters of 1580 reveal Monte's attempts to overcome his discouragement by a continued cultivation of two other important figures at the Imperial Court. The Ninth Book for Five Voices is dedicated to Rudolf's brother Ernest:

To the Most Serene Prince, the Archduke Ernest:

Since ingratitude is considered by men of judgment to be an enormous sin, I would certainly number among the most ungrateful of men, if I failed to demonstrate to Your Highness how much I am aware of my enormous obligation to you not the least for being the son of the Emperor Maximilian of glorious memory and the brother of my most clement lord the Emperor Rudolf, from both of whom I have received many favors, but also for the favors which Your Highness never fails to bestow upon me on every occasion.

But since, on account of my feeble powers, I cannot give a suitable sign of my gratitude, still I must not fail to do what I can, and give some honor to myself at the same time, by dedicating this book of madrigals to the glorious name of Your Highness, who besides having other rare qualities is both a great lover of music, and a perfect listener and judge of it. For this reason, I hope that Your Highness deigns to accept (as I humbly beg you to do) this most trifling gift, with that kind spirit with which Your Highness is accustomed to favor all the virtues.

Prague, 20 September, 1580

Your Serene Highness' most humble and devoted servant,

Filippo di Monte[4]

Although Monte's comments here are quite conventional, his reference to Ernest's devotion to music is worth noting: it is a standard kind of statement which is nevertheless conspicuously lacking from all of Monte's dedications to

Rudolf. Indeed, the extent of Rudolf's affection for music is unclear; none of his biographers has paid much attention to his patronage either of music generally, or of Monte and other composers at the court more specifically. Rudolf's biographers have emphasized his love of the visual arts, and the energy he displayed in amassing one of Europe's finest collections. He took a personal interest in wood carving, and pursued this pastime in his own private workshop, where he could escape from pressing matters of state. He seems not to have played any musical instrument. From what is known, music apparently did not exert as strong a hold on his imagination as the other arts.[5]

Monte's other book of 1580, the Fourth Book for Six Voices, is dedicated to Wolfgang Rumpf, an important minister in Rudolf's court. Rumpf was evidently a man of some learning, and what is more, a lover of music: a catalogue of his library prepared in 1583 lists "over one thousand volumes in all fields of learning, with a particularly rich assortment of printed and manuscript music."[6] Monte writes:

> To the Most Illustrious and Esteemed Lord Wolfgang Rumpf, Baron of Wielross, Counselor and Chamberlain to His Sacred Majesty:
>
> If all, or the greater part of those men, who exceed others in valor, goodness, or wisdom were judged by our predecessors with inscriptions or with other worthy memorials immortalizing their names, this then offers the occasion to their descendants to imitate them.
>
> I, who am one of those who for every good reason admires the most worthy qualities of Your Illustrious Lordship (qualities which are and which always shall be vivid in the minds of men, on account of good and faithful writers), have wished to dedicate these madrigals of mine to your most honored name, hoping that they might be of a kind which can refresh those spirits, which, the more they are wearied by assiduous good works, the less they are satisfied, particularly in the service of His Imperial Majesty, and in working for the universal tranquillity of Christians.
>
> I beg, therefore, that Almighty God grant your Illustrious Lordship a very long and happy life, so that good men might enjoy it more, and I rejoice at its happy successes.
>
> Venice, 20 September, 1580
>
> Your Most Illustrious
> Lordship's most affectionate
> servant,
>
> Filippo de Monte[7]

The most revealing phrase here is the reference to those who "the more they are wearied by assiduous good works, the less they are satisfied." Though ostensibly a reference to such hard-working ministers as Rumpf himself, the comment in fact reads suspiciously like a description of Monte's own difficulties.

One might expect, coming from these dedications, to find Monte's music of 1580 embodying a new style. Yet this is not the case; none of these three books breaks new ground. They reflect Monte's continued commitment to the serious, affective madrigal which he had cultivated for so many years. In this light, his comments in the dedication of the Eighth Book take on a different meaning. Significantly, his reference to a new style is part of an impersonal description of the current scene: "*everyone* is doing his best to lead music to greater perfection...." When he then describes his own efforts, he mentions no new style, but merely states his desire to do what he can to give more pleasure to his patrons. On the basis of the music, it is clear that Monte was not yet willing to alter his style drastically, and his rather vague statements in this dedication reflect that unwillingness. Perhaps this helps to account for his sense of failure: feeling the need to change, yet ambivalent about forsaking a respected tradition, he was no doubt inclined to look upon his music with a certain chagrin.

In the following year, at the age of sixty, Monte published his Tenth Book for Five Voices. Again, he addresses the issues of taste and style, once more dedicating his work to Rudolf. It is the most important dedication Monte ever wrote, and prefaces a book which stands on the threshold of a new period for the composer:

To the Most Sacred Imperial Majesty, the Emperor Rudolf II, my most Clement Lord:

Since one sees and knows from experience, Sacred Imperial Majesty, that in the same way that men are dissimilar both in their physiognomy and in all the parts of their bodies, they are also different in thought, taste and action, it follows that things made by nature as well as by man's artifice, since they are in greater or lesser conformity with [other] things made by nature or man, will be more or less appreciated or abhorred by these men.

Speaking now of music, which is my profession, I can say that since the harmony which music renders can only be appreciated because of that conformity which it has with those who listen to it, every one who would give a judgment in these matters can say with more reason, "this music pleases me," than say, "it is *good* because it pleases me." This is because one is accustomed to making judgments concerning the quality of music, and of the variety of proportions with which composers are accustomed to arrange the intervals of their music, and [even] of the considerable trouble that it might have taken to compose—all things hardly demonstrable at all.

It appears, then, that this diversity of opinion clearly demonstrates the imperfection of both the art and its practitioners, since it can still be seen and shown that men of great judgment customarily take delight in that manner of music which does not normally please many of those who compose it. And since there is so much room for error in all this, and even more if one sought to force men's nature into making something which is contrary to their own nature seem good to them; I have tried, and I am still trying, by a change in style, to give some pleasure to those who have been little pleased with my other compositions. For that reason I have wished to publish the present works, which whatever their quality, I dedicate to Your Majesty's most happy name, with that humility and devotion with which I have dedicated myself and other things of mine to you.

Vienna, 26 June, 1581

> Your Sacred Imperial Majesty's
> most humble and devoted servant,
>
> Filippo di Monte[8]

Monte addresses the issues here in broad, even obscure language, and never refers in personal terms to anyone but himself. Yet the flavor of his comments suggests that his feelings have their origin in his inability to please Rudolf, and perhaps other patrons at court. Much, if not all, of what Monte couches in impersonal terms may refer specifically to his patron. With this in mind, the state of Rudolf's health, both mental and physical, becomes a matter of interest. We know that Rudolf suffered a prolonged illness in 1580-81, and that he had already begun to manifest that profound melancholy which marked his personality deeply in later years. One of the earliest descriptions of Rudolf's malaise comes in a letter of 27 July, 1581, written by George Gilpin, an Englishman, to Sir Francis Walsingham, back in England. Although evidently not based on a first-hand acquaintance with the Emperor, Gilpin's comments are worth quoting, as they suggest just how difficult it may have been for Monte (or anyone at Court) to maintain a relationship with Rudolf during the ten-month period described in the letter (roughly September 1580-July 1581):

> ... The Emperor is still so ill at ease that he keeps his chamber, and has not stirred abroad nor given audience to any these ten months. His disease is diversely reported of, and has been "extremely handled" not without danger of life. It neither is, nor, as some think, can be clearly cured, so that the grief of mind and remembrance is so great as has driven such a melancholy into his Majesty that no pleasure, company, or exercise delights him, but he leads a solitary and pensive life. This as I credibly heard is the course of it: he rises commonly by seven o'clock, at which time the physicians visit him; and after he is ready and has somewhat exercised himself by walking in his chamber, and Mass has been said at another place, which he beholds afar off through a wicket, he dines at ten. After this he is used to subscribe letters, reads a book, or hears those of his Chamber or Council report what passes in affairs of state, with which he troubles himself little. He sups at four and afterwards commonly paints or works in iron, wherein he has most delight; and so spending the day in this sort, goes to bed at 8, after conference with the physicians and their opinions heard.[9]

Seen in the context of a troubled and disrupted court environment, Monte's comments in the dedications to Rudolf seem to reveal his fear of exclusion from the Emperor's favor, or possibly even some fear of being dismissed. Whether such a hypothesis is correct or not, we can now return to the dedication itself with some idea of the circumstances in which it was written.

Monte begins by lamenting the fact that since people are so demonstrably different from one another in "thought, taste and action," it follows that there can be no agreement between them concerning the merits of a work of art. He wishes that men would distinguish between their freedom to say that this or that kind of music pleases them (a right which he accords them) and their desire to say that this or that music is *good* because it pleases them (a right which he would deny them). And he looks critically at those who offer judgments on the technical aspects of music without, we are to infer, sufficient understanding.

All these comments may well refer to difficulties Monte has had with his immediate patrons.

Oddly, after making so strong a case for an almost relativistic theory of art in which people are free to like or dislike whatever they choose, Monte uses this demonstration as proof of a much more traditional notion: that such a diversity of opinion actually reveals the current state of imperfection in the art.

His next comment is tantalizingly vague: "men of great judgment customarily take delight in that manner of music which does not normally please many of those who compose it." Might we infer from this that Monte had recently been commissioned by someone at court to compose in a genre or style that was unattractive to him? He might, for example, have been asked for some canzonette or villanelle, two kinds of music which he never condescended to include among his published works, though he might, after all, have been induced to write some for private circulation.

In the following statement, he reverts to his earlier theme, that it is useless to attempt to persuade others of the value of this or that music which might be "contrary to their nature." With this comment, he reveals his unwillingness to be drawn into a discussion of the relative merits of different styles in the madrigal. Seeing the futility of defending an older style from the attacks of its detractors, he announces his resolve to change his style, and "give some pleasure to those who have been little pleased with my other compositions." As we shall see, there are indeed a number of external as well as internal changes in the Tenth Book. It does contain several pieces in a new style. Yet the book remains committed to the tradition of the serious madrigal, and most of its pieces (as well as its best ones) belong to that tradition. For a much more far-reaching change in style, we must wait until 1586, and the Eleventh Book for Five Voices.

Einstein viewed Monte's statements in these dedications to Rudolf as evidence of the composer's growing isolation in Vienna and Prague, which caused him to "lose touch with the beneficent native soil of the madrigal and with the changes in Italian taste."[10] At the same time, Einstein interpreted the entire body of Monte's post-1568 madrigals as addressed "primarily to the international world of the friends of the madrigal."[11] According to this interpretation, Monte had begun to fear that his long-established relationship with a broadly-based European audience was threatened by his inability to keep abreast of new musical trends. Such an explanation undoubtedly accounts in part for Monte's anxious tone. Yet we must not lose sight of his immediate environment. The emphasis I have placed on Rudolf's character and Monte's presumed interaction with this reclusive and melancholy patron is not intended to replace Einstein's interpretation but to qualify it: Monte's predicament in 1580-81 is not only stylistic but personal, arising from his relationship with a difficult and unpredictable patron.

The other dedications from these years offer rather less insight into Monte's troubles. The Fourth Book for Four Voices, his last book in this series, is dedicated to Count Georges de Monfort, a patron of music to whom Jacob Regnart also dedicated a book in the same year.[12] The dedication is dated July 30, only a little more than a month after the dedication of the Tenth Book. It seems unlikely that he could have written all the pieces in so short a time, though it is certainly possible. The letter is flattering to Monfort, but tells us nothing about the music itself.[13]

The dedication of the First Book for Three Voices is more intriguing. This is, after all, Monte's only publication of three-voice madrigals, and was the result of a commission from his publisher, as Angelo Gardano himself explains in his dedication of the book of Madalena Casulana, a composer (ca. 1540 - ?).[14] In his dedication, Gardano writes:

> Seeing that the genre of three-voice madrigals was almost extinguished (a kind of music so delightful and natural, and, when it comes from a good hand, so perfect and excellent), I decided to resuscitate it and return it once again to the world. For this reason I turned to our most excellent Lord Filippo di Monte and asked him if he would wish to be of some help in fulfilling my intention. This he did most liberally, as is customary with his gentle nature, and he has sent me a good-sized book of them. Now printed, it is dedicated to the great virtue and merit of Your Ladyship, who is a great connoisseur of this and all other forms of gentility.
>
> It will happen, perhaps, that seeing these [madrigals] made welcome in the world, I shall gradually turn to some other excellent musicians and ask them, by favoring me with some similar compositions of theirs, to help this honorable idea of mine, just as I already ask Your Ladyship, a woman of such estimation and reputation in things such as these. For thus did that one judge you, who in his poetry worthily called you "the Muse and Siren of this our age." Like him, I give you every reverence, kiss your hand, and recommend myself to you forever.
>
> Venice, 20 August, 1582
>
>   Your Ladyship's servant,
>
>   Angelo Gardano[15]

Gardano may be exaggerating slightly when he states that the three-voice madrigal was almost dead as a genre; in fact, only seven years earlier, Gardano himself had published a book of three-voice madrigals by Andrea Gabrieli. It is instructive, then, that Gardano did not turn to Gabrieli to keep the form alive, but to an older, more conservative master. Gardano evidently counted upon Monte to uphold the madrigal tradition, and to compose in a style untainted by the villanella and canzonetta. Gardano's hopes were (as he himself states) admirably fulfilled by Monte: all the pieces in this book (as we shall see) are most emphatically madrigals, and not three-voice villanellas.

Finally, Monte's dedication of his Fifth Book for Six Voices (1584) to Rudolf suggests, in its bland and standard language, that Monte's relationship with his patron has settled down, after the confusion and uncertainty of 1580-81. The dedication is short, and cast in the matter-of-factly obsequious tone of most dedications:

> To the Most Sacred and Invincible Emperor Rudolf II, My Most Clement Lord:
>
> Your Majesty's kindness has been so continuously shown to me, not only by finding my humble service agreeable, but in accepting my efforts which have gone out into the world under Your Majesty's most glorious name, that it would seem to be a great sin, and a failing on my part, were I to neglect the opportunity which presents itself to me, to proclaim in the way that I can the enduring obligation I owe to your infinite and heroic courtesy, and so increase it still more. For this reason I now offer to you this book of six-voice madrigals, confident that Your Majesty's magnanimity, which will look more at the spirit in which they are offered than at the smallness of the gift, might be ready to receive it with that promptness which has received other greater efforts of mine. I...dedicate it to Your Majesty as testimony of my devotion, which if not magnificent and splendid, is at least true and constant, praying that Our Lord God may conserve for a long time and increase your happy state.
>
> [no date]
>
> Your Sacred Majesty's humble servant,
>
> Filippo di Monte[17]

This is Monte's last dedication to Rudolf of a madrigal book; indeed, he only turned to the Emperor once more, to dedicate his first book of masses, which came out in 1587. It is not known whether Monte's relationship with Rudolf deteriorated as the Emperor became even more withdrawn in the 1590s. In any case, Monte turned elsewhere during the last fifteen years of his life for support and encouragement in his madrigalian efforts. While a few younger composers continued to dedicate occasional madrigal books to the Emperor, Monte had effectively given up on Rudolf after 1584.

It is always dangerous to infer a personal statement from a sixteenth-century composer's textual choices, yet one poem here fairly cries out for such interpretation. In this, Monte's last book dedicated to Rudolf, the composer sets a diatribe against court life. The poem is a rather dreadful sonnet in which an anonymous poet mercilessly repeats only two words, *inferno* and *corte,* at the end of each line:

> Ho sempre inteso dir che ne l'inferno
> Così si sta come si vive in corte;
> E che la vita di chi vive in corte
> È come de dannati ne l'inferno.
>
> E che le pene grande de l'inferno
> Son come i dispiaceri de la corte,
> Onde l'huom che gran tempo è stato in corte,
> Si può dir che sia stato ne l'inferno.

Così la corte è simile a l'inferno,
Che non ha amor l'inferno, ne la corte;
Ne carità la corte, ne l'inferno.

Ma quand'io penso a la cort'e a l'inferno,
Son differenti, perchè i buoni in corte
Son tormentati, e i tristi ne l'inferno.

(I have always heard it said that hell is like the life at court, and that the life of one who lives at court is like that of the damned in hell. And that the great sufferings in hell are like the displeasures of court, so that a man who has been at court for a long time can say that he has been in hell. Thus, court life is like a hell, for there is no love in hell, or at court, nor charity at court, or in hell. But when I think of the court, and of hell, [I see that] they are different, because at court good people are tormented, but in hell, wicked people.)

Only one other setting of this poem is known, by Lodovico Agostino (Third Book for Six Voices, 1582). While it is perhaps not so extraordinary that Monte would set such a poem, it does seem remarkable (to say the least) that he would include it in a book dedicated to Rudolf. Even more remarkably, Monte does not seem to take the poem at all seriously; his setting is in a cheery Mixolydian mode. Whatever Monte's intentions were, this piece (which concludes the book) marks the end of one phase of Monte's relationship with Rudolf.

The Poetry

The poetry which Monte set in these five years shows that he was still broadly committed to the serious neo-Petrarchan poetry typical of the large mid-century anthologies. At the same time, he began to seek out more fashionable poetry, though he remained unaware of Guarini and Tasso lyrics.[18] (See Tables 4.1-4.7, which give the poetic contents for the seven secular publications under consideration in this chapter).

In chapter 3, we saw Monte turning in his Seventh Book to an unusual narrative poem of eighteen ottava stanzas which dominate the book. In 1580, he returned emphatically to the sonnet: in the three books of this year, there are twenty-five sonnets. In contrast, the books of 1581 and the following years, though each contains several sonnets, do not rely so heavily on the form as do the books of 1580.

There are only two poems by Petrarch in all these books, both in the Eighth Book; Bembo and Sannazaro are entirely absent. Rather, Monte relies more than at any other time on his two two-volume anthologies (see chapter 1). Monte's dependence on these two anthologies reaches its high point in the Fourth Book for Four Voices (1581) and the First Book for Three Voices (1582); in each of these, only one poem cannot be traced to either anthology. The three-voice book is remarkable for its concentration of ottava stanzas.

Table 4.1   The Poetic Contents of the Eighth Book of Madrigals for Five Voices (1580)

	TITLE*	POETIC FORM	AUTHOR
1.	*O sia la voglia ardente*	madrigal	?
2.	*Fugga pur io dove*	sonnet (set in one part)	?
3.	*Se mi toglie la speme*	madrigal	?
4.	*Già verde e forte* *Nel fin de gl'anni 2p*	sonnet	?
5.	*Io mi rivolgo indietro* *Talhor m'assale 2p*	sonnet	Petrarch (15)
6.	*Com'esser può, donna* *Rispose humana 2p*	sonnet	?
7.	*Occhi, cagion ch'ardendo*[1] *Occhi del viver mio*	sonnet	Britonio
8.	*Al dolce suon*	madrigal	?
9.	*Voi sete occhi*	madrigal	?
10.	*Amor m'accende*	madrigal	?
11.	*Perch'al viso d'amor*	Petrarchan madrigal	Petrarch (54)
12.	*Caro pegno del cielo*	madrigal	?
13.	*Ahi chi m'ancide*	madrigal	?
14.	*Se le lunghe fatiche*[1]	sonnet (set in one part)	Lionardi
15.	*Quando nel cor*	madrigal	?

*Poems with superscript 1 appeared in the *Secondo Volume* (see Table 1.4).

Table 4.1   (cont.)

	TITLE	POETIC FORM	AUTHOR
16.	*Hora che gl'animale*[1] *Così sia l'una 2p*	sonnet	B. Tasso
17.	*Da le due chiare* *Così quel pianto 2p*	sonnet	?
18.	*Caro dolce ben mio perche* *fuggite*	ottava stanza	Celiano (?)
19.	*Ben ch'io più arda*	madrigal	?
20.	*Non m'è grave per voi*	madrigal	?
21.	*Come senza timor*	irregular ottava stanza	?
22.	*Come fido animal*[1] *Cosi temendo 2p*	sonnet	B. Tasso

Table 4.2   The Poetic Contents of the Ninth Book of Madrigals for Five Voices (1580)

TITLE*	POETIC FORM	AUTHOR
1. *La pastorella mia l'altr'hier*	irregular ottava stanza	?
2. *Se tu mi dessi, amor* *Ma mentre io taccio 2p*	sonnet	?
3. *Occhi strali d'Amor*	madrigal	?
4. *Deh, chi più rende hor*	madrigal	?
5. *Questa fera gentil*[1] *Fortunato colui 2p*	sonnet	Rinieri
6. *Io son si stanco a riprovar*[1] *Tal ch'io non provo mai 2p*	sonnet	B. Tasso
7. *Lasso me che più m'arde*[2]	ottava stanza	Gandolfo Porrino
8. *Dunque è pur ver cor mio*[2] *Crudel hor queste son 2p* *Perfido ove mi lasci 3p*	ottava stanza	Bernardino Martirano

*Poems with superscript 1 appeared in the *Primo* or *Secondo Volume* (see Table 1.4). Poems with superscript 2 appeared in the *Stanze* (see Table 1.5).

Table 4.2 (cont.)

	TITLE	POETIC FORM	AUTHOR
9.	*Soffri cor doloroso Nulla val contra il ciel 2p*	sonnet	?
10.	*Si dolce è'l foco mio[1] Dolce fiamma d'Amor 2p*	sonnet	B. Tasso
11.	*Chi vi mira e non v'ama Qual poi del tutto 2p*	sonnet	?
12.	*Stratiami pur Amor[1] Non fia mai 2p*	sonnet	G. B. Rinaldi
13.	*Lagrime false[1] Celar più non poteasi 2p*	sonnet	A. Terminio
14.	*Chi crede, amor*	irregular ottava stanza	?
15.	*Di sì cocente fiamma*	madrigal	?
16.	*Amianci, poi che qui cosa Presche lusinghe 2p*	sonnet	?
17.	*Come esser può[1] Se ciò non basta 2p*	sonnet	Politano

Table 4.3   The Poetic Contents of the Fourth Book of Madrigals for Six Voices (1580)*

TITLE	POETIC FORM	AUTHOR
1. *Lunge da voi, con voi* *Lasso quanti sospir 2p*	sonnet	?
2. *Lasso me, se cortese* *Così presso e lontan 2p*	sonnet	?
3. *Qual fugge a l'apparir* *Et qual al dipartir 2p*	sonnet	?

4. *Se voi deste al mio mal*
  O se sapeste
  O se fermaste
  Ma poi vostr'alto orgoglio
	canzone	?

5. *De l'Arno in su le sponde*	madrigal	?
6. *Lagrime care* *Già sarei sotto 2p*	sonnet	?
7. *Se per la mia vita* *Ma se volgete altrove 2p*	sonnet	?
8. *Alma d'amor gioiosa*	madrigal dialogue	?

9. *Coppia gentil, ch'un dolce foco*
  Qual cagion mai
  Sì potess'io mostrarti il cor
  Vero amor, vera speme
  Morte m'è presso
  Grave è più ch'altr'il duol
  Tempra homai l'ira
	canzone	attributed to Rinuccini in the *New Vogel* (highly doubtful)

*According to the Index to the *New Vogel*, only one of these texts, *Alma d'amor gioiosa*, had been previously set to music.

Table 4.4   The Poetic Contents of the Tenth Book of Madrigals for Five
Voices (1581)

TITLE *	POETIC FORM	AUTHOR
1. *Amor m'impenna l'ale*[1] *Che s'altri 2p*	sonnet	Tansillo
2. *Quand'io talhor*	madrigal	?
3. *Hor guerra hor*	madrigal	?
4. *Come vago augellin*	irregular ottava stanza	?
5. *Occhi vaghi amorose*[1] *Occhi leggiadri 2p*	sonnet	Mozzarello
6. *Che piangi*	madrigal	?
7. *Dolci amorose parolette*[1]	sonnet quatrains	G. B. Giraldi
8. *Amor chi m'assicura*	madrigal	?
9. *Dhe qual fero destin* *Ahi desir cieco 2p*	sonnet	?
10. *Nasci e venendo*[1] *Ella di neve 2p*	sonnet	Varchi
11. *Questi gigli*	madrigal	?
12. *Tu mi piaghisti*	madrigal	?
13. *Dolcissima cagion* *Verde e viva 2p*	sonnet	?
14. *Scipio l'acerba caso*	madrigal	?

15. *Già havea l'eterna man*
    Parea dicesse
    Et perch'io torni
    Credei mentre io
    Nasce il gran piacer
    Non sia più meco
    O dolce sonno
    Qual sonno
	chain of eight
	   ottava stanzas
		?

*Poems with superscript 1 appeared in the *Primo* or *Secondo Volume*
(see Table 1.4).

Table 4.5 The Poetic Contents of the Fourth Book of Madrigals for Four Voices (1581)

	TITLE*	POETIC FORM	AUTHOR
1.	*Deh Flori*[1] *Sola te cerco 2p*	sonnet	Montenero
2.	*Deh fata homai*[2]	ottava stanza	Gandolfo Porrino
3.	*O fastiditi già*[1] *Tempo sarebbe 2p*	sonnet	G. B. Giraldi
4.	*Quando Filli potrà*[1] *Poscia pien di furor 2p*	sonnet	Benedetto Varchi
5.	*Dolce mio caro*[1] *Qui trar del petto 2p*	sonnet	Domenico Veniero
6.	*Porta il buon villanel*[1] *Ma i pomi un tempo 2p*	sonnet	Coppetta/Beccuti
7.	*Fa ch'io riveggia*[2]	ottava stanza	Gandolfo Porrino
8.	*Se l'anime piu belle*[1]	madrigal	Remigio Fiorentino
9.	*Quanto di me più*[1]	madrigal	Remigio Fiorentino
10.	*Non fuggì Febo*	madrigal	Molino (*New Vogel*)
11.	*Sotto quest'edra*[1] *O! Quanta ho già 2p*	sonnet	Benedetto Varchi
12.	*Mentre piena d'orgoglio*[2] *Vedrai mutata 2p* *Se dunque è ver 3p*	ottava stanza ottava stanza ottava stanza	Gandolfo Porrino
13.	*Deh, s'io potessi*[2]	ottava stanza	Gandolfo Porrino

*Poems with superscript 1 appeared in either the *Primo* or *Secondo Volume* (see Table 1.4). Poems with superscript 2 appeared in the *Stanze* (see Table 1.5).

Table 4.6 The Poetic Contents of the First Book of Madrigals for Three
Voices (1582)

TITLE*	POETIC FORM	AUTHOR
1. *Amor che sol dei cor*[2]	ottava stanza	Lodovico Martelli
2. *O beata colei*[2]	ottava stanza	Lodovico Martelli
3. *Ohimè, dov'è'l mio ben*[2]	ottava stanza	B. Tasso
4. *Chi non sa com'altrui*[2]	ottava stanza	Vendramini
5. *Vostro fui, vostro son*[2]	ottava stanza	B. Tasso
6. *Non pur sì duro*[2]	ottava stanza	Luigi Alamanni
7. *Mentre ameranno*[2]	ottava stanza	Luigi Alamanni
8. *Vago monte*[2]	ottava stanza	Gandolfo Porrino
9. *O mia lieta ventura*[1] *Io so che non m'inganna 2p*	sonnet	G. B. Piccolomini
10. *Non vedete voi donna*[1]	madrigal	P. Barignano
11. *Volontier canterei*[1]	madrigal	P. Barignano
12. *O chi potrà*[1]	ottava stanza	Gandolfo Porrino
13. *S'io odo alcun*[2]	ottava stanza	Angelo Costanzo
14. *Vissimi un tempo*[2]	ottava stanza	Vincenzo Quirino
15. *Ohimè, cha da quel punto*	ottava stanza	?
16. *Dolce mia vita*[2]	ottava stanza	Molza
17. *La bocca, onde l'asprissime*[2]	ottava stanza	Bentivoglio

*Poems with superscript 1 appeared in the *Primo* or *Secondo Volume*
(see Table 1.4). Poems with superscript 2 appeared in the *Stanze*
(see Table 1.5). (I was unable to locate *Ohimè, che da quel punto*
in the *Stanze*, but it is undoubtedly there, somewhere.)

Table 4.6   (cont.)

	TITLE	POETIC FORM	AUTHOR
18.	*Poi ch'or è dolce*[2]	ottava stanza	Bentivoglio
19.	*Spesso a consiglio*[2]	ottava stanza	Angelo Costanzo
20.	*Ahi dove lasso*[2]	ottava stanza	?
21.	*Qual più scontento amante*[2]	ottava stanza	Vincenzo Quirino
22.	*Ove lontan da la mia fida*[1] *Così d'un olmo* (2p though not indicated)	sonnet	Remigio Fiorentino
23.	*Quel desir c'hebbi*[2]	ottava stanza	Angelo Costanzo
24.	*Piango ch'Amor*[2]	ottava stanza	?
25.	*Satiati Amor*[2]	ottava stanza	?
26.	*Ardo, sospiro e piango*[1] *E son del mio languir* 2p	sonnet	Remigio Fiorentino

Table 4.7   The Poetic Contents of the Fifth Book of Madrigals for Six Voices (1584-5)

	TITLE	POETIC FORM	AUTHOR
1.	*Alma Susanna*	madrigal	?
2.	*Barbara mia gentil* *Il fier dolor 2p*	sonnet	?
3.	*Mi havete amor*	ottava	?
4.	*Scrivo che morto sono*	madrigal	?
5.	*Poi che le tue ragione* *E se già vaga 2p*	sonnet	?
6.	*E questa la man bianca*	sonnet (set in one part)	?
7.	*O felice animal*	ottava	?
8.	*O che mia bella aurora*	madrigal	?
9.	*Qua giu volo dal terzo ciel*	madrigal	?
10.	*Cara mia vita*	madrigal	?
11.	*Pastor che legg'in questa* *scorz'in quella* *L'altr'hier menando 2p*	sonnet	?
12.	*Cio che il Tag'e'l Patholo* *Formo le rose e i gigli 2p*	sonnet	?
13.	*Voi mi tenest'un tempo*	madrigal	?
14.	*Sogliono i chiari spirti*	madrigal	?
15.	*Lascio nel vostro libro* *Mentre cosi la man 2p*	madrigal	?
16.	*In veder che mia donna*	madrigal	?
17.	*Io che gia tropp'audace*	madrigal	?

Table 4.7 (cont.)

TITLE	POETIC FORM	AUTHOR
18. *Tu puoi ben come suole*	madrigal	?
19. *Vivo raggio lucente*	madrigal	?
20. *Vita de la mia vita*	ottava	B. Tasso
21. *Ahi dispietata amor*	ottava	B. Tasso
22. *Ho sempre inteso dir Cosi la corte 2p*	sonnet	?

The two six-voice books reflect other literary sources, as yet unidentified. In the Fourth Book, not a single poet has been identified convincingly,[19] and in the Fifth Book, only the work of Bernardo Tasso can be identified. It seems likely that the many unidentified sonnets from these years (and from the preceding decade as well) will ultimately be traced to other large printed anthologies.

Most of the sonnets and ottavas come from printed sources, then. It is more difficult to propose a source for the other principal poetic type, the madrigal. Most poetic anthologies printed before 1580 tend to contain only a few madrigals; rather, they are typically filled with sonnets and other standard forms. One is tempted for this reason to propose that Monte found his madrigals either in manuscript sources, or in other composers' madrigal books. Though it seems that in a few instances one can point to a particular madrigal book as a likely source for this or that poem, the evidence is slim and not worth considering in detail.[20]

The sonnets and ottavas in these books tend to be serious, even melancholy, though this is by no means always the case.[21] The madrigals are decidedly less serious, and in some the tone of hedonism which triumphs later in the decade begins to emerge. Yet the prevailing impression of Monte's poetic choices from 1580-84 is one of considerable variety: now serious, now frivolous, his poems give the first indication of the ambivalent stylistic stance of these books.

The Music

Introduction

The three five-voice books of 1580-81 embody a number of significant stylistic changes. The books which follow—the last four-voice book (1581), the three-voice book (1582), and the six-voice book (1584)—are less central to Monte's development. The changes in these years are both external and internal; we can begin with the former. Since Monte continued to cultivate quite self-consciously both a lighter and a serious style, we can then examine several examples of each genre. The chapter ends with a consideration of a single piece which points the way towards the style of 1586.

Mensuration

One of the most important external developments in this period is the sudden change of mensuration from ₵ to C, which comes in the Tenth Book (see Table 4.8). The table shows that ₵ prevails in the majority of his books published before 1581: only six of the sixteen books which appeared before that year have

Table 4.8   Monte's Use of C and ₵

	TITLE OF PUBLICATION	MENSURATION SIGN AND COMMENTS
1.	I.5(1554)	Entirely in ₵.
2.	I.4(1562)	Both in C and ₵; this is the only book of Monte's published before 1581 in which more than half of the pieces are in C.
3.	I.6(1563-69)	Entirely in ₵.
4.	II.5(1567)	Entirely in ₵.
5.	II.6(1569)	Entirely in ₵.
6.	II.4(1569)	Only the two previously published pieces (the opening cycle, *La dolce vista*, from 1568[3], and *Quando mi vene*, from I.4) are in C.
7.	III.5(1570)	Entirely in ₵.
8.	IV.5(1571)	With the exception of the concluding sestina, *Quand'al grato spirar*, which is entirely notated in C, the book is notated in ₵.
9.	V.5(1574)	Only two pieces, *Quando il voler* and *Chi vuol veder*, are notated in C (there is some confusion in the parts of these two pieces); the remainder of the book is in ₵.
10.	VI.5(1575)	Entirely in ₵, with the sole exception of the Latin motet, *Augustis Erneste*.
11.	III.6(1576)	Entirely in ₵.
12.	III.4(1569-76)	Entirely in ₵, with the exception of the two Latin pieces, *Europam puera*, and *Nymphae virgines*.
13.	VII.5(1578)	Entirely in ₵.

Table 4.8   (cont.)

	TITLE OF PUBLICATION	MENSURATION SIGN AND COMMENTS
14.	VIII.5(1580)	Entirely in ₵.
15.	IX.5(1580)	Entirely in ₵.
16.	IV.6(1580)	Entirely in ₵.
17.	X.5(1581)	Entirely in C.
18.	IV.4(1581)	Entirely in C.
19.	I.3(1582)	The first eight madrigals are in ₵; the remainder of the book is in C.
20.	V.6(1584)	Entirely in C, as are all subsequent madrigal books.

pieces notated in C. In only one of these six (the First Book for Four Voices, 1562) is a majority of the pieces notated in C; in the remaining five books, the pieces in C are quite exceptional. It is noteworthy, too, that pieces in C become less rather than more common as 1581 approaches; the three books of 1580 are exclusively in ₵. The switch to C in 1581, then, is sudden and remarkable. Only one later book, the First Book for Three Voices (1582) still has pieces written in ₵; after this, all of Monte's subsequent madrigal books are written exclusively in C.

The significance of this sudden change is difficult to assess. In chapter 2, we remarked that even in his First Book for Four Voices, the distinction between the rhythmic styles of C and ₵ pieces was occasionally ambiguous. Throughout the 1560s and 1570s, Monte employed ₵ in pieces which more and more took on the animated *note nere* style associated with the C mensuration. Contrasts of tempo may generally be less bold in pieces in ₵, but this is not always the case: *Lasso ben so che dolorosa prede* (from the Second Book for Five Voices, 1567) has a very broad opening statement in breves and semibreves, yet includes (for word-painting purposes) a passage in which the text is rapidly declaimed in fusas. Though unusual, this variety of text-setting and tempo (two intimately related matters) remains a resource of ₵ pieces which Monte continued to draw upon right up to 1580, as can be seen from his setting of the words *che ben che mille volte il dì,* from *Sì dolce è'l foco mio* (see example 31).

Thus, Monte's change to C in 1581 systematizes or perhaps legitimizes the dominant rhythmic stance of his music: its tendency to move in smaller note values, and its tendency towards a greater variety of tempo. The pieces in C now regularly avail themselves of rapid text declamation in fusas, as can be seen from example 32, which gives the opening page of the Tenth Book's first piece, *Amor m'impenna l'ale.* To be sure, Monte's pieces in C do not always use this variety of rhythmic levels; some pieces in the Tenth Book might have been written in ₵ (*Che piangi,* and *Scipio, l'acerbo caso,* for example). In most, however, the rhythmic variety which C makes possible is an indispensable part of the style.

Monte was apparently largely indifferent to the concept of mensuration as a subtle kind of style determinant or designator. In this, his attitude is quite different from that of Marenzio, Wert, and other late sixteenth-century madrigalists. For example, each of Marenzio's books of the early 1580s contains a few pieces notated in ₵; these are always more serious pieces which move in larger note values than pieces in C. Marenzio remained committed to this sensitive distinction between C and ₵ right up to his last publication in 1599, the Ninth Book for Five Voices.[22] Wert, too, continued to distinguish between the two mensurations.[23]

The last indication of any interest on Monte's part in the distinction between C and ₵ comes in his First Book for Three Voices, which, as we have

Example 31. Monte: The Ninth Book for Five Voices (1580)
Sì dolce è'l foco mio mm. 4-8

Example 32. Monte: The Tenth Book for Five Voices (1581)
Amor m'impenna l'ale mm. 1-5

already noted, contains pieces written in both mensurations. In fact, Monte distinguishes quite clearly between the rhythmic styles of both groups of pieces, as can be seen in examples 33 and 34.

Vocal Scorings

Another important innovation in the Tenth Book is Monte's choice of vocal scorings. For the first time in any book of his, he moves emphatically in the direction of brighter vocal colors, writing several pieces in which the two equal voices are sopranos. This is perhaps the single most innovative feature of the Tenth Book. To quote Einstein:

> In the last third of the century, what might be called a "shifting" of the voices takes place in the five-voiced madrigal: the pair of voices having the same clef wanders from the lower register into the soprano. . . . Not even as conservative a master as Filippo di Monte can ignore this change. It affects his work quite suddenly: in his ninth book of madrigals (November 20, 1580) every voice has its own clef in every piece, but in the tenth book (June 26, 1581) the two sopranos are paired in most of the numbers. . . . This, too, belongs to the *variato stile,* the "changed style" that Monte announces in the dedication of his tenth book.[24]

Einstein goes on to cite one of the most influential madrigal publications of the early 1580s:

> What has happened? Just the year before (August 8, 1580) Luca Marenzio had come forward with his *Primo libro,* and in some of the madrigals of this epoch-making book the duet-like conduct of the two sopranos is, as it were, announced as a principal.[25]

Monte may well have been aware of Marenzio's First Book, though it should be noted that other composers before Marenzio had already begun to explore this shift in texture; as we saw, Monte himself had used it in *Amor m'accende,* one of his contributions to *Il primo fiore della ghirlanda musicale* (1577). Yet the Seventh Book has not a single piece for two sopranos; the Eighth Book has only *Amor m'accende;* the Ninth Book has only *Amianci poi* (which Einstein overlooked). All the other pieces in these three books have either equal-voiced altos or tenors, or no equal voices at all.

It should be instructive to observe both the similarities and the differences between Monte's and Marenzio's manner of treating the pair of equal voices. Marenzio's First Book for Five Voices has six madrigals in which the equal voices are the top ones.[26] His manner of projecting the "duet-like conduct of the two sopranos" can be seen most vividly in the opening of *Cantava la più vaga pastorella* (see example 35).

More typically, however, these six pieces tend to be filled with a series of brief, pseudo-canonic imitations which are tossed back and forth between the sopranos. Typically, the lower voices also take part in the canonic writing;

Example 33. Monte: The First Book for Three Voices (1582)
        Amor che sol mm. 1-9

Example 34. Monte: The First Book for Three Voices (1582)
Volontier canterei mm. 1-9

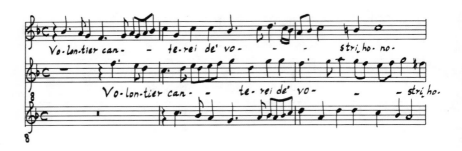

Example 35. Marenzio: The First Book for Five Voices (1580)
        Cantava la più vaga pastorella

often a kind of harmonic-motivic ostinato results. The effect (which Marenzio relies upon almost too much in his early prolific years as a madrigalist) is, in the best pieces, rather like some shimmering and revolving jewel, as can be seen in a passage from *Spuntavan già* (see example 36). Pieces like this were apparently without precedent, and made a lasting impression: Pietro della Valle, writing around 1640, affectionately recalls hearing *Liquide perle* in his youth.[27]

Monte's formulation in the Tenth Book of the two-soprano texture is rather different from Marenzio's, whose light and facile kind of canonic writing (as shown in examples 35 and 36) Monte generally eschews. Rather, he uses the high scoring to shift the textural density still typical of his style from the middle to the top of the texture. The opening of *Amor m'impenna l'ale,* the first piece, shows this (see example 32); all the voices enter quickly, and the imitation is soon close and dense, particularly at the words *e tanto in alto.* Pseudo-canonic writing for the sopranos tends to come only at the beginning of a piece (as here); the technique is generally then dropped. This, too, is different from Marenzio, who loves to return to pseudo-canonic writing again and again in the course of a two-soprano piece.

Monte's twin affections in this book for high sopranos and full textures come together in a unique piece, *Quand'io talhor mi doglio,* for four sopranos (four G clefs) and a high tenor (c^3 clef). The madrigal is evidently something of an experiment, and one which he never repeated. The four equal voices constantly overlap in a hyperactive texture (see example 37).

Occasinally, however, Monte opens up the texture in a gradual and more expansive way, highlighting the duet between the two sopranos, and showing a keen awareness of his textural resource. The opening of *Nasci e venendo* demonstrates these features (see example 38).

The Lighter Style

While each of Monte's books from these years is dominated in varying measure by the serious style, each also contains several madrigals marked by the lighter style. In the Eighth Book, Monte included the two pieces from 1577[1] *(Caro pegno del cielo* and *Amor m'accende),* by far the lightest pieces in the book. Yet the Eighth Book also contains *Caro dolce ben mio,* an oft-set ottava stanza; Monte's treatment, to be discussed shortly, deftly evokes the lighter style, while remaining elegant and sentimental. The Ninth Book, even more serious than the Eighth, nevertheless opens with *La pastorella mia,* a piece with clear references to the villanella and canzonetta. The Tenth Book has the most successful essay in the lighter style, *Occhi vaghi amorosi,* one of the only two pieces from these three books which appeared in a later anthology. Let us look at each of these three pieces.

Example 36. Marenzio: The First Book for Five Voices (1580)
Spuntavan già mm. 47-58

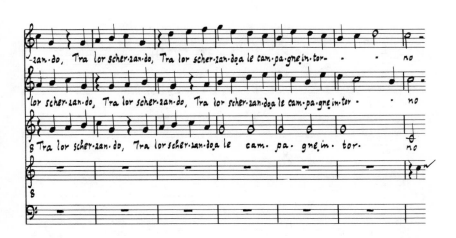

Example 37.   Monte: The Tenth Book for Five Voices (1581)
          Quand'io talhor mi doglio mm. 1-6

Example 38. Monte: The Tenth Book for Five Voices (1581)
            Nasci e venendo mm. 1-6

Ex. 38 (cont.) mm. 7-12

With *Caro dolce ben mio,* Monte hit upon a text which appealed to many other madrigalists at the end of the century. The stanza is attributed to Livio Celiano, and was set at least fifteen times between 1572 and 1611:[28]

Caro dolce ben mio, perche fuggite
Chi v'ama, e per amar languisce e more?
Se vi piace il mio pianto e'l mio martire,
Eccovi il petto, e ne cavate il core.
Che quand'io deggia per dolor morire,
E far del viver mio piu brevi l'hore,
L'alma lieta de ma sara partita,
Se di man vostra lasciarò la vita.

(My dear sweetheart, why do you flee one who loves you, and one who languishes and dies for love? If my weeping and suffering please you, here is my breast—take away my heart! When I might have to die of suffering, and so make shorter the hours of my life, my soul shall happily depart from me, if I leave life by your hand.)

Monte's setting evokes a lighter world by its more straightforward melodic style, by its clear and balanced phrase shapes, by its Canto-dominated texture, and by its bright F Ionian mode (see example 39). The music for lines 1-2 is particularly attractive. Monte begins with a Mixolydian inflection (for the word *dolce,* m. 1), which gives unexpected weight to the subdominant right at the beginning of the piece. He then moves towards the dominant (mm. 3-4) to balance the subdominant gesture. What is most attractive about these opening measures is the carefully controlled Canto line, which gradually expands from its opening statement, rising to a high point (mm. 5-6), and falling gradually to a cadence (m. 9). The lyric elegance of this line is supported in the lower voices not so much by the imitative treatment as by the expressive harmonies which underpin the Canto melody (see particularly the unusually spaced 6-5-3 in m. 6).

The setting of lines 3-6 (mm. 9-23) are less Canto-dominated than the preceding measures, and more consistently imitative. Now it is the harmonic aspect which recalls the lighter forms: the cadences have a balanced and rhythmically settled quality which is almost unusual in the context of Monte's normally effervescent style. Lines 3 and 5 (with the same rhyme, be it noted) both end on half-cadences, which touch respectively on the dominant chords of ii (m. 14) and vi (m. 20). In contrast, line 4 moves unequivocally to a cadence on V (mm. 16-17). The setting of line 6 gaily reinstates the tonic key (mm. 23-24).

The music for the final two lines returns to the opening style: attention shifts back to the Canto line, which is given the most expansive phrase of the whole piece, a line which reaches up an octave and then beyond (m. 28) for the same expressively handled d" heard in m. 6. Again, the clear inflection of V at the end of line 7 (m. 26) is typical of the harmonic clarity of the piece. The light

Example 39. Monte: The Eighth Book for Five Voices (1580)
   Caro dolce ben mio (complete) mm. 1-6

Ex. 39 (cont.) mm. 7-12

Ex. 39 (cont.) mm. 13-18

Ex. 39 (cont.) mm. 25-30

Ex. 39 (cont.) mm. 31-36

scalar figures which fill out a fifth (Canto, Quinto, mm. 25-26) are typical of Monte's style in these years, both in his light and serious pieces.

This piece is far from being old-fashioned, and yet its manner seems to evoke the period of the "classical madrigal" and the style of, say, Arcadelt's *Il bianco e dolce cigno.*[29] In his choice of mode, his clear phrase shapes, his unusually clear harmonic plan, and even in his opening Mixolydian inflection, Monte may have wished to call up in his listeners' minds a memory of the lyric elegance and gently ironic sentimentality associated with the madrigal of the late 1530s.

The Ninth Book opens with *La pastorella mia,* an ottava stanza of an irregular rhyme scheme. Einstein was much offended by the poem's hedonistic tone; his *Notes* characterize it as "on the border of lasciviousness" and conclude with a rhetorical address to the composer: "Old man, what have you come to?"[30] Einstein felt that with such poems as these, Monte was forsaking a nobler poetic tradition. Considered on its own, the poem seems harmless enough:

La pastorella mia, l'altr'hier mirando
Col mio capro cozzar la sua cervetta,
Rise, e sfidommi a lotar seco a prova
E ver me mosse, in dolci atti scherzando,
Ond'io la presi ne le braccia stretta
Ne molto andò che d'una in altra prova
Mentre ella meco pugna, io'l pie l'allaccio;
Vinti cademmo de l'herbetta in braccio.

(The other day, my little shepherdess, watching my goat sporting with her little deer, laughed and challenged me to battle with her, and moved towards me with frolicsome, sweet actions. Whence I took her tightly in my arms, and she went to it from one to another test. While she fights me, I trip her up with my foot. Beaten, we fall into the grass, in each other's arms.)

Monte's setting may first strike the eye as wholly serious, and untouched by the lighter forms: its Dorian mode, and its swift changes of texture, motive and tempo initially confirm this impression (see example 40). Yet, probably in response to the poem's obsession with physical action, the music is filled with the sophisticated metrical play associated with the lighter forms, in which continually shifting patterns of triple meter are superimposed over the notated duple meter. These triple patterns occur at three rhythmic levels: $\frac{3}{4}$, $\frac{3}{2}$, and $\frac{3}{1}$. Triple meter inevitably conjures up the dance, and it was doubtless Monte's intent to convey the poem's erotic connotations by means of these stylized dance rhythms. Example 40 leaves the original notation intact, but also supplies an interpretation of these superimposed triple patterns. Not all of them are as obvious as others; part of Monte's technique here is to move back and forth among various levels of metrical clarity. The triple-time setting of line 1 is unambigous, though, and sets the tone right at the beginning. Equally unambiguous (to my ears) is the metrical handling of line 8. Here we find two

Example 40. Monte: The Ninth Book for Five Voices (1580)
La pastorella mia (complete) mm. 1-4

Ex. 40 (cont.) mm. 5-8

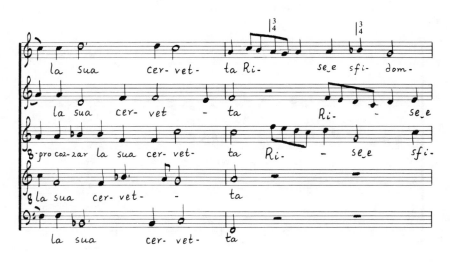

Ex. 40 (cont.) mm. 9-12

Ex. 40 (cont.) mm. 13-16

Ex. 40 (cont.) mm. 17-21

Ex. 40 (cont.) mm. 22-24

measures of $\frac{3}{2}$, followed by a hemiola (that is, a measure of $\frac{3}{1}$), which brings the final cadence. Harmonic rhythm, melodic shapes, and textual accents all conspire to make these superimposed triple patterns quite convincing. Such metrical play is not unusual for Monte; we have already observed another example of it in the Seventh Book (see chapter 3). What is new here is the subtlety of the treatment, and its clear evocation of the dance, albeit in stylized form.

Occhi vaghi amorosi, from the Tenth Book, is Monte's most successful essay in the lighter style of the early 1580s; not surprisingly, it is one of only a very few pieces from these years to be included in a later anthology. It also appeared in two intabulations. Oddly enough, it is not one of the two-soprano pieces, but one with a more traditional two-alto scoring. Its text is an innocuous sonnet in praise of the lady's eyes.

Occhi vaghi amorosi is filled with homophonic passages, dressed out in sprightly, almost dance-like rhythms. Indeed, homophony appears to a greater degree in this madrigal than in any other in the book. When imitation is used, the point is an airy figure resembling the diminution patterns we have already observed. Monte places these figures prominently at the beginning of the *seconda parte,* for the words *Occhi leggiadri.*

The piece is in the Mixolydian mode, which is handled here with a new and quite striking harmonic clarity. This is a symptom of a broader development which took place in the last thirty-odd years of the century, which Einstein referred to as "the clearing-up of the harmonic style."[31] He relates the development to the influence of the lighter forms, an interpretation also made by Edward Lowinsky in his *Tonality and Atonality in Sixteenth-century Music.*[32] In *Occhi vaghi amorosi,* this harmonic clarity is conveyed by short, repetitive, and formulaic harmonic patterns and by a texturally distinct and obviously functional lower voice (see example 41).

A single detail from the *prima parte* shows how close this style is to the lighter style which Marenzio also cultivated in his First Book for Five Voices (1580). At the words *occhi soavi e cari* and *d'eterno honore,* Monte writes two homophonic passages in which the chords of G, F and D major are swiftly juxtaposed, an effect drawn from the Mixolydian cadence formula of the lighter forms (see example 42A). The expressive effect is flippant and ironic. Passages in a similar vein abound in Marenzio's madrigals of the early 1580s; Example 42B is taken from *Che fa oggi il mio sole,* from the First Book.

The apparent ease with which Monte mastered this lighter style makes it all the more odd that this should be the only example of this style in the Tenth Book, or indeed in any of the books of 1580-81. Einstein's reaction to the piece (voiced in his *Notes*) sums up its importance: "Monte has really accommodated himself to the new and lighter style; the first part [is] almost completely homophonic; the second part [has] that agile, airy, and finely chiselled motivic

Example 41. Monte: The Tenth Book for Five Voices (1581)
Occhi vaghi, amorosi (*seconda parte*, mm. 50-60) mm.
50-55

Ex. 41 (cont.) mm. 56-60

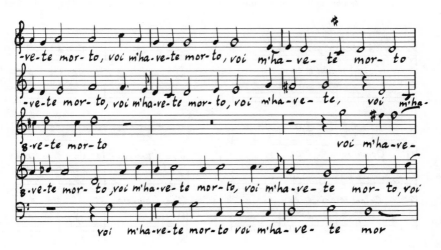

Example 42a.   Monte: The Tenth Book for Five Voices (1581)
Occhi vaghi amorosi, mm. 13-14, and mm. 17-18

Example 42b.   Marenzio: The First Book for Five Voices (1580)
Che fa oggi il mio sole mm. 27-30

style of the younger Italians: it appears as though Monte already might know Marenzio's madrigals. *And this piece was a success!*"[33]

The Serious Style

All of Monte's publications from these years abound with excellent serious pieces. Yet the culmination of his serious manner comes in the Tenth Book, and there in a few remarkable pieces, most notably *Scipio l'acerbo caso,* and the concluding cycle, *Già havea l'eterna man.* Both present fascinating poems as well as extraordinary settings. In the discussion which follows, both works will serve as examples of Monte's finest achievements in his serious vein.

Scipio l'acerbo caso is an unusual lament on the death of a certain Scipio:

> Scipio, l'acerbo caso
> Onde'l lucido sol de giorni tuoi
> Fu sospinto a l'occaso
> Sul primo lampeggiar de raggi suoi
> Piangerà eternamente
> Sospirando sua sorte
> Più ne ne piaghe tue che la tua morte.
>
> Tu, morendo innocente,
> Da crudel ferro anciso,
> Volasti in paradiso
> Ove l'eterno ben godi presente.
> Ella, in tenebre avolta
> D'oscura nebbia d'immortal dolore,
> Priva del tuo splendore,
> In perpetuo martir resta sepolta;
> Perchè l'empia ferita
> Che ti tolse la vita,
> Quando del sangue tuo la terra tinse,
> Nella tua morte ogni sua gloria estinse.

(Scipio, your native land will mourn forever the cruel fate by which the bright sun of your days was driven out to the west at the first glimmer of its rays, and will lament its fate more for your wounds than for your death.

You, who died innocent, slain by cruel steel, flew to heaven where you now enjoy eternal peace. Your native land, wrapped in a gloomy fog of unending sadness, deprived of your splendor, remains buried in perpetual suffering, because the evil wound which took your life, when your blood stained the ground, extinguished all her glory with your death.)

The authorship of this poem has not been established, nor when or for whom it was written. Clearly, the poem laments the violent death of a young man whose greatness had just begun to reveal itself, as the reference in lines 1-4 makes clear. Possibly the poem refers to P. Cornelius Scipio Aemilianus Africanus

Minor of ancient Rome.[34] It has also been suggested that it may refer, more topically, to Don Juan of Austria (1547-1578).[35] The poem was also set by the following composers:

Soriano	First Book for Five Voices	1581
del Mel	First Book for Five Voices	1584
Marenzio	Fourth Book for Five Voices	1584
Moscaglia	Third Book for Five Voices	1585
Ingegneri	Fifth Book for Five Voices	1587

The dedication of Soriano's book precedes Monte's by several months.[36] Monte may have taken the text from Soriano's book, or may have acquired it from an independent source; there is some evidence for the former supposition.[37] In any case, Monte's setting is utterly different (except for its ending) from Soriano's. Evidently the excellence of Monte's *Scipio l'acerbo caso* helped set in motion the typical process of emulative settings, which lasted for several years.

In *Scipio l'acerbo caso*, Monte calls upon all the resources of the serious madrigal: the Phrygian mode; a dark two-tenor scoring; vivid contrasts of texture, rhythm, and melodic figure; and even a sparing use of harmonic color, a feature now rare in his music (see example 43). (Monte even indulges in a rare moment of eye-music; see mm. 43-44). In its application of these techniques, and in its utter seriousness, this madrigal allies itself firmly with the tradition of Willaert, Rore, and Lasso.

Monte shows his mastery of that tradition by his sensitive handling of a few key motivic and harmonic relationships. The setting of lines 1-2, one of the most colorful passages Monte wrote in these years, establishes the grave tone which permeates the whole piece, and at the same time exposes a motive with both melodic and harmonic implications. That motive, initially only hinted at by means of a cross-relation between Tenore and Alto in m. 4, is a rising chromatic line, here B-C♮-C♯-D (see example 44A). In his second half, Monte uses the skirmish between C♮ and C♯ to fashion two imitative points (see example 44B and C). More importantly, Monte returns again and again to the juxtaposition of the triads of C and A major (which first occurs in m. 4), using that juxtaposition to give point to the homophony at *sul primo lampeggiar de raggi suoi* (see example 44D), and to give the ending of the first half its distinctive quality (see example 44F). Transpositions of this juxtaposition occur as well, as example 44E and 44G demonstrate. Note how both example 44E (with its juxtaposition of G and E major triads) and example 44G (with its F and D major juxtaposition) retain the initial triad in first inversion, a feature drawn from m. 4. Other examples of Monte's attention to detail could be adduced.

Example 43. Monte: The Tenth Book for Five Voices (1581)
Scipio, l'acerbo caso (complete) mm. 1-6

Ex. 43 (cont.) mm. 7-12

Ex. 43 (cont.) mm. 13-18

Ex. 43 (cont.) mm. 19-24

Ex. 43 (cont.) mm. 25-28

Ex. 43 (cont.) mm. 29-34

Ex. 43 (cont.) mm. 35-40

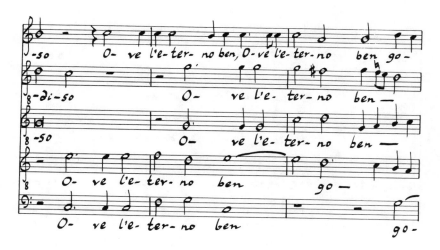

Ex. 43 (cont.) mm. 41-46

Ex. 43 (cont.) mm. 47-52

Ex. 43 (cont.) mm. 53-58

Ex. 43 (cont.) mm. 59-64

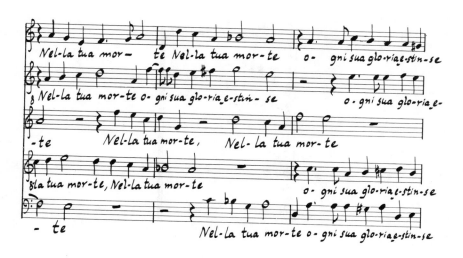

Ex. 43 (cont.) mm. 65-68

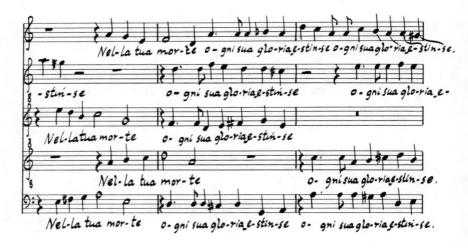

Example 44. Monte: The Tenth Book for Five Voices (1581)
            Thematic Interrelationships in *Scipio, l'acerbo casa*

Ex. 44a. mm. 2-5

Ex. 44b. mm. 52-54   Ex. 44c. m. 64

Ex. 44d. mm. 11-13

Ex. 44e. m. 16

Ex. 44f. mm. 26-28

Ex. 44g. m. 51

The most unusual passage in this madrigal is its conclusion. In the final measure, the music disintegrates in a vivid representation of the closing line: *nella tua morte ogni sua gloria estinse*. No firm cadence is reached, and the standard harmonic close of a Phrygian mode piece (A minor-E major) is only darkly implied. The Alto alone is left singing, its last two notes a ghostly echo of the Canto's preceding phrase.

Endings such as these, though certainly rare, were not without precedent in the madrigal literature. Probably Monte knew Rore's four-voice *Amor ben me credevo*, published in 1550;[38] like *Scipio, l'acerbo caso*, it too is in the Phrygian mode, and has a similarly tenuous close (see example 45). A comparison of these two moments is instructive: Monte's is much more extreme, rhythmically and texturally, than Rore's. Though Monte borrows an expressive detail from the serious mid-century tradition, he elaborates that detail in an inventive and bold manner. In such ways, he shows himself to be not merely an older proponent of the serious tradition, but one who continued to explore its expressive possibilities into the 1580s.

Actually, a similar ending can also be seen in Soriano's setting of the same year, in Marenzio's of 1584, though not in Ingegneri's of 1586. Soriano's setting is available in Ruth de Ford's dissertation, where the author finds the piece technically inept and inexpressive (a judgment with which I can only concur).[39] Yet Soriano's ending is of interest if only because of its similarity to Monte's. Soriano too chose to end with an unusual cadence, yet the staid rhythm and the inexpressively handled mode make for a tame and lifeless ending in comparison with Monte's (see example 46).

The Tenth Book closes with an ambitious cycle, *Già havea l'eterna man*, eight melancholy ottava stanzas on the theme of sleep and the pain and delusion which come with "bitter waking." As a work of lyric poetry, these stanzas may evoke little interest,[40] but their underlying structure is intriguing, for they form a cento based upon a single stanza in the *Orlando Furioso*. Each of these stanzas ends with a line drawn successively from Ariosto's single stanza, *Il dolce sonno* (33:63). This stanza, and an English translation drawn from Sir John Harrington's version of the epic printed in London in 1594 are given below.

Il dolce sonno mi promise pace,
Ma l'amaro veggiar mi torna in guerra:
Il dolce sonno è ben stato fallace,
Ma l'amaro veggiare, ohimè! non erra.
Se'l vero annoia, e il falso sì mi piace,
Non oda o vegga mai più vero in terra:
Se'l dormir mi dà gaudio, e il veggiar guai,
Possa io dormir senza destarmi mai.

Example 45. Rore: First Book for Four Voices (1550)
Amor, ben mi credevo (concluding measures)

Example 46. Soriano: The First Book for Five Voices (1581)
    Già havea l'eterna man (stanza prima) mm. 1-6

Sweet dream did promise me a quiet peace,
But bitter waking turneth all to war;
Sweet dream deluded me and soon did cease,
But bitter waking plagues and doth not err;
If falsehood ease and truth my pain increase,
I wish myself from truth I still might bar;
If dreams breed joy and waking cause my pain,
Aye might I dream and never wake again![41]

Here is the Tenth Book's eight-fold elaboration:

Già havea l'eterna man d'ogni sua stella
Fatto il sereno ciel lucente e adorno,
E di Febo la candida sorella
Facea parer la notte un chiaro giorno;
Stanca già s'en dormia la pastorella
C'havea il dì scorso il monte e'l piano intorno,
Quando con quella che m'ancide e sface
"Il dolce sonno mi promise pace."

(Already the eternal hand had illuminated and adorned the serene sky with all its stars, and Phoebus' shining sister had made the night appear as clear day. The tired shepherdess, who in daytime had scurried across mountain and plain, went to sleep, when, with that one who slays me and is my undoing, "Sweet dream did promise me a quiet peace.")

"Parea," dicesse, con aperte braccia,
"D'haverti usato torto; hor mi pent'io.
Stringemi forte, e dolcemente abbraccia,
Che tu sei la mia vita, e il cor mio.
Succia 'ste labbia e questa fronte baccia,
E tempra hormai l'ardente tuo desio."
Al'hor mi tenn'io sol felice in terra,
"Ma l'amaro vegghiar mi torno in guerra."

("It seems," she said with open arms, "that I have abused you; now I repent. Squeeze me tightly, embrace me sweetly, for you are my life and my heart. Drink from these lips, and cool your burning desire." I held myself then to be the only happy man on earth, "but bitter waking turneth all to war.")

Et perch'io torni a le mie usate pene,
Sparve il sonno qual nebbia a un fiero vento;
Ond'io pien d'ogni duol, fuor d'ogni speme,
Svegliato mi trovai, solo e scontento.
O breve gioia! O fuggitivo bene!
Come lieve t'involi in un momento!
Ben posso dir, Amor, con la tua pace:
"Il dolce sonno è ben stato fallace."

(And so that I should have to return to my usual suffering, sleep was scattered like a cloud in a fierce wind. Full of every woe, without any hope, I found myself awakened, alone, and discontented. O brief joy! O fleeting happiness! How lightly you fly away in a moment! I can rightly say, Love, with your permission: "Sweet dream deluded me and soon did cease.")

Credei, mentre io dormia, ch'egli, gia satio
Del mio dolor, de le miserie mie,
(Fatto havendo di me si lungo stratio)
Havesse anco oggi mai voglie più pie;
Ma, svegliato, m'accorsi in breve spatio,
Che si facean maggior mie pene rie.
Il duolo falsamente il sonno atterra,
"Ma l'amaro vegghiar, ohimè, non erra."

(I believed, while I slept, that Love, already sated with my unhappiness and my miseries (having tormented me for so long), would yet have today more compassionate wishes. But, awakened, I quickly perceived that my wretched pains were made greater. Sleep falsely knocks my suffering down, "but bitter waking plagues and doth not err.")

Nasce il gran piacer mio da van gioire,
Che si mi fugge in un tratto, com'ombra;
Se da vera cagion nasce il martire,
Ch'ogni piacer fin dentro il cor mi sgombra,
Così quiete non trova il mio desire,
Se non nel falso che l'anima ingombra.
Fugga dunque da me cosa verace,
"Se'l ver m'annoia e'l falso sì mi piace."

(My great pleasure is born of a vain joy which flees from me in a moment, like a shadow. If my suffering is born of a true cause, so that every pleasure is swept away from my heart, thus it is that my desire finds no quiet, other than in that falseness which burdens my soul. May anything true then flee from me, "if falsehood ease and truth my pain increase.")

Non sia più meco quel ch'io odo vero,
Ma quel soave falso eternamente.
Poi che di sì dolce esca il mio pensiero
Pasce la mesta e travagliata mente,
Fugga da me il venen mortal e fiero,
Che le mie gioie eternamente ha spente.
E poi ch'ogni mio ben mi toglie e serra,
"Non odo o veggia mai più vero in terra."

(May what I hear as truth be no more with me, but forever that sweet falseness. Since my sad and troubled mind feeds my thoughts with such a sweet allurement, may that fierce and deadly venom, which has extinguished all my joys, flee from me. And since it [the venom] takes from me, and excludes me from all my happiness, "I wish myself from truth I still might bar.")

O dolce sonno, più di vera vita
Compagno, ch'assomiglia fiera morte!
Sonno, per cui da l'hora infinita,
Godo del mio bel sol beata sorte!

Sonno, che con l'amara dipartita,
Ogni contento mio teco ne porti!
Chiude questi occhi eternamente hormai,
"Se'l dormir mi dà gaudio e'l vegghiar guai."

(O sweet sleep, companion to me more than real life, which resembles fierce death! Sleep, by whom I enjoy for an infinite hour a blessed fate with my beloved! Sleep, whose bitter leaving takes away all my happiness! May these eyes forever be closed, "if dreams breed joy and waking cause my pain.")

Qual sonno hebb'io giami lieto e tranquillo,
Da poi ch'entrai ne l'amoroso mare;
Quant'onde, ohimè, per questi fonti stillo;
Quante spargo ad ogn'hor lagrime amare;
A la più ardente bruma, ardo e sfavillo;
E' al più cocente sol, soglio agghiacciare.
S'io debbo dal vegghiar sempre trar guai,
"Possa dormir senza destarmi mai."

(What a sleep I had, never happy or tranquil, since I entered the sea of love; how many waves, alas, do I distill from these fountains; how many bitter tears do I shed at all hours! In the most searing fog, I burn and sparkle. In the most fiery sun, I am accustomed to freeze. If I must always find pain in waking, "aye, might I dream and never wake again!")

James Haar has admirably treated another example of this kind of literary amplification in a case also involving music.[42] To recount briefly his findings: Palestrina's fourteen-stanza cycle, *Da fuoco così bel nasce il mio ardore,* is textually the result of a process of creation identical with that of *Già havea l'eterna man:* each of its fourteen ottava stanzas ends with a line drawn successively from a Petrarch sonnet (*Pace non trovo,* 132). What is more, Palestrina quotes the music of an independent setting of *Pace non trovo* at the final Petrarchan line of each ottava stanza. As Haar remarks, "A whole set of topics... is created by this combination of literary and musical borrowing."[43] In this context, one is disappointed to find that (as far as is known) Monte does not quote the music of an independent setting of *Il dolce sonno* in the final lines of *Già havea l'eterna man*'s eight stanzas.

Both *Da fuoco così bel* and *Già havea l'eterna man* reflect an approach to literary parody quite characteristic of sixteenth-century Italian writers. Haar discusses the extreme vogue for Petrarchan imitation both as it affected the sonnet *Pace non trovo* and Petrarch's *œuvre* in general:

Pace non trovo was, then, spiritualized, travestied, and paraphrased; and, along with the rest of Petrarch's Italian verse, it was dismantled and used a line at a time in innumerable pastiches. Petrarchism being the common disease it was in 16th century Italy, it is not surprising that whole poems, even whole collections of poems, were made simply out of rearrangements of Petrarchan lines and nothing more.[44]

Petrarch was not alone in having his work subjected to such scrutiny and dissection. Ariosto's epic, first published in 1516, quickly attained the reputation of a classic, and was not only endlessly reprinted and translated, but was also taken as the starting point for numerous pastiches.[45] All of these copy Ariosto's language and imagery in varying degrees, but a special category must be reserved for those pastiches which include schematic centonization. One example of just how extreme such centonization could be will suffice. The *Discorso sopra tutti i primi canti d'Orlando Furioso, fatto per la S. Laura Terracini* (1550) has been described in the following way:

> The title of the book ... does not clearly explain the content or the construction of this little work, which is composed of forty-six cantos [there are forty-six cantos in the *Orlando Furioso*] ... each of seven ottava stanzas, in which the corresponding cantos of the *Furioso* are summarized. The first six lines of the first ottava stanza in each of Ariosto's cantos form the last lines of the first six stanzas of Terracini's cantos. The last two lines of Ariosto's ottava stanza appear as the closing lines in the last stanza of Terracini's cantos.[46]

Già havea l'eterna man, then, is a poem which embodies a current literary passion of considerable dimensions. If the extreme artificiality of this centonizing craze strikes modern readers as absurd, we can at least take comfort from the fact that some contemporary writers were equally unimpressed. Pietro Aretino, writing to his friend Lodovico Dolce, had this to say about empty poetic imitation:

> And I tell you plainly that Petrarch and Boccaccio are properly imitated by the writer who expresses his ideas with the beauty and skill which they used to employ when they so beautifully and skillfully expressed their own ideas, and not by someone who plunders them not only for "hence's" and "thence's" and "oftimes" and "graciles" but for whole verses.[47]

Finally, Miguel de Cervantes, in his Don Quixote (1614), wickedly parodies the centonizing vogue in an amusing episode in which a young would-be poet avidly reads aloud his most recent *glosa,* or cento, a patently grotesque poem.[48]

Let us return to *Il dolce sonno.* It is Bradamante, one of the epic's central characters, who speaks in this stanza. In Ariosto's scheme she is destined by her union with Ruggiero to found the illustrious Este dynasty. This couple plays a central role, since one of Ariosto's aims is to sing the praises of his patrons, and to provide their mythological ancestors with adventures on a Homeric scale.

Ariosto contrives to separate the lovers, and then draws an affecting portrait of Bradamante's miserable and inconsolable state. In two impassioned outbursts (32:18-25, and 32:37-43) she gives vent to her grief. In the following canto, she gives a briefer and more restrained expression to her continuing sorrow (33:62-64). In these three stanzas (of which *Il dolce sonno* is the second), she speaks of the deceptive peace which sleep brings, and the bitter waking which shatters that sleep.

The author of *Già havea l'eterna man* shows neither respect for the original context of this stanza, nor much originality in his eight-fold elaboration of it. *Già havea l'eterna man* has nothing to do with Bradamante's predicament; rather, it is a lovesick man who speaks here. The pastoral setting of stanza 1 and the erotic dialogue of stanza 2 are new features, yet they are gracelessly abandoned in the remainder of the poem. To fill out the remaining six stanzas, the poet turns to Ariosto and Petrarch for help. From the stanza immediately following *Il dolce sonno* (33:64), he takes images from lines 1-3:

> O felice animai ch'un sonno forte
> Sei mesi tien senza mai gli occhi aprire:
> Che s'assimigli tal sonno alla morte...
>
> (O happy wights whom sleep doth so possess
> As in six months you never open eye;
> For sure such sleep is like to death, I guess...)[49]

These lines reappear in stanza 7 as:

> O dolce sonno, più di vera vita
> Compagno, ch'assomiglia fiera morte...

The Petrarchan echoes are few, but quite clear: for example, the closing line of Petrarch's canzone 23 *(Ogni men bel piacer del cor mi sgombra)* is glossed in stanza 2, line 2 *(Ch'ogni piacer fin dentro il cor mi sgombra.)*

Whether written as *poesia per musica,* or merely as some kind of academic exercise (by the likes of Don Quixote's young poet friend), these stanzas are, as Einstein said in another connection, beneath Monte's *niveau.* Yet their desperate tone provides him with the material for some of the most expressive music he ever wrote. His setting of the cycle as a whole achieves an extraordinary flexibility and variety of tempo, rhythmic figure, texture, and style. The volatility of the poetry is aptly mirrored by such treatment—even though a nervous and unsettled quality in the music is the result. At the same time, no other piece of Monte's seems to be so obsessed with certain imitative procedures, particularly the simultaneous exposition of a point and its inversion, or the simultaneous exposition of two mildly contrasting points (perhaps one or both of them stated in inversion as well).

Something of this variety of approach can be seen if we look closely at the first and second stanzas. The *stanza prima* begins, as do all but one of the eight stanzas, with an imitative exposition (see example 47). Monte carefully respects the enjambment of lines 1 and 2, and moves to a luminous C major for

Example 47. Monte: The Tenth Book for Five Voices (1581)
    Già havea l'eterna man (stanza prima) mm. 1-6

Ex. 47 (cont.) mm. 7-12

Ex. 47 (cont.) mm. 13-18

Ex. 47 (cont.) mm. 19-23

Ex. 47 (cont.) mm. 24-28

Ex. 47 (cont.) mm. 29-33

the words *lucento e adorno.* Line 3 unequivocally brings the villanella to mind, and the Mixolydian inflections in the following line (mm. 14-15) recall the lighter forms as well. This light touch, and almost veiled or neutral approach to the text is maintained for the remainder of this stanza. None of the following stanzas is quite like this, though again and again they call upon the tone established here to pull away from a too expressive treatment.

The second stanza also begins with an imitative exposition of an almost neutral quality (see example 48). Such a style may seem inappropriate here, for the stanza opens with a quotation (the shepherdess's words). For the end of line 2, however, Monte suddenly pulls the texture together, for a dark Phrygian cadence (mm. 4-5). The commands of the following line *(stringemi forte...)* are also set homophonically, and an expressive B♭ highlights the single word *dolcemente.* Monte returns to an active polyphonic texture for lines 4-5, though the declamatory rhythms of line 4 *(succia 'ste labbia...)* recall those of line 2. Line 6 begins polyphonically, but gradually coalesces into a speaking style for the climax of the shepherdess's speech (mm. 14-15). That climax is achieved by the homophonic focus of the phrase, the lovely pitch peak (e″) in the Canto, and the firm cadence. The following line ("I held myself then to be the only happy man on earth") is set to a point of imitation and its inversion, which crumble to a weak half-cadence (mm. 17-18): the music tells us before the poetry can that this line is mere self-delusion. Finally, the Ariostean quote of line 8 is set off stylistically from what precedes it, both by its deliberate tempo, and by a more elaborate treatment of its imitative material. The Canto dominates the final measures, by returning to the high e″, and then expressively leaping down the octave. The other voices are arranged so as to support the Canto's finely shaped phrases.

Besides revealing the flexibility and variety alluded to, these stanzas also reveal that Monte's music in 1581 has continued to develop along quite idiosyncratic lines: not only is this series of *ottave* an odd kind of poem to set, but Monte's music for it could not possibly be confused with the work of any other madrigalist publishing in 1581—whether a beginner of Marenzio's generation or a twenty-five year veteran of Lasso's.

Towards 1586: *Qui dove un verde lauro*

This chapter can end by considering one quite unusual piece. *Qui dove un verde lauro* is a sonnet setting which first appeared in print in Monte's Eleventh Book for Five Voices, of 1586. Yet it also appears in a manuscript anthology of madrigals, now in Verona. The provenance and probable dating of this manuscript are the subject of some disagreement among scholars. Egon Kenton first proposed that the manuscript was compiled for the wedding of Laura Peverara, a court singer of Ferrara, which took place in early 1583.[50]

Example 48. Monte: The Tenth Book for Five Voices (1581)
Parea dicesse (stanza seconda) mm. 1-4

Ex. 48 (cont.) mm. 5-8

Ex. 48 (cont.) mm. 9-12

Ex. 48 (cont.) mm. 13-16

Ex. 48 (cont.) mm. 17-21

Ex. 48 (cont.) mm. 22-26

Anthony Newcomb takes issue with this hypothesis, and proposes instead that the manuscript was "compiled by the members of the Accademia Filarmonica of Verona, probably in late 1580 and in order to honor Peverara upon her relatively sudden departure from the area of Manuta and Verona in the middle of that year."[51] Because of the appearance in the manuscript of Marenzio's *Ridean già* (which appeared in his Third Book for Five Voices, dedication dated December 1582), Newcomb proposes this date as "a *terminus ante quem* for the presentation of the manuscript anthology."[52] Newcomb goes on to briefly discuss *Qui dove un verde lauro,* one of the few contributions in the anthology from an *oltremontano,* praising its "uncommon excellence." He sums up his view of the piece by stating: "If *Qui dove un verde lauro* is indeed from 1580, it is one of the most modern pieces of its day: it should stimulate us to reassess the position of Monte the madrigalist during the last quarter of the century."[53]

Qui dove un verde Lauro is certainly an attractive piece, yet it would appear on stylistic grounds alone (not taking into account the problems of dating the Verona manuscript) that it is not a product of 1580, if we hold it against the standard of Monte's three other books from that year. Its most prominent features place it in either 1581 or 1582. These features (which Newcomb ably analyzes) are: a high scoring, a virtuosic handling of high textures, and lengthy clusters of eighth-note melismas. Example 49A gives the opening of the piece, which shows the deft handling of high textures, combined with lightly dissonant details typical of Monte's work after 1581. More compelling evidence for why this piece dates from 1581 or 1582 can be seen in Monte's setting of the words *hor va spargendo* (see example 49B). Here, Monte writes the lengthiest melismas yet observed in any of his music. Though passages of this kind appear sparingly in the Tenth Book, they are not as forcefully carried out as here.

Monte's contribution to the Verona manuscript may have been one of the last ones to reach the compilers. (They must have been prepared for some delay in soliciting a piece from someone so far away.) In his contribution, Monte evidently took great care in fashioning a piece which showed his mastery of the most recently developed styles. As such, it must have seemed appropriate for Monte to include it in his next five-voice publication, and one in which that new style has won an overwhelming victory.

Example 49a. Monte: The Eleventh Book for Five Voices (1586)
Qui dove un verde lauro mm. 1-3

Example 49b. Monte: The Eleventh Book for Five Voices (1586)
Qui dove un verde lauro mm. 28-33

5

The Crisis Resolved: 1586-1603

Philippo de Monte y Lucas Marenzio tienen muy lindos y muy suaves passos chromáticos, o per dezirlo mas propriamente, passos moles, lacivos, y affeminados. . . .

Pietro Cerone, in his *Melopeo* (1613)

Introduction

Between 1586 and 1603, Monte published the following eighteen madrigal books, fifteen of them secular (those marked with an asterisk do not survive complete):

The Eleventh Book for Five Voices	1586
The Twelfth book for Five Voices	1587
The Thirteenth Book for Five Voices	1588
The Second Book of Spiritual Madrigals for Six and Seven Voices	1589
The Fourteenth Book for Five Voices	1590
The Third Book of Spiritual Madrigals for Six Voices*	1590
The Sixth Book for Six Voices*	1591
The Seventh Book for Six Voices*	1591
The Fifteenth Book for Five Voices	1592
The Sixteenth Book for Five Voices	1593
Eccelenze di Maria Vergine [for six voices]*	1593
The Eighth Book for Six Voices*	1594
The Seventeenth Book for Five Voices	1595
The Eighteenth Book for Five Voices*	1597
The Nineteenth Book for Five Voices*	1598
The First Book for Seven Voices *(La Fiammetta)*	1599

The Second Book for Seven Voices
  (Musica sopra il Pastor Fido)   1600
The Ninth Book for Six Voices*   1603

In the Eleventh Book for Five Voices, a publication remarkable for its break with Monte's past manner, he wholeheartedly adapts the textures of the canzonetta to the purposes of the madrigal. Homophony is ubiquitous, and a lighthearted and witty expressive cast prevails. In this chapter, we begin by examining the music of this book, a watershed in Monte's career. A brief consideration of other madrigalists connected with the Imperial Court will demonstrate the relationship of Monte's new style to broader contemporary currents. In the years after 1590, Monte slowly retreats from this extreme position, returning to a more contrapuntal style, and renewing his contact with his previous more serious manner, with its affective dissonance treatment, its volatile changes of tempo and texture, its fluid rhythmic language, and its chromatic figures. His later poetic choices no doubt largely account for this stylistic retrenchment: he returns to darker, more melancholy verse, rather than the clever, concettist poetry of 1586 and the years immediately following. In the final decade or so of his life, Monte's abiding interest in contrapuntal intricacy manifests itself in his growing love for fuller vocal scorings: in 1591 alone, he published two books of six-voice madrigals, and in 1599 and 1600 two books of seven-voice madrigals. These works signal Monte's final rapprochement between the canzonetta-madrigal and the more serious style.

The Eleventh Book for Five Voices

Monte's first five-voice publication in five years is dedicated not to a patron in his immediate Imperial environment, but rather to a famous Italian connoisseur of the madrigal, Count Mario Bevilacqua of Verona (1535-1593). Bevilacqua was a prominent member of the Accademia Filarmonica, and the founder of a brilliant *ridotto,* or musical salon, whose fame spread far beyond Verona. An impressive list of madrigalian publications dedicated to Bevilacqua in the 1580s attests the widespread reputation of this *ridotto.* To judge from the variety of music dedicated to him, Bevilacqua favored no particular species of madrigal more than any other: on the one hand, Orazio Vecchi dedicated a book of canzonettas to him in 1580; on the other, Lasso dedicated to him his Fifth Book for Five Voices (1585), and Marenzio his Madrigals for Four, Five and Six Voices (1588)—both extremely serious publications. In choosing to favor Bevilacqua with his first book given over to a new and much lighter style, Monte may have relied on the Count's broad tastes for an enlightened acceptance of his new music. The dedication itself is an important document, and gives evidence of a more confident attitude towards his art:

To His Most Illustrious Lordship, My Most Esteemed Lord Count Mario Bevilacqua:

Among all the delights and pleasures which I have always greatly savored (and which I still savor) when often I find myself taken up in conversation with the Muses—in whose gracious company my soul has always found much stimulation, both because of natural inclination and through many years of study—my greatest pleasure has come when I have needed to present those fruits (which I have sometimes been allowed to gather in the Muses' spacious and perpetually verdant garden) to some honored person, who is not only visibly delighted by music, but who by the continual and affectionate practice of music, takes special pleasure in it.

It appears to me that the consonance, or rather conformity which such a person has with my spirit and thoughts might be enough to awaken in my soul a perpetual and gentle harmony of consolation. And if an encounter which is so pleasant to me should ever succeed favorably, I can say most happily that it has done so today, since it happens by my good fortune that I should make this encounter with the valorous person of Your Illustrious Lordship. For I know not only by reputation how much Your Lordship, by natural inclination, holds all musical compositions in esteem, I have also been assured that Your Lordship sometimes takes pleasure in my own (such as they are). Since you most courteously have already given me some forewarning of your favor, I have wished that, by whatever means, this book of my madrigals, which I have just sent to the presses, might come from them to communicate to you the gratitude which I owe you for the kind recollection which it may please you to have of me. For the great distance, added to the debility of my age, forbid me to present my necessary compliments in person. Now, since I have taken the greatest pleasure in composing these madrigals in the most animated and lively style which I have been permitted to discover, so that they might offer to others the material for some lively singing, so also, with happy sentiments entirely in conformity with these [madrigals], I dedicate them to the generous name of Your Illustrious Lordship, assured that, as your soul is not at all dissimilar from mine, they will be received and enjoyed until a greater opportunity presents itself, that I might show in a more vivid way the esteem in which I hold your most honored qualities. And I kiss your hands.

Prague, 15 November 1586

Your most devoted servant,

Filippo di Monte[1]

Monte's confidence is particularly striking, and contrasts markedly with the diffidence of his dedications to Rudolf earlier in the decade. The incidental imagery is indicative of this new confidence: in his evocation of the Muses' "spacious and perpetually verdant garden" we see the composer reveling in his productive powers, rather than doubting his ability to please his patron.

Indeed, this book stands at the beginning of a new period in Monte's relationship with Emperor Rudolf. In dedicating new madrigalian works, Monte no longer turns to the Emperor, but rather to Italian patrons or connoisseurs of music at the Imperial Court. Evidently aware that the Emperor took little interest or delight in music, Monte turned away from this increasingly melancholy figure.

At the same time as he discovers a lighter style, he also discovers the poetry of Guarini and Tasso, which abounds in the Eleventh Book. He was not in the vanguard in this: by 1586, many Italian composers had been setting the poetry of Tasso and Guarini for a half dozen years or so. Marenzio, for example, included settings of a few poems by either author in eight of the nine books which appeared from 1580 to 1585. His range was broad: he set Guarini's lascivious *Tirsi morir volea* in his First Book for Five Voices (1580), as well as four powerfully dramatic stanzas from Tasso's *Gerusalemme Liberata* in his Fourth Book for Five Voices (1584). These same books reveal Marenzio's love for Petrarch, Ariosto, Sannazaro, and other "classical" authors. In the preceding chapter we saw that, by 1580, Monte's devotion to these poets was largely spent.

When Monte came across the lyrics of Tasso and Guarini, he must have realized that he had finally made contact with a new touchstone of taste in madrigal poetry, and he devoted the greater part of the Eleventh Book to these two poets (see Table 5.1). There are twenty-one poems here, plus two secular Latin motets. Of these twenty-one, ten are by Guarini, and five are by Tasso (including his *risposta* to Guarini's *Ardo si, ma non t'amo*). Only six poems are anonymous (including a *contra-risposta* to the Guarini-Tasso *Ardo si / Ardi e gela* pair).

The poetry here is remarkably homogeneous in tone: a certain sanguine feeling prevails in these amorous, pastoral, and concettist madrigals. There are no laments, no long melancholy disquisitions on the lover's fate such as we encountered in the Tenth Book.

The music of this book, from the expressive point of view, is also remarkably homogeneous, since all the madrigals here are deeply colored by the world of the canzonetta. This means, principally, that homophony is present to a degree unparalleled in any previous publication of Monte's. Other elements drawn from the world of the lighter forms include: clear and forcefully projected rhythms, sometimes dance-like; frequent cadences; high and transparent scorings; and an overall emphasis on diatonic harmony. Even in Dorian and Phrygian pieces, there is an overwhelming tendency for the music to emphasize major triads, and cadences in which the triad is major. All the madrigals are notated in C, and unlike the Tenth Book, there are no pieces here in which this mensuration could be mistaken for ₵. Semiminim movement predominates, with few extended passages in minims, much less semibreves. For the first time in any of Monte's publications, the Quinto has either the same clef as the Canto (in eleven of the twenty-one pieces), or one close to it, which is always above the Alto (the remaining ten pieces). Again, the contrast with the Tenth Book, with its much greater variety of vocal scoring, is remarkable. Monte's conception here weights the texture unequivocally toward the upper voices.

Despite the overwhelming presence of canzonetta traits here, these pieces remain madrigals, and would not have been taken for canzonettas. This is so

Table 5.1 The Poetic Contents of the Eleventh Book of Madrigals for Five Voices (1586)

TITLE	POETIC FORM	AUTHOR
1. *Perfidissimo volto*	madrigal	Guarini
2. *In un bel bosco* *O dolce laccio 2p*	sonnet	Tasso
3. *Tirsi morir volea*	madrigal	Guarini
4. *Donna se ben le chiome*	sonnet	Tasso
5. *Splende la fredda luna*	madrigal	Guarini
6. *Tutto eri foco, Amore*	madrigal	Guarini
7. *Ove a diporto eletto*	madrigal	?
8. *Langu'al vostro languir*	madrigal	Guarini
9. *Al tuo vago pallore*	madrigal	?
10. *Non più guerra*	madrigal	Guarini

11. *Ardo si ma non t'amo*
    Ardi e gela 2p
    Ne ardor ne gelo 3p
	madrigal
	madrigal, *risposta*
	madrigal, *contra-risposta*
		Guarini
		Tasso
		?

12. *A che tanto dolersi*	madrigal	?
13. *Verde laur'e'l mio core*	madrigal	?
14. *Qui dove un verde lauro* *E al credendo 2p*	sonnet	?
15. *Con che soavità*	madrigal	Guarini
16. *O come è gran martire*	madrigal	Guarini
17. *Anima dolorosa*	madrigal	

Table 5.1 (cont.)

	TITLE	POETIC FORM	AUTHOR
18.	*Che dura legge*	madrigal	Guarini
19.	*Odi, Filli, che tuona* *Ben folle 2p*	sonnet	Tasso
20.	*A che piu squarci* *Ahi che son tutto sangue 2p*	sonnet	?
21.	*Laeta Sigismundo veniant*	secular Latin motet	?
22.	*Mille vias dum blanda*	secular motet	?

for a number of reasons: the poems are all madrigal, not canzonetta texts, and the pieces here never use the clear-cut musical repetitions typical of canzonetta and balletto. More importantly, Monte calls upon the techniques of the serious tradition—a sudden slowing up of the tempo, a deft imitative point, a delicacy in the harmony—whenever he is moved to, and never with parodistic intent. The term canzonetta-madrigal is particularly appropriate for this style, then. Einstein's encapsulation of what we find here is an apt one: "Everything must be short, light and nimble; the piling up of seven-syllable lines has changed Monte's thematic and motivic language from the ground up."[2]

The opening madrigal, a setting of Guarini's *Perfidissimo volto,* presents Monte's *più vivace et allegro stile* in its most concentrated form. The poem is vigorous, filled with conceits, yet has a playful and ironic detachment from its theme typical of much of Guarini's verse:

Perfidissimo volto!
Ben l'usata bellezz'in te si vede,
Ma non l'usata fede.
Già mi parevi dir quest'amorose
Luci che dolcemente
Rivolgo a te sì belle e sì pietose,
Prima vedrai tu spente,
Che sia spento il desio ch'a te le gira.
Ahi! che spent'è'l desio!
Ma non è spento quel per cui sospira
L'abbandonato core.
O volto troppo vago e troppo rio!
Perche, se perdi amore,
Non perdi ancor vaghezza?
O non hai pari a la belta fermezza?

(O most treacherous visage! One sees the usual beauty in you, but not the usual faithfulness. Once it seemed to say to me, "These loving eyes which (so beautiful and full of pity) I turn to you, you will see extinguished [by death] before the love which turns them towards you is extinguished." Alas, that love is extinguished, but not that [face] for which my abandoned heart sighs. O too lovely face, and too wicked! Why is your beauty not lost, as is your love! Have you no constancy as you have loveliness?)

The clarity and simplicity of texture, harmony and rhythm make an immediate impression (see example 50). The treatment of line 1 announces the canzonetta style: here, as elsewhere in the piece, the homophony is absolutely homorhythmic. The text is set syllabically throughout, with the exception of formulaic scalar passages filling out a fifth (m. 4, 8, etc.). Imitation is always lightly handled; the points are short, sharply profiled, and we find none of the clever double-points so ubiquitous in Monte's music from earlier in the decade.

Throughout, Monte favors light textures, setting most lines for either three or four voices; he reserves the full five-voice texture for line 7 (mm. 10-12)

Example 50. Monte: The Eleventh Book for Five Voices (1586)
Perfidissimo volto (complete) mm. 1-6

Ex. 50 (cont.) mm. 7-12

Ex. 50 (cont.) mm. 13-18

Ex. 50 (cont.) mm. 19-24

Ex. 50 (cont.) mm. 25-30

Ex. 50 (cont.) mm. 31-34

and line 15 (mm. 33-34). In short, there is more "air" in these textures than in anything Monte has yet composed. Each line of poetry has its own distinct scoring; there are no textural modulations. Rather, the music continually lays itself out in discrete textural blocks.

Rhythmically, *Perfidissimo volto* is dominated by a startlingly limited range of figures, as example 51 shows.

Example 51. Rhythmic similarities in *Perfidissimo volto*.

Line 4:	Già	mi	pa	- re	- vi	dir	
Line 8:	Che	sia	spen	- to il	de	- sio	
Line 10:	ma	non	e	spen	- to	quel	
Line 11:	L'ab	- ban	- do	- na	- to	co	- (re)
Line 12:	O	vol	- to	trop	- po	va	- (go)
Line 13:	Per	- che	si	per	- di a	- mo	- (re)

| Line 7: | Pri | - ma | ve | - drai | tu | spen | - te |

| Line 9: | Ahi | che | spen | - t'è'l | de | - si | - o |

A crisp figure, with semiminim upbeat and dotted rhythm, appears in six of the poem's fifteen lines; every line of the poem has at least one dotted semiminim in it. The single tempo contrast in this piece (which augments a previously announced rhythm, as example 51 shows) is particularly effective, then, in this otherwise uniformly bouncy context.

Harmonically, too, the style is indebted to lighter models. Every line of poetry—already texturally distinct from its surroundings—ends with a clear-cut cadence. In this style, Monte shows little (if any) interest in the continual cadential evasion typical of his earlier serious writing. Over and over again, clear cadences signal the end of a poetic line, and many of the cadences resolve to a bare octave (mm. 6, 10, 22, 23, 24, and 26), a new feature. The treatment of dissonance is generally straightforward, with none of the unusual 6-5-3 or 6-4-2 sonorities associated with the serious style. There are a few fleeting dissonances, though, carefully placed for expressive purposes: the augmented triad in m. 23, and, more interestingly, the parallel sevenths, and complex dissonance above the Basso's f♮ in m. 21.

An odd technical feature in this style merits some attention: Monte's penchant for cadences brings with it a continually recurring syncope pattern in which the text is often improperly accented (Quinto, m. 10; Alto, m. 13; Quinto, m. 23, etc.). This seeming insensitivity to correct word-setting is unusual for Monte, but it is characteristic of the lighter style that he is assimilating. If a melisma is set in motion prior to the syncope pattern (Tenore, m. 21), then all is well; if not, this inelegance occurs.[3]

In his handling of line 7 (mm. 10-12), Monte returns to the technique of pseudo-canonic imitation at the unison between upper voices, which we found in a few of the equal-voiced pieces in the Tenth Book. Here, his handling of this device has all the virtuosity and deftness of Marenzio: with stretto-like compression, the three upper voices ring out the descending syncopated line, until the Canto rises up grandly to a half-cadence, with what seems like an inversion of the descending point. Moments later, after deftly setting line 8, Monte returns to this descending point, altering it slightly, transposing it up a fourth, and augmenting it. Yet its close relationship with the previous point cleverly underscores Guarini's concettist toying with the word *spento,* some version of which comes in four lines in succession. At line 7, the piling up of the texture and the powerful half-cadence underscore (ironically) the lady's protestation of faithfulness; at line 9, the suddenly slower tempo and the gradual collapse of the texture signal the poet's dismay at his lady's loss of interest.

It seems significant that *Perfidissimo volto* is placed at the beginning of the book: it presents Monte's new style in its most unequivocal form. While some pieces in the book are nearly identical with it in style, others are more active contrapuntally, rhythmically, and texturally. Yet every piece is touched by the lighter style; there are no wholly serious madrigals here. In a piece like *Che dura legge,* Monte calls upon the serious style to set Guarini's opening line (see example 52). The greater rhythmic fluidity, the double-point, the cross-relations (mm. 1-2), and the expressive dissonance (m. 4) all evoke the serious madrigal, just as Guarini's text begins by invoking a famous line from Petrarch's *Trionfo d'Amore* (III, 148: *Dura legge d'Amor...*). Yet in the remainder of the piece, Monte abandons the serious style, returning to the dance-like homophony of *Perfidissimo volto.*

Other Madrigalists Who Dedicated Books to Rudolf

Why did Monte effect so remarkable a change and embrace the lighter style so wholeheartedly? The answer seems to be twofold. First, the hybrid- or canzonetta-madrigal was the most influential development in secular music in these years, or, in Newcomb's words, "the predominant type in Italy and ... the major style at the end of the century."[4] The more individual and eccentric styles of the late Marenzio, the late Wert, Gesualdo, and the younger Monteverdi— all in varying measure atypical of the stylistic mainstream—were fostered in the academies of northern Italy and in the courts of such men as Duke Alfonso d'Este, where they thrived more than in any other environment. Second, the

Example 52. Monte: The Eleventh Book for Five Voices (1586)
            Che dura legge (complete) mm. 1-6

Ex. 52 (cont.) mm. 7-12

Ex. 52 (cont.) mm. 13-18

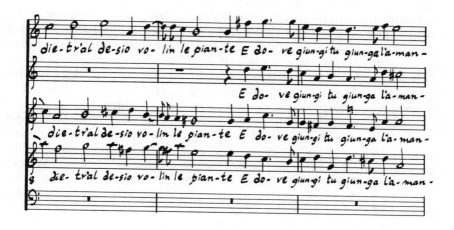

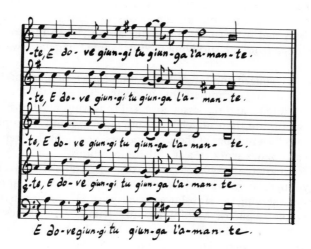

canzonetta-madrigal, and even more so the undiluted forms of canzonetta, villanella and balletto had a European-wide vogue at the end of the century. Kerman demonstrates that the Elizabethan madrigal is an altogether lighter development than its Italian model;[5] the same is true of Italian music composed in southern Germany and Austria. Significantly, when composers in this region chose to "naturalize" Italian music, it was to the lighter forms of canzone, villanella, and balletto that they turned, as we shall see. Paradoxically, the stylistic vocabulary of the serious Italian madrigal was adapted by German and Austrian composers primarily for sacred, not secular purposes.[6]

The evidence strongly suggests that composers, both Italian and Netherlandish, in the service of Habsburg rulers were quick to adopt and promulgate the lighter canzonetta style. Some of these composers dedicated books to Rudolf, or other members of the Imperial family; some were Monte's personal colleagues. A brief survey of the more prominent composers in this Imperial environment seems in order; it will place Monte's stylistic development in a broader perspective.

Table 5.2 lists all the known madrigalian publications dedicated to Rudolf. The list is not a lengthy one—ten dedications, four of which come from Monte. No Italian master dedicated a book to Rudolf solely on the basis of his reputation as a music patron: all the books dedicated to him come from composers who had at least once been in his service, and most of whom received (to judge from the surviving records) some financial reward for their efforts.[7]

Einstein recognized the interest and importance of this small group of Italian and italianizing composers involved variously with the Imperial Court at Vienna and Prague, and the lesser courts of Innsbruck and Graz.[8] Typically, his interest was more than matched by his industry, and he copied several complete books by a number of these composers, and published representative samples of each man's work in a useful compendium.[9]

Jacob Regnart (ca. 1540-1599) was one of Monte's most prolific and successful younger contemporaries and colleagues.[10] Born apparently in Douai, he began serving the Habsburgs as early as 1557, singing in the Imperial Choir during the reigns of Maximilian and Rudolf. His earliest published works are motets in anthologies, and in the 1570s he published two books of motets, one of them *(Sacrae aliquot cantiones,* 1575) dedicated to Maximilian. (Monte had already dedicated two books of five-voice motets to Maximilian earlier in the decade.) A period of study in Italy (1568-70) evidently sparked his interest in secular music, and in the 1570s he produced a body of music whose popularity lasted into the seventeenth century. He dedicated his first secular book, *Il primo libro delle canzone italiane a cinque voci,* to Rudolf, then not yet emperor, and only twenty-two years old. This he followed with a remarkably successful and influential set of three-voice *"teutsche lieder"*—villanellas in

Table 5.2 Madrigal Books Dedicated to Rudolf

	COMPOSER	TITLE, PLACE AND DATE OF PUBLICATION
1.	Regnart	*Il Primo Libro delle Canzone italiane.* *Cinque voci.* Vienna, 1574.
2.	Monte	*Il Settimo Libro delli Madrigali a cinque voci.* Venice, 1578.
3.	Monte	*L'Ottavo Libro delli Madrigali, a cinque voci.* Venice, 1580.
4.	Monte	*Il Decimo Libro delli Madrigali, a cinque voci.* Venice, 1581.
5.	della Gostena	*Il Primo Libro de Madrigali a cinque voci.* Venice, 1584.
6.	Monte	*Il Quinto Libro de Madrigali a sei voci.* Venice, 1584-5.
7.	Orologio	*Il Primo Libro de' Madrigali a cinque voci.* Venice, 1586.
8.	Zanotti	*Il Primo Libro de Madrigali a cinque voci.* Venice, 1586.
9.	Zanotti	*Il Primo Libro de Madrigali a sei voci.* Venice, 1589.
10.	Galeno	*Il Primo Libro de Madrigali a sette voci.* Venice, 1598.

German, in fact. Published in three sets (1576, 1577, and 1579), they were almost immediately gathered together and reprinted in two omnibus editions (Munich, 1583; Nuremberg, 1584). In 1579, he succeeded Alard Gaucquier as vice-Kapellmeister under Monte. In 1581 his *Secundo Libro delle Canzone italiane a cinque voci* came out, dedicated to Count George de Montfort, to whom Monte also dedicated his Fourth Book for Four Voices (1581). In 1583, he was enticed away to Innsbruck by the Archduke Ferdinand (son of the late Emperor Ferdinand, and Rudolf's uncle) where he was appointed Kapellmeister in 1585. There, he evidently focused his energies on sacred music, and saw his *Mariale* published by an Innsbruck printer (1588). He remained there until Ferdinand's death in 1595; in the following year, he returned to Prague, where he again took up the position of vice-Kapellmeister, which he held until his death in 1599.

Regnart's secular production contrasts vividly with Monte's in almost every conceivable aspect. He cultivated, indeed invented, the German counterpart of the villanella, describing his *"teutsche lieder"* as *"nach Art der Neapolitanen."* He retains the coarse or lowly texts of his models, as well as the frequent parallel fifths. Monte eschewed the villanella utterly; even his serious and melancholic compatriot Lasso was moved to publish a book of stylized villanellas in 1581.[11] While Monte's popularity fell off considerably after 1580, Regnart's works were extremely popular and often reprinted. This is attested in a number of ways: in 1579, Leonhard Lechner published a set of twenty-one arrangements of Regnart's three-voice *deutsche lieder;* these attempt to lift Regnart's works to a higher artistic sphere by expunging the parallel fifths, dressing them out in the classical five-voice texture, and enlivening the counterpoint.[12] Another example of Regnart's remarkable success can be seen in the two German language editions of his two madrigal books, which appeared in 1595. Such a distinction was never bestowed on Monte's madrigals, though one suspects that Regnart's close ties with publishers in Munich and Nuremberg help to account for these remarkable prints.

These two books of *canzone italiane* are dominated by the lighter style of Ferretti, yet also contain (as Einstein is careful to point out) a few serious pieces. All in all, however, Regnart's secular *œuvre* offers considerable evidence for the enormous success of the lighter style in southern Germany and Austria.

Next to Regnart, the most interesting composer of secular music with ties to the Imperial Court is Camillo Zanotti (ca. 1545-1591).[13] An Italian from Cesena, he became vice-Kapellmeister under Monte in 1587. There is some disagreement among scholars as to how long he had been in Imperial service, though to judge from his statement in the dedication to Rudolf of his First Book for Five Voices (1587), it cannot have been very long. In the last four years of his life, he apparently cultivated the patronage of Rudolf and other court figures with a zeal matched only by Monte's in 1580-81. In 1588, Zanotti dedicated a book of masses to Rudolf (the *Missarum liber primus*). (Monte had dedicated his first book of masses to Rudolf in the preceding year.) In 1589, Zanotti published his First Book of Madrigals for Six Voices, once again dedicated to Rudolf; in his dedication he mentions that the Emperor was greatly pleased with his First Book for Five Voices.[14] The remark may merely be self-serving, though Walter Pass suggests that Zanotti was "much esteemed, to judge from his monthly salary... and from the gratuities he received in 1587 and 1588 from the emperor, mainly in return for the dedication of madrigals and masses."[15] Zanotti's *Terzo Libro de Madrigali con alcune Villotte a cinque voci* (1589) is dedicated to an Italian patron, but in his last work, the *Madrigalia tam italica...* (1590), he once again turns to his immediate environment, dedicating the book to Guilhelmo Ursino, a privy councillor to the Emperor.[16]

Zanotti's First Book for Six Voices opens with a madrigal in praise of Rudolf *(O di Progenitori Eccelsi Augusti).*[17] His last publication has a number of dedicatory pieces, and several more which have been interpreted as serving occasional purposes. The contrast between Zanotti's assiduous cultivation of imperial patronage in the same years as Monte's apparent indifference to it is striking. As Einstein remarked, "Zanotti fulfills the requirements of courtly music which Monte ignores, preferring to direct his attention to broader horizons."[18]

In his madrigals, Zanotti reveals an easy mastery of the lighter style. He can write serious pieces, though even these tend to be colored by the lighter vein (see *Giacea la mia virtù,* from his First Book for Five Voices).[19] He is most at home with the lighter style, and his setting of *Tirsi morir volea* (from the First Book for Five Voices), besides slyly quoting from the settings of Marenzio and Wert, is a delightful piece in its own right.[20]

Finally, his *Madrigalia tam Italica* includes a setting of Guarini's *Donò Licori a Batto,* which Monte had set only a few years earlier in his Twelfth Book for Five Voices (1587). Zanotti's setting clearly pays homage to Monte's, as we shall see shortly.

We can now turn to the rather more obscure (and much less prolific) madrigalists who appear in Table 5.2. Giovanni Battista della Gostena (ca. 1540-1598) was a student of Monte's, as we remarked in chapter 1—though it is unclear when. In the dedication of his First Book for Five Voices (1584) to Rudolf, della Gostena tells us that he largely acquired his talent at the court of Maximilian II, through Monte's instruction.[21] This book, written after the composer's return to Genoa, does not survive complete; its musical relationship to Imperial taste cannot be presently judged.

Alessandro Orologio (ca. 1550-?1633) is something of a cipher: Eitner believed that there were two composers with this name, both working in the

North.[22] Einstein accepted this hypothesis and attempted to divide the various publications and single pieces between the "Dresden Orologio" and the "Viennese or Prague Orologio."[23] More recently, it has been suggested that these scholars were mistaken, and that we are dealing with a single composer.[24]

This controversy need not concern us, though it appears in this instance that Einstein was led astray. Orologio dedicated his First Book for Five Voices (1586) to Rudolf, having apparently served the Imperial Court as "trumpeter and musician" since just before 1580.[25] His dedication is even more long-winded and flowery than demanded by convention, but it prefaces a delightful set of pieces in which Orologio's mastery of the hybrid style is readily apparent. From this book, Einstein chose to include *Occhi miei, che vedeste* in his useful anthology.[26] Even this single piece shows that Orologio's refinement, and his subtle blend of elements drawn from a broad stylistic spectrum equals Monte's—if it does not actually excel it. Orologio received a special payment from the Emperor for this book, though he apparently had to wait a year for it.

With Giovanni Battista Galeno (ca. 1550-1555; d after 1626) we come to the last figure to dedicate a madrigal book to Rudolf.[27] In the dedication of his First Book for Seven Voices, Galeno states that he has served the house of Habsburg from early youth.[28] He sang first as an alto in the Graz court chapel of Archduke Karl II. After a period in his native Italy (1573-1584), he returned to Graz, where he served as court chaplain until 1590 and the death of the Archduke. Apparently he then became senior court chaplain to Rudolf's brother, the Archduke Ernest, regent of the Netherlands. He dedicated his First Book for Five Voices (Antwerp, Phalèse et Bellère, 1594) to Ernest, signing the dedication in Antwerp. After Ernest's death in the following year, Galeno became court chaplain and alto in the Imperial Chapel in Prague. In 1598, he dedicated his First Book for Seven Voices to Rudolf, expressing the hope that the Emperor might "sometimes kindly lend an ear to the harmony of those voices by which these madrigals are favored...."[29] Galeno remained in his position as court chaplain until the Emperor's death in 1612; after this, little is heard from him.[30]

Monte followed Galeno's seven-voice book almost immediately with two of his own. On this basis, Einstein hypothesized that madrigals with this rich scoring were particularly favored at the Imperial Court. Yet it is odd that Monte chose to dedicate his two seven-voice books neither to the Emperor nor to any other court figure. Rather, he turned to Italian patrons, dedicating his First Book for Seven Voices *(La Fiammetta)* to Cardinal Pietro Aldobrandini, and his Second Book *(Musica sopra il Pastor Fido)* to Ferdinand Medici, Grand Duke of Tuscany. In the latter dedication, Monte mentions the kindness shown him in Florence in 1566. That Monte would address a work to a patron with whom he had (apparently) last had contact thirty-five years earlier exemplifies once more his desire to remain in touch with a broad network of patrons and admirers.

A more detailed exposition of the textual choices and musical styles of the composers just enumerated would reveal that both the lighter forms (as promulgated by Regnart, and later by Hans Leo Hassler) and the pastoral canzonetta-madrigal triumphed unequivocally in southern Germany and Austria in the last two decades of the century. Zanotti, Orologio, Galeno (and a few other figures who, though they did not dedicate books to Rudolf, were active at the courts in Innsbruck and Graz)[31] all cultivated the canzonetta-madrigal to the apparent exclusion of the serious, or experimental madrigal. There can simply not have been an audience for the more esoteric styles being explored in northern Italy in these same years.

The Books for Five Voices: 1587-1595

Monte's music of the late 1580s conforms with the broad stylistic picture just outlined. The Twelfth Book[32] and the Thirteenth Book for Five Voices are still dominated by the style set forth in the Eleventh. A single piece from the Twelfth Book not only demonstrates Monte's continuing cultivation of the canzonetta style, but also offers an opportunity to compare Monte's setting with Zanotti's, published only a few years later in his *Madrigalia tam italica* (1590).[33] (Monte's setting is given in example 53.)

Donò Licori a Batto sets a delightful Guarini madrigal:

Donò Licori a Batto
Una rosa cred'io di paradiso;
E sì vermiglia in viso
Donandola si fece, e sì vezzosa,
Che parea rosa che donasse rosa.
All'hor disse il Pastore
Con un sospir dolcissimo d'amore:
"Perchè degno non sono,
D'haver la rosa donatrice in dono?'

(Licori gave Batto a rose, I believe from paradise; and giving it to him she was so crimson-hued, and so charming, that it seemed a rose was giving a rose. Then the shepherd said, with the sweetest sigh of love: "Why am I not worthy to have the giving rose as gift?")

Zanotti's setting is modelled rather closely on Monte's: both are in the Ionian mode, and both are set in a light, predominantly syllabic manner. The similarities run deeper than this, however, as example 54 shows. Zanotti's setting of line 1 clearly quotes Monte's, and his descending phrase for line 2 inverts Monte's rising one. Like correspondences appear consistently in the remainder of Zanotti's brief piece; his frequent use of two dotted figures in succession (see example 54E) recalls Monte's use of the same figure. Zanotti's harmonic plan, however, does not follow Monte's, with the single exception of

Example 53. Monte: The Twelfth Book for Five Voices (1587)
Donò Licori a Batto (complete) mm. 1-6

Ex. 53 (cont.) mm. 13-18

Ex. 53 (cont.) mm. 19-22

line 6, where Zanotti borrows Monte's Phrygian cadence on E (see example 54D). Finally, Zanotti's ending freely inverts Monte's imitative point (see example 54E).

Zanotti's madrigal is obviously a kind of homage to Monte, which may have had its origins in personal as well as purely musical reasons. It demonstrates that Monte's music was considered worthy of imitation by a gifted composer of the younger generation. Indeed, it is not impossible that, were it not for the younger composer's death in 1591, a pattern of "friendly emulation" might well have developed beween the two figures.

The Thirteenth Book appeared in the following year, dedicated to Chiara Gabri, the daughter of an Antwerp lawyer, and a musician of some repute.[34] It is evident that Monte was personally acquainted with her, for she is mentioned in a letter from Plantin to Monte concerning the publication of his masses.[35] In his dedication, Monte praises her skills as a musician, mentioning that she both plays and sings, though it is clearly her skills as a singer which earned her reputation. Monte includes, as the penultimate piece, a four-part cycle on a French text, *La Déesse Vénus avecque Polymnie* (published in the old *Opera Omnia*).[36] In the guise of a pastoral and mythological setting, it sings Claire's praises, ending with the line: *"Quant à moi, je demeure avec la belle Claire!"* This poem had already been set by Séverin Cornet, and published in his *Chansons francoyses à 5. 6. et 8. parties . . .* (Antwerp, 1581).[37]

This is Monte's only madrigal publication to include a French text. Evidently, Monte's willingness to include a non-Italian piece opened up further horizons: the book ends with a Spanish madrigal (!), *Se bien balle, mudador—* a unique occurrence in Monte's books.[38]

One other piece from this book, a setting of Luigi Groto's *Sottile e dolce ladra,* has been published in modern edition.[39] In selecting this piece, Einstein evidently wished to give an idea of Monte's canzonetta-madrigal of this period. The choice was rather unfortunate, however; here the lighter style seems hardly to have engaged Monte's creative energies at all. It is perhaps not to be wondered that Groto's poem does not stir Monte to much effort:

> Sottile e dolce ladra
> Che con mano sì accorta e sì leggiadra
> Ancor con gl'occhi mi rubaste il core,
> Qual merita supplicio il vostr'amore?
> Merta che dolce laccio al collo un nodo
> Vi faccia e, per serbar più giusto modo,
> Ch'io, che'l rubato fui, sia quel che'l faccia;
> E'l farò se ti par, di queste braccia.

> (Subtle and sweet thief, who with your hand so fair and crafty, and with your eyes as well, stole my heart, what torture does your love deserve? It deserves that a sweet rope shall make a knot around your neck, and, to serve justice more properly, that I, the one who was robbed, be the one to make it, and if you agree, with these arms I shall do it.)

Example 54. Similarities between the Monte and Zanotti settings of
            Donò Licori a Batto

Ex. 54a.   Monte

            Zanotti

Ex. 54b.   Monte

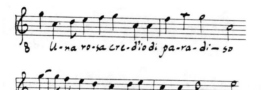

            Zanotti

Ex. 54c.   Monte

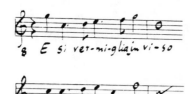

            Zanotti

Ex. 54d. Monte

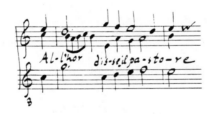

Zanotti

Ex. 54e. Monte

Zanotti

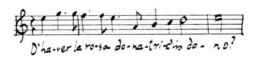

Despite the counterpoint and the textural variety, the piece makes a remarkably vapid impression, perhaps because of its comparatively impoverished rhythmic and melodic material. For a composer of Monte's gifts, the setting is adequate, and little more.

That Monte could still respond to a more expressive text can be seen in his setting (also in this book) of *Lagrime triste,* the tercets of Petrarch's sonnet *Perch'io t'abbia guardata* (see example 55). This is Monte's first Petrarch setting in eight years. Though deeply colored by the rhythmic and melodic gestures of the canzonetta-madrigal, *Lagrime triste* still recalls his earlier serious style in a number of ways. Outwardly, it conforms to the serious genre: it is in the Phrygian mode on A, and has a two-tenor scoring. It opens broadly in semibreves and minims, its first phrase ending with a sudden quickening of the tempo—all this solidly evoking the serious style.

Yet other features immediately call up associations with the lighter forms: the crisp rhythmic figures at line 2 (mm. 7-10); the playful canon between Canto and Tenore at line 3 (mm. 10-12); and even more obviously, the isolation of the words *E voi* (m. 13) with a perky upbeat motive.

To end the piece, Monte returns to the serious style, signalled by a crunching dissonance for the words *angoscia e duolo* (m. 19). The descending point for the penultimate line (mm. 20-22), followed by a syncopated rising one (mm. 23-28) brings the piece to an effective conclusion.

As we turn to Monte's music of the 1590s, our purpose cannot be to illuminate it from all possible angles. We shall concentrate on tracing the most important development in these years: Monte's gradual return to and reformulation of a serious style. Though he continues to write lighter canzonetta-madrigals throughout the decade, he gives more and more prominence to pieces which reaffirm an older and more serious tradition, typically placing a serious piece at the head of each publication. The following discussion seeks only to trace this development, and is based on a close study of a number of pieces transcribed from these books (and a broader acquaintance drawn from Einstein's transcriptions).

Einstein characterized Monte's new stylistic direction in this way:

> From the Sixteenth Book (1593), Monte turns away from the all-too-facile stance of his recent works. He returns to a certain extent to his former self. Again, he cultivates a richer animation through imitation, without renouncing the "stil vivace"; the development is unmistakable.[40]

That development is already evident in the Fourteenth Book for Five Voices (1590), dedicated to Duke Alfonso d'Este. After much flattery, Monte expresses his admiration for the Duke's musical establishment, which he knows (according to his own account) only by reputation. Monte has heard of "music which shines with splendid harmony amidst your royal customs, divided

Example 55. Monte: The Thirteenth Book for Five Voices (1588)
   Lagrime triste (complete) mm. 1-6

Ex. 55 (cont.) mm. 7-12

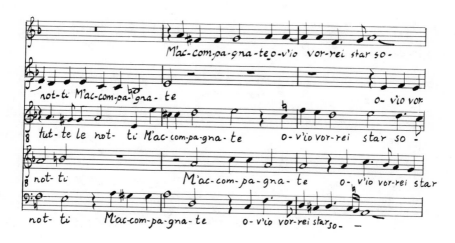

Ex. 55 (cont.) mm. 13-18

Ex. 55 (cont.) mm. 19-24

Ex. 55 (cont.) mm. 25-28

among angelic voices, and sung by such rare spirits that whoever finds himself there believes that he is already in paradise."[41] Monte goes on to express his hope that his madrigals might find a place in the Duke's musical entertainments.

By 1590, the luxuriant madrigal, which had largely been fostered in Alfonso's court in the early 1580s, had become a widely imitated commodity. (In chapter 4, we saw Monte's first effort in this style in his contribution to the Verona manuscript.) Newer, more esoteric styles of composition and performance, emergent in the Ferrarese court of the 1580s, were more jealously guarded. Only gradually and in incomplete form did these styles become known through prints.[42] Yet it is now clear that across the late 1580s and early 1590s a new genre of madrigal emerged in Ferrara, cultivated principally by Luzzasco Luzzaschi, Carlo Gesualdo, and (to a lesser degree) Alfonso Fontanelli, which has been described as expressionistic. Here, extreme disjunctures of rhythm, melody, texture, harmony, coupled with a new and almost reckless treatment of dissonance led to an entirely new sound in the madrigal, and the emergence of its final, decadent form.

In 1590, Monte cannot have had a precise notion of the Duke's particular tastes, or of these remarkable developments. Nevertheless, it is possible that Monte's decision to include a number of darker pieces in this book, and to place them prominently at the beginning may reflect an effort to attract the Duke's attention with a more dense and complex style.

The appearance later in the book of one of the earliest known settings of lines drawn from Guarini's *Pastor Fido* shows Monte's awareness of Guarini's most recent literary accomplishment. The play had only just appeared in print; in fact, Monte's version of the lines he sets strongly suggests that he had access to a manuscript of the play. Guarini had begun it in the early 1580s, and it had indeed circulated in manuscript well before its publication in late 1589 (arousing a considerable literary controversy).[43]

Monte opens the book with four madrigals in the Phrygian mode: *Per questi alpestri monti; Con pietà vi rimiro; Come sì m'accendete;* and *Piango che'l mio bel sol.* I know of no other publication of Monte's which places its Phrygian pieces so prominently at the outset. The first and fourth of these have the more melancholy texts, of a kind we have not encountered for some time in Monte's books. *Per questi alpestri monti* reads like a reworking in madrigal form of the pessimistic ottava stanzas of 1578 (VII.5) or those of 1581 (X.5):

Per questi alpestri monti,
Per quest'horride selve,
Tane di fiere belve,
Lunge da voi mio bene,
Provo noios'e insopportabil pene;
Onde due caldi fonti
Cavo di questi lumi,

Anzi due largh'inessiccabil fiumi;
Ben bramerei la morte
Per finir così fiera iniqua sorte,
Ma tropp'ohime mi preme
Giunger senza vedervi à l'hore estreme.

(Through these wild mountains, through these horrid forests, and lairs of fierce beasts, far from you my beloved, I feel burdensome and unbearable pain, whence I draw out from these eyes two hot streams—nay, unstoppable rivers. Well might I desire death, and thus put an end to so fierce and unjust a fate, but I am too burdened [by the thought of] reaching my last hour without seeing you.)

This theme of alienation from one's beloved in a wild and inhospitable landscape is one to which Monte regularly, if sparingly, returns in the 1590s; in its inversion of the pastoral motif it offers some thematic relief in books otherwise clogged with more vapid expressions of the genre. Monte's approach to these texts is always rather more interesting than his way of handling the standard ones.

His success with these more expressive texts can be seen in his setting of *Per aspre horride vie,* a poem possibly by the same author as *Per questi alpestri monti.* It too is in the Phrygian mode, here transposed to A:

Per aspre horride vie,
Boschi et alpestri sassi,
Luoghi conformi à le miserie mie,
Muovo gl'infermi passi;
Quivi allentando il freno
A miei gravi martiri,
Cavo dal mesto seno
Angosciosi sospiri;
E poi, dolente e d'ogni gioia casso
Dico à me stesso: "ahi, lasso!
Che premio unqu'haveran tuoi casti amori?"
Ma cruda voce mi risponde: "Mori!"

(Amidst these horrid paths, woods, and wild rocks—places in conformity with my miseries—I move with infirm steps; then, loosening the rein upon my grave sufferings, I draw out anguished sighs from my sad breast. And then, sorrowful, and empty of all joy, I say to myself. "Oh, alas! What reward shall your chaste loves have?" But a cruel voice answers me: "Die!")

Monte is able to make a skillful blend of the canzonetta style of his Eleventh Book with some of the techniques of his older serious style (see example 56). The rhythmic and textural focus in the settings of lines 7 and 11 comes from the lighter style: these moments are here largely because of Monte's experience with the canzonetta idiom. But the speaking homophony of mm. 1-8, the dissonant cluster in m. 2, and the harmonic disjuncture between C and A

Example 56. Monte: The Fourteenth Book for Five Voices (1590)
        Per aspre horride vie (complete) mm. 1-6

Ex. 56 (cont.) mm. 7-12

Ex. 56 (cont.) mm. 13-18

major (m. 5) are all drawn from the serious style. The thematic and harmonic relationship between the setting of lines 1 and 2 (compare the Tenore, mm. 1-2, with the Basso, mm. 4-5), and the almost nervous tempo contrasts which come later evoke the care which Monte typically devoted to the serious pieces of the early 1580s.

Monte's setting of the final line (mm. 32-35) provides something like a *catalogue raisonée* of his serious techniques: the descending tetrachord; the theme in both syncopated and unsyncopated form; the double suspensions which result in a particularly expressive series of dissonances (m. 33); the sudden increase in tempo; the cross-relation of m. 34; and finally, the extraordinary final measure, whose rhythmic violence immediately recalls Monte's setting nine years earlier of the final line of *Scipio l'acerbo caso*.

Also in the Phrygian mode on A is Monte's *Pastor Fido* setting, drawn from Act I, sc. ii. Oddly, Monte's text, the earliest known setting of this scene, does not begin with the famous opening words, *Cruda Amarilli, che col nome ancora*, but with its fifth line, *O, d'aspido più sorda*. As suggested earlier, Monte's version of the scene diverges sufficiently from the printed version to suggest that he had access to a manuscript of the play (see example 57). His version deletes entire lines and parts of lines, and is clearly corrupt. Monte's later settings from the play (in his two seven-voice books of 1599 and 1600) display a similar divergence from the printed source, suggesting that he continued to rely on his own source.

Example 57. Two versions of Guarini's *Il Pastor Fido*, Act I, sc. i.

Guarini's published version

Ma de l'aspido sordo
E più sorda, e più fera, e più fugace
Poi che col dir t'offendo,
Io mi morrò tacendo;
Ma grideran per me le piagge, e i monti
E questa selva, a cui
Sì spesso il tuo bel nome
Di risonare insegno:
Per me piangendo i fonti,
E mormorando i venti,
Diranno i miei lamenti;
Parlerà nel mio volto
La pietade, e'l dolore;

E se fia muta ogn'altra cosa, al fine,
Parlerà il mio morire,
E ti darà la Morte il mio martire.

From Monte's Fourteenth Book

O d'aspido più sorda e più fugace,

Poi che col dir v'offendo,
I mi morrò tacendo;
Ma grideran per me le piagg'e i monti;

E gl'antri, e i boschi, e mormorando i fonti
E sospirando i venti
Diranno i miei lamenti;
Parlerà nel mio volto
L'aspro dolore accolto,
Parleran gl'occhi lagrimosi e mesti,
E se non bastan questi
Parlerà la mia morte e col morire
Vi dirò il mio martire.

In 1591, Monte published two books of six-voice madrigals (the Sixth and Seventh);[44] neither of these survives complete. In their choice of texts, the books are markedly different from one another: the Sixth Book relies heavily on Guarini and Tasso (particularly the latter), while the Seventh Book has mostly anonymous pieces.[45] Since nothing from either of these books appeared in a contemporary anthology, not a single piece can be reconstructed.

The Fifteenth Book for Five Voices appeared in the following year, dedicated to Camillo Caetano, who was for a brief time (1591-1592) the Papal Nuncio in Prague. Evidently a friendship quickly developed between the two; Monte's dedication tells us that Caetano was greatly pleased with these pieces, having played them himself on his viola da gamba.[46] The book opens with a Petrarch sonnet *(La donna che'l cor nel viso porta),* the first complete Petrarch poem Monte has set in twelve years, and the last complete one he would ever set. His choice of Petrarch is instructive: rather than turn to a gloomy sonnet or sestina stanza, he turns to a lighthearted sonnet which no major composer had previously set. This single genuflection to Petrarch is quite anomalous in this book, which is otherwise filled with Guarini and with the pastoral and amorous verse of Celiano, to whom Monte turns for the first time.

Monte's setting of *La donna che'l mio cor nel viso porta* (see example 58) displays a remarkable lightness of touch, in keeping with the predominant character of the poem. Its airy scoring, rapid declamation and occasionally clear homophonic textures are all indebted to the lighter style, but its predominantly contrapuntal cast, and particularly its slow-moving, dissonance-laden conclusion rely upon the serious tradition.

Significantly, each of the serious pieces discussed so far strikes its own unique balance between the opposing worlds of the lighter and more serious styles. It is always the text which dictates the particular equilibrium of each piece: here, faced with Petrarch, Monte relies upon counterpoint to achieve a dignified tone, allowing the lightness of texture and the deftness of his rhythms to strike a modern, up-to-date chord.

As Einstein suggested, the return to a more serious style fully arrives with the Sixteenth Book (1593). Monte dedicated it to Diego de Campo, described on the dedication page as *protonotario apostolico,* canon of Santa Maria Maggiore (Rome), and a *"camarier secreto di sua Santità."*[47] Monte speaks of having become personally acquainted with de Campo "upon his return from Poland." He mentions the delight which de Campo takes in music, and states: "I send this Sixteenth Book of Madrigals for Five Voices to Your Most Reverend Lordship . . . to satisfy your desire to see something new of mine."[48] De Campo, evidently resident principally in Rome during these years, was also the dedicatee of Marenzio's Seventh Book for Five Voices (1595). Marenzio too speaks of the interest which de Campo has taken in his works.[49]

Example 58. Monte: The Fifteenth Book for Five Voices (1592)
La donna che'l mio cor nel viso porta (complete) mm.
1-6

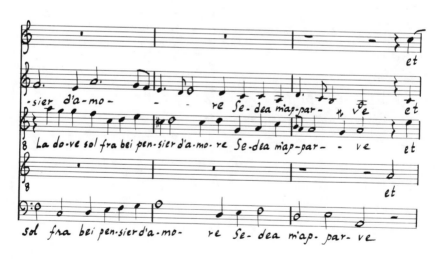

Ex. 58 (cont.) mm. 7-12

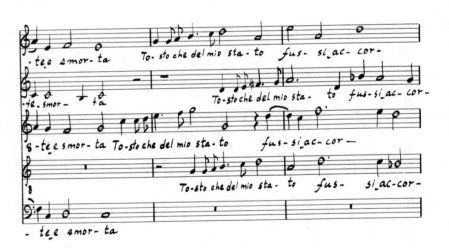

Ex. 58 (cont.) mm. 13-18

Ex. 58 (cont.) mm. 19-24

Ex. 58 (cont.) mm. 25-30

Ne'l dol- ce sfa- vil-lar de gl'oc-chi suo- i   Hor mi ri-

dol-ce sfa- vil-lar de gl'oc-chi suo-   i

Ne'l dol- ce sfa-vil-lar de gl'oc- chi   suo- i   Hor mi ri- tro-

Hor mi ri-tro-   vo

mi ri-tro- - vo pien di si di-ver- si Pia-ce- ri   in quel sa-lu-to

-tro- vo pien di si di-ver- si Pia-ce- ri   in quel sa-lu-to

-vo pien di si   di-ver-   si Pia-ce -ri in quel sa-lu-to ri-

pien di si di-ver- si

Ex. 58 (cont.) mm. 31-36

ri-pen-san-do   Che   duol

ri-pen-san-do   Che duol non

Che duol non sen-   to   ne

-pen-san-do   Che   duol   non

Che   duol   non   sen-

non sen-   to   ne sen- ti mai po-

sen-   to   ne   sen- ti   mai po-

sen- ti   mai   po   -

sen-   to   ne   sen- ti   mai   po-

to   ne   sen- ti mai po-

Ex. 58 (cont.) m. 37

Once again, Monte places a serious piece at the head of the book. It is a brief anonymous poem of the kind which appears regularly in the late five-voice books:

Se pur il ciel consente,
Che fian le gioie mie del tutto spente,
A che più mi riserba,
In questa vita acerba?
Ahi, ben dovrei morire,
Per sottrarmi a sì grave, aspro martire.

(If even heaven consents, that my joys might be entirely extinguished, what more is left to me, in this bitter life? Alas, I might as well die, and so put an end to such heavy, sharp suffering.)

What is immediately striking in Monte's setting is its seeming return to a much older style (see example 59). Rhythmically, the piece evokes a much earlier notational practice; though notated in C, the text is most often declaimed in semiminims. Both the melodic and rhythmic styles are much smoother than what we are now accustomed to, with continual step-wise motion and few tempo contrasts or syncopations.

Other features recall Monte's serious style, as well: the leisurely exposition of an imitative point, and the deep textual (and thematic) overlapping of line 1 and 2. For both lines 3 and 4, Monte states his point of imitation simultaneously with its inversion, a technique reminiscent of his serious style, particularly of the Tenth Book. And he skillfully elides lines 3 and 4, and so avoids the rather poor effect which these two rhyming seven-syllable lines make when merely read. Line 4 dissolves texturally to a weak half-cadence (m. 19), preceded by several remarkable dissonances: the abandoned C♯ in the Quinto (m. 17) and the grating $^6_5$ in the same measure.

Even more effective is Monte's setting of the following line. Few moments in Monte's earlier music have the almost soloistic weight of the Quinto's entrance on the single word *ahi* (m. 19), with which the penultimate line opens. There is something new, too, in the harmonic restraint yet intensity of expression which characterize Monte's setting of this line. The slow unfolding of his imitative point, which expands from a high trio to the full texture, incorporates the Canto's dramatic pitch peak (mm. 25-26), and then rushes headlong towards a cadence on C, which is thwarted—all this vividly calls to mind older style, yet simultaneously impresses us as fresh and new.

In the final line, we find the same expansive treatment of the contrapuntal material as in the preceding line, and the same textural expansion from a high trio to full texture. Oddly, a point and its inversion stated in m. 28 are soon abandoned for a new point (first stated in the Tenore, mm. 29-31). Again, the textural expansion brings the climactic a″ in the Canto, in a phrase whose shape

Example 59. Monte: The Sixteenth Book for Five Voices (1593)
Se pur il ciel consente (complete) mm. 1-6

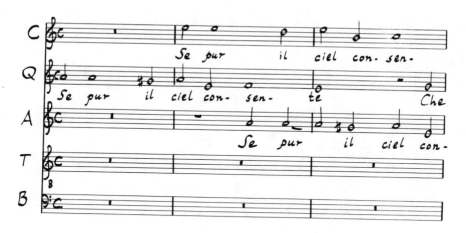

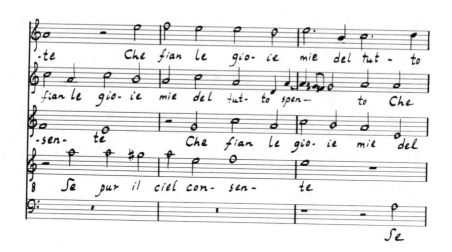

Ex. 59 (cont.) mm. 7-12

Ex. 59 (cont.) mm. 13-18

Ex. 59 (cont.) mm. 19-24

Ex. 59 (cont.) mm. 25-30

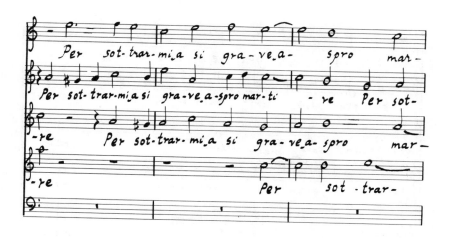

Ex. 59 (cont.) mm. 31-36

recalls the Canto line in mm. 10-11, here in augmentation. As in the old, serious style, dissonances pile up near the final cadence.

The Seventeenth Book (1595) is the last five-voice book which survives complete: for the Eighteenth Book we have only the recently discovered Canto partbook and Einstein's transcription of the Basso; the Nineteenth Book lacks only its Quinto partbook.

Monte dedicates his Seventeenth Book to Sigismondo Bathori (1572-1613), Prince of Transylvania. Typically, Monte refers to the delight which the Prince takes in music, and mentions that the Prince's *maestro di capella,* Giovanni Battista Mosto, has assured him that his own compositions "are not unattractive" to the Prince. He closes by invoking the Prince's enormous reputation principally for being, "in this time so calamitous for Christianity, one of the main champions of the holy faith."[50]

The Seventeenth Book not only reveals a continued cultivation of the serious style alongside the lighter one, but a new factor as well. Not content to rely on the technical and expressive techniques of the 1580s, Monte now explores a number of new ones. *Solingo in selve e'n boschi,* the opening piece, displays some of these features (see example 60). Once again, its text is a brief and melancholy madrigal:

Solingo in selve e'n boschi,
Passo i miei giorni foschi;
E non è quercia annosa
Che non sappia mia vita aspra e noiosa;
Ne fonte, o fiume, o rio
Che non cresc'al versar del pianto mio.

(Alone in the forests and woods, I spend my gloomy days. And there is no gnarled oak, which does not know of my bitter troublesome life; nor spring, nor river, nor stream which does not rise at the shedding of my tears.)

Monte sets lines 1-2 very quickly (mm. 1-5), and then sets them again, freely reworking his material (mm. 5-10). The freedom in the rhythmic treatment (with its frequent syncopations and contrasts of tempo), and the marvelously sensitive text-setting give these two poetic lines a lyrical shape which they hardly possess if simply read. Once again, Monte's music redeems the banality of these short-breathed *setenarii* with an almost excessive subtlety. He treats the following lines in the same manner.

The final lines are set once (mm. 19-29) and then literally repeated (mm. 29-39). Such literal repetitions, generally avoided since the Eleventh Book, return frequently in the late works. (As we shall see in his setting of *Già fu chi m'hebbe cara* from *La Fiammetta,* they can be made to serve a broad structural purpose.) Also new here is the bold declamation on repeated notes for the first half of the final line *(che non cresc'al versar).*

Example 60. Monte: The Seventeenth Book for Five Voices (1595)
Solingo in selve e'n boschi (complete) mm. 1-6

Ex. 60 (cont.) mm. 7-12

Ex. 60 (cont.) mm. 13-18

Ex. 60 (cont.) mm. 19-24

Ex. 60 (cont.) mm. 25-30

Ex. 60 (cont.) mm. 31-36

Ex. 60 (cont.) mm. 37-39

To close the discussion of the Seventeenth Book, we can turn to a setting of a more standard love lyric, rather than the melancholy species which we have dwelled upon:

Fui preso, fui ferito, arsi e gelai;
Effetto non d'amore,
Che tant'egli non ha forza e valore,
Fu la forz'e'l vigor ne le parole
Che cortesi mi disse il mio bel sole
E nel soave sguardo
Fu il ghiaccio e'l foco e la prigion e'l dardo.

(I was captured, I was wounded, I burned and I froze—not from the effect of love, for love has no such force and courage. The force and strength were in the words which my sweetheart kindly spoke to me, and in her gentle glance were the ice, the fire, the prison and the dart.)

This piece is in a new style for Monte—perhaps the closest he comes to the *seconda prattica* (see example 61). Stylistic novelties appear in the opening measures: in response to the three-part statement in line 1, Monte invents a remarkably discontinuous and fragmented polyphony. Three imitative strands are present, not strongly contrasted with one another, but individually discernible nonetheless. In mm. 1-4, the three fragments are set out rather deliberately; in mm. 4-6, the last two appear in a more compressed space, and are precipitously focused on C major, which arrives on a curiously weak beat in m. 6. These odd metrical displacements recur several times (see m. 7, 13, and 17).

Equally novel is Monte's treatment of the final couplet, for which he writes an imitative point which prominently displays a leapt diminished fourth (to paint the lady's *soave sguardo*). Though madrigalists had turned to this interval as an expressive resource at least since the 1580s, we have not seen it in Monte until now. He states his imitative point at three different pitch levels, and the result is more colorful harmonically than anything we have encountered in Monte for some time. His music for the words *e la prigion e'l dardo* also highlights the diminished fourth, though here that interval is filled in with stepwise motion. That this piece is by no means an isolated experiment can be seen from *Ne per varcar torrenti,* in this book, which also highlights a leapt diminished fourth in its opening measures.

Monte's treatment of cadences is intriguing as well. He approaches C major (mm. 21-22) in an almost bizarre way: the dominant triad is preceded by a first-inversion f♯-minor chord. His final cadence contains one last surprise, a chromatic tension between the triad of A major (which sounds prominently in m. 25 and the first half of m. 26) and the A-minor triad which must inevitably precede the final Phrygian E-major chord. Once again, the detail is drawn from

Example 61. Monte: The Seventeenth Book for Five Voices (1595)
Fui preso, fui ferito, arsi e gelai (complete) mm. 1-6

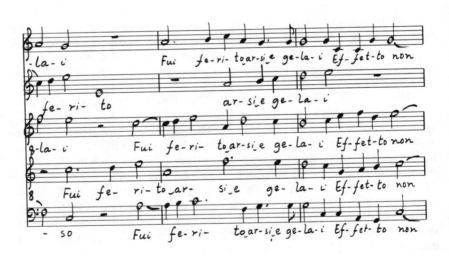

Ex. 61 (cont.) mm. 7-12

Ex. 61 (cont.) mm. 13-18

Ex. 61 (cont.) mm. 19-24

Ex. 61 (cont.) mm. 25-30

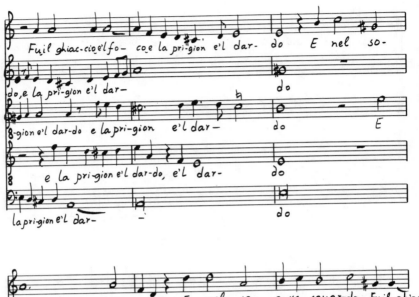

Ex. 61 (cont.) mm. 31-35

his experience as a serious composer, and resurfaces here as he formulates his own response to contemporary trends.

The foregoing several examples together reveal the extent to which Monte in his music of the 1590s tempered the canzonetta-like style of the years after 1586 with a more serious and contrapuntally elaborate style. Though this is no doubt only one aspect of his stylistic development during these years—a complete picture will only emerge from the New Complete Edition—still, it is the most important one. And, even at this stage in our knowledge, it is evident that in returning to his former seriousness, Monte remained in touch with broader developments in the madrigal as well. The 1590s saw a turning away from the canzonetta style of the 1580s, as the works of Wert, Marenzio, Gesualdo, Luzzaschi, and Monteverdi attest. Monte's more serious style of the 1590s should certainly be seen as his appreciation of this stylistic turn in the contemporary madrigal.

The Final Years: *La Fiammetta*

In 1599, the First Book for Seven Voices appeared, fancifully titled *La Fiammetta.* (In chapter 1, I suggested that this title was probably not Monte's invention, but his publisher's effort to boost lagging sales.) The title draws attention to the opening piece, a four-part cycle on words drawn from Boccaccio's *Decameron.* The poem in question, *Niuna sconsolata,* comes at the end of the *Giornata Terza,* yet it is not Fiammetta who sings this ballatta, but rather another of Boccaccio's characters, Lauretta: strictly speaking, the book should have been titled *La Lauretta!*

Monte dedicated the book to Cardinal Pietro Aldobrandini, one of the most powerful and highly placed churchmen of this time. Monte had already dedicated his Eighth Book for Six Voices (1594) to the Cardinal; in that dedication, Monte states that he has heard not only second-hand that his works were approved by the Cardinal, but that he even showed his delight in them with "most gracious letters."[51] In the dedication of *La Fiammetta,* Monte mentions having dedicated the Eighth Book to the Cardinal, and simply adds that this book is yet another indication of his devoted service.[52] It should be noted that Aldobrandini was also the dedicatee of at least three other madrigal books, including Ruggiero Giovanelli's Third Book for Five Voices (1599) and Luzzaschi's famous *Madrigali . . . per cantare, et sonare . . .* of 1601.[53]

This was not Monte's first attempt at seven-voice writing. Already in 1576, he had concluded his Third Book for Six Voices with a seven-voice setting of della Casa's *Stolto mio core.* In his next six-voice book (1580), fully a third of the pieces are for seven voices; the same is true of his Second Book of Spiritual Madrigals for Six and Seven Voices (1589). In the 1590s, he published three books of six-voice madrigals, two in 1591, one in 1594. In this context, his turn to the seven-voice texture in 1599 and 1601 seems logical, even inevitable. Yet there may also have been external reasons why Monte should have turned to so rich a vocal scoring. We have already mentioned Galeno's First Book for Seven Voices, dedicated to Emperor Rudolf in 1598. One may hypothesize that Galeno's book was enough of a success at court to induce Monte to show what he could do with the same ensemble. Einstein felt that these works were designed to satisfy a taste at the Imperial Court; he referred to Monte's *Musica sopra il Pastor Fido* as a "Viennese, Imperial work."[54] Perhaps further research will bear out our hypothesis, though it must be borne in mind that both of Monte's books were dedicated to Italians.

Monte's treatment of Boccaccio's poem is unusual, even unique in his career. He sets only two of Boccaccio's five stanzas, and places the poet's opening *ritornello* as a refrain at the end of his own second and fourth stanzas. The original poetic form is thus entirely ignored, and a free madrigal-like succession of stanzas emerges. I can think of no other occasion on which Monte sets a poem (for which we have a literary source) in so heavily edited and rearranged a fashion. Boccaccio's original poem is given below,[55] followed by Monte's adaptation.

Niuna sconsolata
Da dolersi ha quant'io,
Che'nvan sospiro, lassa!, innamorata.

Colui che muove il cielo e ogni stella,
Mi fece a suo diletto
Vaga, leggiadra, grazïosa e bella,
Per dar qua giù ad ogn'alto intelletto
Alcun segno di quella
Biltà, che sempre a lui sta nel cospetto:
E il mortal difetto,
Come mal conosciuta,
Non mi gradisce, anzi m'ha dispregiata.

Già fu chi m'ebbe cara, e volentieri
Giovinetta mi prese
Nelle sue braccia, e dentro a' suoi pensieri,
E de' miei occhi tututto s'accese.
E'l tempo, che leggieri
Sen vola, tutto in vagheggiarmi spese;
E io, come cortese,
Di me il feci degno;
Ma or ne son, dolente a me!, privata.

Femmisi innanzi poi presuntuoso
Un giovinetto fiero,
Sé nobil reputando e valoroso,
E presa tienmi, e con falso pensiero

Divenuto è geloso;
Laond'io, lassa!, quasi mi dispero,
Cognoscendo per vero,
Per ben di molti al mondo
Venuta, da uno essere occupata.

Io maladico la mia sventura,
Quando, per mutar vesta,
Si dissi mai; sì bella nella oscura
Mi vidi già e lieta, dove in questa
Io meno vita dura,
Vie men che prima reputata onesta.
O dolorosa festa,
Morta foss'io avanti,
Che io t'avessi in tal caso provato.

O caro amante, del qual prima fui
Più che altra contenta,
Che or nel ciel se' davanti a Colui
Che ne creò, deh pietoso diventa
Di me, che per altrui
Te obliar non posso: fa ch'io senta
Che quella fiamma spenta
Non sia, che per me t'arse,
E costà su m'impetra la tornata.

Here is Monte's reworking of the text:

Prima parte

Già fu chi m'hebbe cara e volontieri,
Giovinetta mi prese
Nelle sue braccia e dentro a suoi pensieri
E de miei occhi sì tutto s'accese
Che'l tempo, che leggieri
Se'n vola, tutto in vagheggiarmi spese.

Seconda parte

Et io come cortese
Di me lo feci degno,
Ma hor ne son dolente, ohime, privata!
Niuna sconsolata
Da doler s'ha quant'io
Che'n van sospiro, lasso, innamorata.

Terza parte

O caro amante, dal qual prima mosso
Fu'l misero mio core
A seguir il tuo amore,

Mentre che tu il gradisti
E nei diletti tuoi meco t'unisti
Fui, più ch'altra contenta,
Deh, pietoso di me hormai diventa,
Che per altrui te obliar non posso.

Quarta parte

Amor, deh fa ch'io senta
Che quella fiamma spenta
Non sia, che per me t'arse
E costassu t'imperi la tornata!
Niuna sconsolata
Da doler s'ha quant'io
Che'n van sospiro, lasso, innamorata.

It has evidently been Monte's intent (or that of whoever made this adaptation) to eliminate Boccaccio's narrative complexity and so transform the poem into a straightforward love lyric. In the process, a typically Boccaccian undertow of realism and satire (in which Lauretta regrets exchanging her widow's weeds for a bride's clothing) is entirely expunged. Monte may have been unhappy, too, with the blend of sacred and profane imagery in Boccaccio's stanza 5; several lines have been removed and replaced by new ones in Monte's *terza parte*.

Monte's version provides him with a poetic refrain which is treated as a musical refrain as well: the *seconda* and *quarta parte* end with the same music for their last three lines. As we shall see, this is a lengthy section, with its own internal repetitions. The *prima* and *terza parte*, though they share no poetic or musical material, also literally repeat their closing two lines. In the *prima parte*, that material accounts for roughly half the length of the stanza; in the *terza parte*, the repeated material accounts for two-thirds of the stanza (see example 62, which shows these proportional relationships).

Monte is quick to exploit the rich variety of scoring possible with seven voices. In this piece, the seven-voice ensemble has a pair of voices in each range save the Bass. In repeating his material, then, he is free to exchange voice parts, though he follows no rigid scheme. In the literal repeat in the *prima parte*, all three pairs exchange material; in the repeat in the *terza parte*, they do not. The situation is rather more subtle in the *seconda* and *quarta parte*. In the *seconda parte*, the refrain is set with a number of brief internal repetitions (see below); none of the voices exchange parts for these. But when the refrain is literally repeated in the *quarta parte*, a different voice in each pair presents the material. Monte has evidently taken some delight in this playful handling of his material.

The refrain is the high point of the cycle, and deserves close attention (see example 63). Here, Monte draws upon some of his accustomed resources: textural virtuosity, nimble canzonetta rhythms, and a remarkable approach to

Example 62. The Formal and Proportional Relationships in
Monte's *Già fu chi m'hebbe cara* (*La Fiammetta*,
1599).

Prima parte

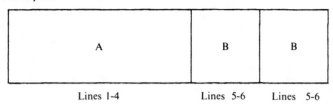

A	B	B
Lines 1-4	Lines 5-6	Lines 5-6

Seconda parte

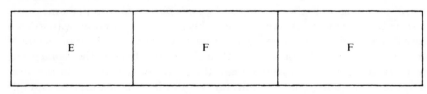

C	D
	a b c a b c′ c′
Lines 1-3	4 5 6 4 5 6 6

Terza parte

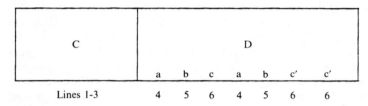

E	F	F
Lines 1-6	Lines 7-8	Lines 7-8

Quarta parte

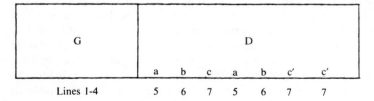

G	D
	a b c a b c′ c′
Lines 1-4	5 6 7 5 6 7 7

Example 63. Monte: The First Book for Seven Voices (*La Fiametta*, 1599)
Già fu chi m'hebbe cara (*Quarta parte*, mm. 12-28)
mm. 12-17

Ex. 63 (cont.) mm. 18-23

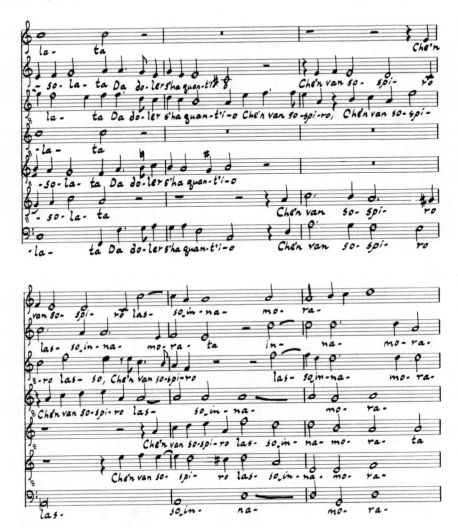

Ex. 63 (cont.) mm. 24-28

dissonance. His setting of *Niuna sconsolata* dips marvelously down the circle of fifths (to a cadence on F) for its expressive effect. (This turn to F is particularly effective in the *quarta parte,* where the preceding phrase has cadenced on D major.) The cadence (m. 13) is achieved by a modern formula (7-5-3 - $^6_4$ - $^5_4$ - $^5_3$) which (oddly) Monte generally avoids, and with which he never ends a piece. The music for the following line *(Da doler s'ha quant'io)* moves rapidly to the other end of the tonal spectrum.

Monte excels himself in his setting of the final line. He immediately signals its greater expressivity by fashioning an imitative point from the descending tetrachord, and by intensifying the rhythmic style (note that the point comes on both a strong and weak part of the minim). The fleeting augmented triad in m. 15 confirms the more anxious tone. Monte now repeats the music of the preceding two lines, and then returns to the final line, expanding it gradually by building up the texture, and by further intensifying the dissonance treatment. Initially, the material of mm. 14-16 is freely transposed: compare the Canto and Quinto (mm. 14-15) with Basso and Sesto (mm. 19-21). Yet he moves immediately beyond simple transposition. The dissonance treatment is more intense: the augmented triad returns, but is preceded by an even more unusual harmony (m. 20, beat 4). Futhermore, the augmented triad is now followed by a momentarily evaded cadence (the brief $^6_3$ in m. 21). The expressive octave leap in the Canto does much to heighten the effectiveness of this passage, too. The textural crescendo in mm. 21-22 is accompanied by a growing harmonic intensity, generated by the continual clash of f and é. Finally, the rhythm broadens for the final cadence.

Monte's virtuosity in the handling of texture, his subtle and quite original ways of treating dissonance, and his sophisticated blend of stylistic elements are all cause for much admiration—not the least when one considers that he was seventy-eight years old when this work was published. Though he went on to publish at least two more madrigal books, and contribute a five-part cycle to an anthlogy,[56] it is perhaps fitting to conclude our consideration of Monte's late style with this splendid madrigal.[57]

The Critical Problem Reexamined

From this piece we may profitably move to a critical reexamination of Monte's last period. In chapter 6 of *The Italian Madrigal* Einstein offered the view, which has never been reconsidered, that Monte's final period represents a capitulation to decadent contemporary tastes—in poetry as well as in music. Since Einstein viewed much of Italian *fin-de-siècle* poetry with indifference (if not disgust), it was perhaps natural for him to see Monte's gradual transformation from serious Petrarchist to Arcadian shepherd as "tragicomic." Here are his own words, once again:

In the end...he forsakes the lofty muse of Petrarch, Bembo, Bernardo Tasso, and Luigi Tansillo in favor of Guarini and Celiano. He is now sixty-five, and it is little short of tragicomic to see the old man become an Arcadian—like Don Quixote at the end of his life, after the collapse of his knightly ambitions.... We repeat: all this is little short of tragi-comic, for this gesture toward modernity and toward the latest fashion was made in vain.[58]

It is unfortunate that Einstein, perhaps for reasons of economy, did not include in this brief chapter any mention of Monte's continuing stylistic growth in this last period. The chapter was evidently written in some haste, and is in essence a conflation of his two earlier articles. Yet in both of these, Einstein had much praise for Monte's late music, as we have seen—praise which is pointedly deleted from the book. Indeed, a clear change of emphasis can be seen when we compare the passage quoted above with his earlier statement, given below:

Monte is sixty-five, when he brings this style-change to completion.... He has become a shepherd in his old age, like Don Quixote.... It is tragic that nevertheless, even now his madrigal books are no longer reprinted.[59]

Where does this tragedy, or tragi-comedy lie, then? In Monte's willingness to follow contemporary taste, or in his failure to maintain an audience?

Einstein ends his 1930 article by affirming the timeless strengths of Monte's music—including his late-period works:

We cannot imagine what might have come after these great manifestations of mastery. They were not of their time...but there is no piece of his, from any period of his career, which is not a masterpiece of style, and for us today, the untimeliness of his late works can no longer hinder us from recognizing and admiring the greatness of his art.[60]

This more sympathetic view seems the more appropriate response to Monte's final period, and we can now abandon the fanciful and picturesque image of Don Quixote, with its attendant tragi-comedy. That Monte should turn to the *Pastor Fido* and other fashionable pastoral verse shows his characteristic willingness to take part in the musical life of his time: from his earliest days as a madrigalist, he set a course which continually responded to changing stylistic currents. Though he never fully abandoned the serious madrigal, and considered the villanella and its companions unworthy of his efforts, he was deeply touched by the canzonetta-madrigal, as we have seen. In the end, however, he achieved a unique *rapprochement* between the stylistic extremes of his age, writing madrigals which combine the complexity and expressivity of the serious genre with the rhythmic deftness and ironic distance of the lighter forms.

Appendix

1. The dedication of the Second Book for Six Voices (1569).

ALLA SACRA CESAREA MAESTA / DEL IMPERATORE MASSIMILIANO /
Secondo mio Signore Clementissimo.

ERA (sacratissimo Principe) comune opinione di tutti i Pittagorici
che i dolcissimi concenti che risultano dall'armonia, havessero
luogo non solo in questo mondo inferiore, ma etiandio tra le sfere
celesti, affermando che derivando il suono grave della tardità,
& l'acuto dalla velocità del movimento, le sfere piu tarde nel moversi
causassero il suono grave, & le piu veloci l'acuto, onde secondo
l'opinion loro corrispondeva cosi proportionatamente il grave con
l'acuto, che da loro necessariamente risultava una soavissima ar-
monia. Altri poi, si come sono stati i Platonici, hanno affermato
ancora l'anima humana ritener in se stessa una certa armonia la qual
risulta, allhora quando la parte rationale dominando gli affetti
sensitivi, gli riduce in una tal proportione, che da loro non nasce
dissonanza alcuna, Onde per due cause dicevano la Musica esser cosi
grata a l'animo humano. L'una perche udendo il concento delle voci
humane, e'l suono de gli istrumenti, si ricordava di quella armonica
melodia, che venendo qua giu per le sfere celesti a vestirsi di
carne humana udita havea: L'altra perche essendo ella composta d'ar-
monia, sentendo il suono riconosceva se stessa, & riconoscendosi ben
proportionata si rallegrava. La onde quanto piu l'animo humano
si diletta de la Musica, tanto piu mostra ricordarsi de le cose
celesti, & divine, Il che non averrebbe se in se stessa non havesse
riservato qualche parte del lume divino, & perche naturalmente ogni

cosa ama tanto il suo simile, quanto abhorrische il suo contrario,
quanto piu l'anima ama questa armonia la qual consiste in una certa
proportionata dispositione, tanto piu mostra d'esser ben disposta
& preparata. Onde essendo V. M. Solita di prender intiera satis-
fattione de l'armonia, ne fa conoscer chiaramente quanto ella sia
partecipe del lume divino, & quanto ancora sia grande la proportione, che l'anima di V. M. in se stessa riserba sottoponendo sempre
le voglie del senso a la ragione. La onde credendo di far cosa
grata a V. M. cosi come sinceramente l'ho consacrato l'animo, cosi
ancora ho voluto dedicarli questi miei madrigali, sperando che hab-
bino da esser con quella benignità intesi dalla M. V. che Iddio
esaudisce le preghiere di tutti quei buoni che non restano di pre-
garli per l'essaltatione di V. M. Di Viena alli 15 di Aprile 1569
D. V. M. C.

      Humilissimo & fedelissimo Servitore

                        Filippo di Monte.

2. The dedication of the Third Book for Six Voices (1576).

ALL'ILLUSTRISS. SIG. MIO OSSERVAND. / IL SIGNOR GIOVAN GRIMALDI.

IN Aversa, mentre io mi truovavo in qualche difficolta, & bisogno
dell'aiuto, & favore de gli amici, & miei Signori. V. S. Illustre
da se stessa si mosse con tanta prontezza à dichiararmi la liberalità,
& grandezza del'animo suo, che aggiunto l'obligo all'inclinatione,
& affetione, che prima le portavo, ne acquistò talmente che dall'-
hora in poi sono stato sempre vegghiando occasione, di poterle sig-
nificare, la gratitudine mia; Ma perche dalle deboli forze, che
sono in me, non possono uscire se non povere dimostrationi, & per
conseguenza molto inferiori al desiderio, & al debito, che le hò;
mi sono risoluto non potendo quel, che vorrei, fare quello, che
posso, sperando, ch'ella havendo riguardo all'animo mio, debba ve-
nire in cognitione anco di quello, che ne con gl'effetti, ne con
parole posso esprimere. Mando dunque & dedico à V. S. Illustre questi
miei Madrigali, quali per scarso testimonio che siano di questa mia
debita, & grata voluntà, tengo nondimeno per certo, che le deb-
bano esser cari, & che approvati dal giudicio suo siano ancora
per fare acquisto appresso gl'alti amatori delle virtu, & com-
parire arditamente innanzi à tutti. Con che resto pregandoli
dal Signor Dio ogni contentezza, & felicità, & nella gratia sua,
quanto piu vivamente posso, mi racomando

> *Di V. S. Illustriss.*
>
> *Deditissimo Servitore*
>
> *Filippo de Monte.*

3. The dedication of the Seventh Book for Five Voices (1578).

ALLA SACRA CESAREA MAESTA / DEL IMPERATORE RODOLFO SECONDNO [sic]
Mio Signore Clementissimo.

PILADE famosissimo Histrione à tempi d'Augusto, importunato da
Hila suo discepolo a concorrer seco, disse a quel temerario &
ingrato giovane, il qual volendo accompagnar co'l gesto, questa
parola: IL MAGNO ATRIDE: si sollevò quanto più puotè con la per-
sona, & co'l braccio: Tu l'hai immitato alto di statura, & non
grande: Et pregato dal Popolo, ch'era giudice della lor controver-
sia, che fosse contento con atto convenevole accompagnar la me-
desima parola, proferendola con la mano alla gota, si arrecò in
atto pensoso, & funne sommamente lodato, comprendendosi percio
ch'egli voleva inferire che la grandezza de' Re consiste in oc-
cuparsi ne' pensieri & nelle cure de' Popoli dalla Divina pro-
videntia, a, lor governo commessi. Ma perche tutte le cose che
con fatica si fanno, hanno bisogno di qualche spatio di tempo
tra loro, & di cosa che in qualche modo conforti la natura afflitta;
che senza questi intervalli non sarebbe durabile, si cerca qual
diletto sia convenevole in cosi fatti bisogni a gran Prencipi,
& concludesi questo esser la Musica, la quale mentre che si es-
sercita, oltre al piacer che porge, ne gli animi humani bene
armonizati, crea quelli divini & mirabili effetti, & affetti,
che gia sono notissimi. Et benche Filippo Macedone dicesse al
grand'Alessandro. CHE assai era, & forse di vantaggio, che il

Prencipe havesse otio di ascoltare gli altri che cantassero, questo

intervenne perche quel saggio Re, zeloso della gloria del figliuolo,

sforzato dall'humana tenerezza, temeva non che vi si applicasse

(che questo harrebbe lodato) ma che egli vi si occupasse & immer-

gesse troppo. Il che non puo avvenire di V. Ces. Maestà, la quale

tutti i diletti, quantunq; virtuosissimi usa con tanta sobrietà,

& discretione, che è cosa meravigliosa à udire & vedere. Per

tutto cio non rimarro io di dedicarle queste mie poche Musiche

Italiane c'hora mi son risoluto mandare alle stampe, si come

ha, molto tempo, le dedicai il cuore, & tutto me stesso, il quale

piu tosto riguardando ella che la debolezza del dono (se dono

è quel che si debbe) spero, tal'è la sua humanità, che restarà

appagata della pure mia volonta, & dell'ardentissimo desiderio ch'io

ho di veder S. Maesta Sereniss. sempre piu gloriosa, & piu felice;

che cosi Iddio la facci. Di Vienna il primo di Febraro 1578.

Di V. M. Sereniss.

Humiliss. & devotiss. Servo Filippo di Monte

4. The dedication of the Eighth Book for Five Voices (1580)

ALLA SACRA CESAREA MAESTÀ / DELL'IMPERATORE / Rodolfo secondo. /
MIO SIGNORE CLEMENTISSIMO.

Se fin qui SACRA CESAREA MAESTÀ si è visto che quanto ogn'uno
può, va cercando di ridur la Musica con nuovo stile à maggior
perfettione; necessariamente ne segue, ch'ella non è ancor giunta
à quella eccellenza, che potrebbe arrivare. Essendo io dunque
uno di quelli, che della Musica fanno professione, se ben quanto
piu hò cercato di trovare strada da poter più dilettare a quelli,
che d'essa debbono, & possono dar giuditio, tanto più forse me
ne sia discostato, Nientedimanco, facendo quant'io posso, &
specialmente per dilettar à quelli, à quali è necessaria per
ristorare gli spiriti affaticati nelle cose più necessarie al
viver politico; Se io non meritasse lode dell'effetto, non pero
merito biasmo della mia intentione. Et perche cosi de gl'effetti,
come dell'intentione buona ciascuno deve render gratie prima
à DIO, & poi alli mezzi, per li quali lui concede le gratie.
Trovandomi io dalla magnanimità di Vostra Maestà, & dalla glo-
riosissima memoria di suo padre talmente rimunerato, che posso
commodissimamente attender à questo studio, non potendo per altra
strada certificar à Vostra Maestà, & al mondo l'obligo grandis-
simo, ch'io le tengo, havendole già son molt'anni dedicata l'hu-
mil servitù mia, le dedico ancora le presenti opere, lequali
si degnarà d'accettare con la solita sua benignità, non guardando
alla debolezza del duono, ma all'animo, & devotissima mia servitù.

Di Praga li 4. Maggio.   1580.

D. V. S. C. M.

Humiliss. & devotiss. servitore.

Filippo di Monte.

5. The dedication of the Ninth Book for Five Voices (1580).

AL SERENISSIMO PRENCIPE / L'ARCIDUCA ERNESTO.

ESSENDO tra gli huomini di giudicio tenuto per peccato enormissimo
la ingratitudine, Io certo sarei nel numero degl'ingratissimi
quando lasciassi di mostrare, & particolarmente a V. Altezza
quant'io conosca l'obligo grandissimo che le tengo, non manco
per esser figliuolo de la gloriosissima memoria de l'Imperatore
Massimiliano & fratello de l'Imperator Rodolfo mio Signor Cle-
mentissimo dalli quali ho ricevuto tante gratie, che per i favori
che in ogni occasione ella non lascia di farmi: Ma poi che per
le mie debili forze non posso mostrarne segno conveniente, per non
mancar di quel che posso, & per honorarmi doppiamente, ho dedi-
cato questo libro di madrigali al gloriosissimo nome di Vostra
Altezza, laquale oltre le altre sue rare qualita è anco grandis-
simo amatore non solamente, ma intendente & di perfettissimo
giudicio nella musica. Il che spero sarà causa che si degnarà
d'accettar (come con ogni humiltà le supplico) questo mio dono
anchor che picciolissimo con quella benignità d'animo, con la
quale suol favorir .tutte le virtù, Di Praga li 20. Setembre 1580.

   Di Vostra Altezza Serenissima

        Humilissimo & devotissimo Servitore

            Filippo di Monte

6. The dedication of the Fourth Book for Six Voices (1580).

ALL'ILLUSTRISSIMO SIGNOR MIO OSSERVANDISSIMO / IL SIGNOR WOLFANGO
RUMF LIBERO BARONE DI WIELROSS. / Consigliere & Cameriero maggiore
della Maestà Cesarea &c.

Se tutti ò la maggior parte di coloro, che di valore, di bontà,
ò di sapere avanzavano gli altri huomeni, fù da i nostri ante-
cessori giudicato deversi con scritti, ò con altre degne memorie
immortalando i nomi loro, porgere occasione alli posteri di do-
verli imitare. Io, che sono un di quei che con ogni ragione am-
miro le degnissime qualità di V. S. Illustrissima, le quali sono
& saranno per cagion de buoni & fedeli scrittori sempre vive nel-
le menti de gli huomini; hò voluto dedicar à l'honoratissimo
suo nome questi miei Madrigali, i quali vorrei che fussero tali,
quali dovriano essere per ricrearli quei spiriti che quanto piu
si stancano per le assidue buone opere, manco si satiano, & par-
ticolarmente per servitio della Maestà Cesarea, & per la quiete
universale de Christiani. Supplico dunque l'omnipotente Dio che
doni à V. S. Illustrissima lunghissima & felicissima vita, acciò
i buoni possano maggiormente godere, & io rallegrarmi de suoi
felici successi. Di Venetia il di 20. di Settembrio. 1580.

Di V. S. Illustrissima

Affettionatissimo Servitore

Filippo de Monte

7. The dedication of the Tenth Book for Five Voices (1581).

*ALLA SACRA CESAREA / MAESTÀ DE L'IMPERATORE / RODOLFO SECONDO /
mio Signor Clementissimo.*

*Vedendosi & provandosi per isperienza S. C. Maesta che cosi come
tutti gli huomini fra essi son dissimili d'effigie, & in tutti
i membri loro, Cosi sono ancora fra essi varij in ogni lor pensiero, gusto, & attione, ne segue, che cosi le cose fatte dalla
natura, come da l'artificio de gli huomini, secondo havranno maggiore ò minor conformità con le cose fatte da essa natura o da
l'arte siano piu ò manco apprezzate o abhorrite da essi huomini
& parlando io hora de la Musica quale è mia professione, dico
che non potendo l'armonia che ella rendesse, esser apprezzata da
altro che dalla conformita che havesse con chi l'ascoltasse,
ciascun che tenesse giuditio parlando d'essa puo con piu ragione
dire questa Musica mi piace, che dire è buona perche mi piace,
perche si suol far giuditio della qualità de la Musica, dalla
diversità delli numeri co i quali sogliono disporre le zifre
di quella, & dal maggior travaglio che fusse andato in conporla,
cose tutte poco ò niente probabilli, parendo dunque che la diversità dei pareri ci dimostra chiaramente l'imperfettion de
l'arte & de compositori, poi ch'ancor si vede & prova che huomini
di gran giuditio sogliono piu ricrearsi di quella maniera di Musica che non è solita piacere a molti di quelli che ne compongono,
& potendosi in cio tanto piu errare, quanto piu si volesse sfor-
zar la natura de gli huomini a farli parer buona, cosa che fosse*

contraria alla propria disposition loro, Ho cercato, & cerco

tuttavia col variar stile dar qualche contento à quelli a chi

havessero poco piacute l'altre mie compositioni, & per tal cagione

ho voluto dar fuori le presenti opere le quali come elle si siano

dedico al felicissimo nome de la Maestà Vostra con quella humiltà

& divotione che gli ho dedicato me stesso & altre cose mie.

Di viena alli 26 di Giugno. 1581.

    D. V. S. C. Maesta

        Humilissimo & divotissimo Servitore.

             Filippo di Monte.

8. The dedication of the First Book for Three Voices (1582).

*ALLA VIRTUOSISSIMA SIGNORA / LA SIGNORA MADALENA CASULANA DI
MEZARII / Signora mia osservandìssima.*

*Vedendo quasi spento il seme de i Madrigali a tre voci (Musica
tanto commoda, & dilettevole, e quando viene da qualche buona
mano tanto eccellente, & perfetta) deliberai di suscitarla, &
quasi di nuovo ritornarla al mondo, & però mi volsi al nostro
Eccellentissimo Signor Filippo di Monte, & lo pregai, ch'egli
volesse dar aiuto a questa mia intentione. Il che (come è solito
della sua gentil natura) ha fatto liberalissimamente, & me n'ha
già mandato un giusto libro: il quale stampato si dedica al molto
valore, & merito di V. S. ottima conoscitrice di questa, & d'ogni
altra honorata gentilezza. Averrà forse, che vedendo questi grati
al mondo mi volgerò di mano in mano à qualch'un'altro di questi
eccellentiss. Musici, e pregarolli, che favorendomi di qualche
loro simili compositioni aiutino questo honorevol mio pensiero,
come di già ne prego V. S. di tanta stima, & riputatione in cosi
fatte cose, di quanta la giudicò colui, che in quella sua poesia
meritamente la chiamò Di questa nostra età Musa, & Sirena, alla
quale, come tale facendo ogni maggior riverenza bacio la mano,
& mi raccomando per sempre. Di Venetia li 20 Agosto 1582.*

      Di V. S.

                         Servitore Angelo Gardano.

9. The dedication of the Fifth Book for Six Voices (1584-5).

AL SACRATISSIMO ET INVITTISSIMO / IMPERATORE RODOLFO SECONDO
&c. / Suo Signore Clementissimo.

La benignita di Vostra Maestà mi si è continuamente mostrata si
grande, non pur in haver à grado la mia humile servitu, ma in
accetar ancora le mie fatiche uscite sotto il suo gloriosissimo
nome, che mi parrebbe di peccar grandemente, & di fare torto a me
stesso, se tralasciassi occasione che mi si presenti, & di pre-
dicar per quella via, che io posso l'obligo immortale che tengo
all sua infinita, & heroica cortesia, & d'accrescerlo tutta via
piu. Per laqual cosa le offerisco hora questo Libro de miei
Madrigali a Sei: confidatomi che la magnanimità della M. V.
risguardando piu all'animo, col quale glie l'offerisco, che alla
picciolezza del dono, sia per riceverlo con quella prontezza, che
ha ricevute altre mie fatiche maggiori. Io certo il dono, & de-
dico à Vostra Maestà come testimonio della mia devotione, se non
ricco & splendido, almeno vero, & constante: pregando N. Sig.
Dio che conservi lungamente, & augmenti il suo felice stato.

   Di V. Sacra Maestà

                Humilissimo Servo

                      Filippo di Monte.

10. The dedication of the Eleventh Book for Five Voices (1586).

ALL'ILLUSTRISS. SIGNORE, MIO SIGNOR COLENDISS. / IL SIGNOR CONTE MARIO BEVILACQUA.

Fra tutti i diletti & piaceri, che grandissimi ho sentito sempre, & tuttavia sento col ritrovarmi sovente a trattar i miei capricci con le Muse, della cui gratiosa compagnia, e per natural mia inclinatione, & per studio di molti anni ho havuto sempre l'animo grandemente acceso. Il maggior mio gusto è stato, qual'hor mi sono abbatuto a dovere de i frutti, che nel spatioso & perpetuamente verdeggiante giardino di queste stesse mi viene concesso alcuna fiata di raccore, far parte a qualche honorato soggetto, cui in vivace apparenza non solamente per se stessa piaccia la Musica, ma che insieme con lodevole effetto del continuo essercitio di quella affettuosamente se ne compiaccia: Parendomi che questa tale proportione o sia conformità, laquale cotesti hanno meco d'animo, e di pensieri, basti sola a destarmi nell'alma una perpetua soave armonia di consolatione, & se scontro cotanto da me gradito mi succedette mai favorevole, hoggi posso dir di haverlo havuto felicissimo, poi che mi accade per mia buona fortuna di farlo nella valorosa persona di V. Sig. Illustriss. però che non solamente so per fama, quanto per natural suo genio ella tenghi in preggio tutte le compositioni Musicali, ma vengo assicurato, che delle mie (quali si siano) ne prende alcuna volta ricreatione. Tàl che havendomi gia la gentilissima sua cortesia prevenuto in favorirmi, ho voluto che per ogni modo questo Libro de' miei Madrigali, che nuovamente ho dato alla stampa, venghino da quella, a darle parte del riconoscimento, ch'io le devo, per

quella si cortese memoria, che le piace tener di me, poi che

la lontananza giunta alla debolezza della età mia, mi vieta di

poter far cotal mio dovuto complimento. Hora si come ho havuto

grandissimo gusto in compor questi Madrigali in quello piu vivace

& allegro stile, che a me sia stato lecito di poter ritrovare,

accio che porghino altrui materia d'esser allegramente cantati,

cosi anco, con lieto affetto, a punto a quegli stessi in ogni

parte conforme, li dedico al generoso nome di V. Sig. Illustriss.

assicurato, che con animo non a punto dissimile dal mio, saranno

ricevuti, & goduti da lei, sin che mi si porghi maggior occasione

di poterle mostrar a piu vivi segni la stima ch'io faccio delle

honratissime [sic] sue qualità, & bacio la mano. Di Praga, il

di 15. Novemb. 1586.

Di V. Sig. Illustriss.

Devotissimo Servitore

Filippo di Monte

11. The dedication of the Twelfth Book for Five Voices (1587).

ALL'ILLUSTRISS. SIGNORE, PADRON SUO OSSERVANDISS. / IL SIGNOR
F. OTTAVIO SPINOLA.

L'Incredibile bontà & benigna natura di V. Sig. Illustriss. fa,
che non pure coloro che la conoscono di presenza, l'amano &
osservano; ma etiamdio coloro a quali n'è pervenuto solo il nome
la riveriscono come padrone commune de' buoni & virtuosi. Onde
come che la nobiltà, il gran valore di V. Sig. Illustriss. & il
loco principale ch'ella tiene in questa Corte la rendano riguar-
devole appresso ogn'uno; nissuna cosa però la fa piu ammirare
della fama universale, che la gratia & auttorità ch'ella ha ha-
vuta già tanti anni & have appresso sua Maestà Cesarea vien im-
piegata da lei con tanta modestia in commodo altrui, che chiunque
ricorre da lei, si parte ò satisfatto di effetto, ò appagato
di buona volontà, & ciascheduno obligato alla sua somma benignità.
Ma fra tanti beneficati da V. Sig. Illustriss. io debbo haverle
tanto maggior obligo, quanto la sua infinita cortesia non cessa
mai d'accrescermi favori à favori, & beneficij à beneficij, si che
s'io pensassi di poterle mai rendere minima parte delle gratie
che debbo, sarei senza dubbio ingratissimo: il qual vitio però
è si alieno dalla mia natura, che non potendo altro, ho voluto
con l'occasione di dar fuori questo duodecimo Libro de miei
Madrigali, dar publica testimonianza di questa mia impotenza,
& dell'immortale obligo & perpetua osservanza verso V. Sig. Il-
lustriss. alla quale prego da Dio ogni felicità.

Di Praga il di 15. Zugno 1587.

Di V. Sig. Illustriss.

Servitore obligatiss.

Filippo de Monte.

12. The dedication of the Thirteenth Book for Five Voices (1588).

ALLA GENTILISSIMA ET VIRTUOSISSIMA / SIGNORA CHIARA GABRI, /
Mia Signora Osservandissima.

Fanno coloro giuditiosamente, iquali per antico costume, per-
venuto à noi da molti secoli adietro, mandano fuori i lor com-
ponimenti sotto nome Illustre di chi per nobiltà, ò per raro
valore risplenda fra noi. Perciò che in questa guisa, come ho-
norano la virtù, laquale non riconosce altro premio degno della
sua grandezza fuor della gloria, & dell'honore; cosi à quella
luce che gli viene da parti del loro ingegno aggiongono nuova
luce, che gli viene dal nome di coloro, à quali, come à cosa
Divina in terra, consacrano i loro componimenti. Di cosi bella
luce spero che habbiano à risplendere i presenti miei Madrigali,
che hora escono illustrati dal chiaro nome di V. Sig. Ma non
so già qual luce potrà ella all'incontro sperare da questo mio
picciol dono, che se pur parrà maggior che non è al mondo, non
per altro sarà, che per quel pregio che gli verrà dal nome di
lei; donde come da chiara lampa, puo ricever accrescimento di
luce, & di splendore. Una laude so io bene che non mi si potrà
negare, di haver con riguardo, & con aviso molto, dedicata à lei
questa parte di Musica ch'io le dono; non solo perche V. Sig.
è rara fra tutte l'altre in cosi bella virtù; ma perche dalla
bellezza de l'animo suo, & de suoi nobili, & signorili costumi,
spira non so come, una vaga, & dolce armonia; che riesche non

meno vaga a gli occhi di coloro che mirano in lei, che quella

che viene dalla voce sua all'orecchie di coloro che l'odono,

mentre canta & suona, il che ella fa con si dolce & soave maniera,

che dove arriva col suo canto, rapisce con dolce inganno, i

cuori de gli ascoltanti, & volge in se stessa, sviati da ogni

altro pensiero: il che pregando Nostro Signore le conceda per

lungo spatio d'anni con perpetua felicità.

Dalla Corte Cesarea il di primo Decembre 1588.

Di V. Sig.

Affettionatiss. Servitore

Filippo di Monte

13.   The dedication of the Fourteenth Book for Five Voices (1590).

AL SERENISSIMO PRINCIPE / DON ALFONSO SECONDO / DUCA DI FERRARA.

Fra molte Illustri heroiche virtù, lequali da grado altissimo

d'honore rendono fra noi glorioso il nome della Serenità vostra,

loderan altri l'altezza dell'animo suo, la sapienza, la giustitia,

dond'ella con uguale temperamento rege in beato, & tranquillo

stato i popoli soggetti al suo imperio: celebreranno altri que'

doni, & quelle gratie, che molti attribuiscono alla fortuna,

ma piu veramente la Serenità vostra riconosce dalla providenza

di Dio, largo donatore delle sue richezze à que' Principi, che

ha ordinati ministri, & conservatori della sua giustitia al mondo:

inalzerano altri la nobiltà, rivocando dall'altra vita à questa

i gloriosi nomi di coloro, che nella Serenissima sua Casa, per

molti chiari, & Illustri fatti consecrorono la lor memoria al-

l'eternità che non spegneran mai tenebre di oblivione ne secoli

à venire: magnificheranno con pari altezza di stilo il Reale

sangue di Francia, donde hà la Serenità vostra l'origine sua

materna, nipote di quel gran Re, il quale contendendo con la

gloria de gli Avi suoi, i quali illustrorono gli annali di tutte

le genti con le vittorie, & co' trionfi loro, aggiunse à quella

gran luce, che da loro pervenne à posteri, molto maggior splendore

lasciando dubbio al mondo se essendo stato grande nell'una for-

tuna, & nell'altra fusse in questa, ò in quella maggiore.   In

questa guisa si faran gli altri scala alla gratia della Serenità

vostra, alla quale aspirando io, & sollevandomi indarno da basso luogo, per arrivar à tanta altezza non dubito punto che ricono-

scendo nel piccol [sic] dono de miei Madrigali ch'io riverente

gli appresento l'animo grande donde viene, non mi porga la mano,

& facendomi iscusar per merito la sua benignità, non mi dia luogo

nella gratia sua. Mi hà invitato a farle dono di questi novi

parti del mio ingegno, la fama, che fra l'altre sue gran virtù

celebra lo studio della Musica, laquale come con maravigliosa

armonia risplende ne suoi Reali costumi, cosi vuole spesso udire,

compartita fra angeliche voci, & cantata da cosi rari spiriti

che chi vi si trova si crede haver certa caparra della beata

vita. Dove se havran luogo questi miei Madrigali, non fia mai

ch'io mi creda questo avenire per merito ch'io conosca in loro,

ma per havergli à ciò graditi V. Serenità; alla quale non potendo

piacere se non quelle cose che sono perfette, & rare, si crederà

per aventura che ne' miei componimenti sia quella perfettione,

che perche vi fusse, tuttavia mi sono affaticato molto; che se per

altro non si dee lodare, si almeno per ciò si dee; che fu sempre

stimato molto il voler fare, quello che si fa perfettamente.

Con che à V. Serenità inchinannandomi [sic] le bacio riverente

la mano. Dalla Corte Cesarea il dì 15. Aprile 1590.

   Di V. A. Sereniss.

               Affettionatiss. Servitore

                          Filippo di Monte.

14. The dedication of the Sixth Book for Six Voices (1591).

ALL'ILLUSTRISSIMO SIGNORE, / MIO SIGNOR COLENDISSIMO / IL SIGNOR

GIACOMO CURTS / Di Senfftenau, Consiglier Secreto di S. M. Ces. /

& Vicecancelliere dell'Imperio, &c.

Quando la molta humanità, & cortesia di V. Sig. Illustriss. non

m'havesse obligato à portarle quella osservanza, che richiedono

gli infiniti favori da lei ricevuti, & che continuamente ricevo;

si m'havrebbe astretto la incomparabile sua bontà, & la sua sin-

gulare virtù & dottrina, tanto piu degna di essere stimata &

celebrata, quanto piu rara in personaggi pari suoi hoggidi ella

si ritruova. Percioche come che V. S. Illus. sia si occupata

nel suo honoratissimo offitio, & ne gli affari di S. M. Ces.

che pare maraviglia, com'ella possa bastar à tanti pesi; nondimeno

quando le vien dato agio di respirar alquanto da essi, si esercita

per modo di diporto si voluntieri nello studio delle buone lettere,

& con tanta laude da tutti gli intendenti, come s'ella non havesse

mai havuto, ne havesse altro per le mani. Si che quello che altri

ha per principale negotio, & per fatica, ella ha per porto di

quiete & di solazzo. Onde ben si conosce la grandezza dell'in-

gegno di V. Sig. Illustriss. nato, & alle ationi civili, & alla

contemplatione delle piu nobili scientie. Fra le quali ella è

si eccellente nelle Mathematiche, come dimostra qualche sua acuta,

& ingegnosa compositione che si è veduta, & come sento predicare

da chi ne può à buona ragione giudicare. Ma quel che è piu,

non bastando à V. Sig. Illustriss. la pura cognitione, ella riduce

ancho alcune d'esse alla prattica, & all'uso. Della Musica certo, della quale mi pare di poter dire alcuna cosa, vedo che V. Sig.

Illustriss. sente molto gusto & piacere non solo in comporre, quando

le sue occupationi il permettono alcuna cosa per trastullo, ma

in ascoltar ancho & giudicare i componimenti altrui. Per la qual

cosa dovendo uscire fuori questo Sesto Libro de miei Madrigali

hò voluto mandarlò a V. Sig. Illustriss. in segno, se ben piccolo,

della mia servitù, & della gratitudine dell'animo mio, per li

molti oblighi che le tengo, & ancho per acquistargli maggior

riputatione dall'honoratissimo nome di V. Sig. Illustriss. alla

quale humilmente bacio la mano, & prego ogni prosperità.

Di Venetia il di 25. Maggio 1591.

Di V. Sig. Illustriss.   *Devotissimo Servitore*

Filippo di Monte.

15. The dedication of the Fifteenth Book for Five Voices (1592).

ALL'ILLUSTRISS: ET REVERENDISS: / SIGNORE, MIO SIGNOR COLENDISSIMO /
IL SIGNOR CAMILLO CAETANO / Patriarcha d'Alessandria, &c. / Nuntio
di N. Sig. appresso sua Maestà Cesarea.

Parrà forse ad alcuno, che poco convenevole dono io presenti
a V. Sig. Illustriss. & Reverendiss. come è questo mio Libro de
Madrigali a Cinque voci; nondimeno dovendo pur questo uscir fuori,
& per Quintodecimo far compagnia a gli altri suoi fratelli, non
ho potuto di non mandarlo in luce sotto l'honoratissimo nome
di lei, percioche sonandosi questi Madrigali li mesi adietro con
le viuole da gamba, mostrò che piacessero tanto a V. Sig. Illu-
striss. che tale giudicio fattone da lei, intendentissima cosi
di questa come di tutte le altre nobilissime arti, io reputo come
patrocinio preso di essi, sotto la cui ombra ardiscano comparire
da pertutto. Per la qual cosa io vengo quasi a presentare a V.
Sig. Illustrissima quel che in certo modo è suo, poi che dall'aut-
torità di lei essi sono per ricevere piu splendore che dal Com-
ponitor istesso. Oltre che io mi conosco si obligato a V. Sig.
Illustriss. per li molti favori, ch'io ogni dì ricevo da lei da
che ha cotesto supremo luogo nella Corte Cesarea, che se io le
presentassi tutto ciò che puo venire dal mio ingegno & dalla mia
industria, mi parrebbe tuttavia non haver satisfatto a minima
parte dell'obligo ch'io tengo alla sua infinita humanità & cor-
tesia, predicata non pur da me, ma da chiunque la conosce. Onde
tanto maggiormente confido che V. Sig. Illustriss. accetterà

volentieri questo picciol dono verso di se, ma grandissimo,

s'ella risguarderà la devotione dell'animo, con che glie l'offero.

& pregando Dio per ogni sua prosperità, le bacio humilmente le

mani.

Di Venetia il dì Primo Maggio 1592.

Di V. Sig. Illustriss. & Reverendiss.

Servitore Devotiss.

Filippo di Monte.

16. The dedication of the Sixteenth Book for Five Voices (1593).

AL MOLTO ILLUSTRE ET REVEREN - / DISSIMO SIGNORE MIO COLENDISS. /
MONSIG. DIEGO DI CAMPO. / Protonotario Apostolico, Canonico di
S. M. Maggiore, &c. / Camarier secreto di sua Santità.

Mando à V. S. Reverendissima il Sestodecimo Libro de' miei Madri-
gali à Cinque, si per sodisfar al suo desiderio di veder alcuna
cosa nuova delle mie, come anco per dare publico testimonio della
servitù & obligo ch'io ho con esso lei. Assai io mi riputava
per avanti & favorito da V. Sig. Reverendissima da che nel ritorno
suo di Polonia io hebbi gratia di conoscerla, & venturato di havere
stretta amicitia & servitù con Signore di si rare qualità, che
non è nissuno che la conosca, il quale insieme non l'ami & osservi:
ma poi che per l'assontione di N. Sig. al Pontificato vien insieme
ad esser cresciuta l'autorita di V. Sig. Reverendissima, che gli
è stata sempre si cara per la bontà & singular virtù sua, ho veduto
con mio gran piacere, che quantunque io le portassi quell'affet-
tione & osservanza ch'io doveva, io l'era nondimeno tenuto più
assai di quel che havrei potuto pensare, poi che ella non solo
ha conservata la sua solita amorevolezza verso di me, ma accre-
sciuta la cortesia sì, che si conosce la vera nobiltà dell'animo
suo non esser soggetta à mutationi di fortuna, come suol avenire.
Per la qual cosa non accade ch'io mi stenda in parole per pregarla
à ricever volentieri questo piccolo dono, sapendo che le sara
grato & per venire da suo Serviotre si devoto come le son io.
Anzi havrei da ringratiarla della benignità sua verso di me,
& dell'amore che mostra alle mie compositioni qualunque elle si

siano, ma non essendo questo ne luogo, ne tempo, ne, dirò anco,

poter mio, mi resterò, contento di professare non pur l'obligo

com'io diceva, ma ancora il desiderio mio d'obligarmi sempre

piu à V. Sig. Reverendiss. alla quale riverentemente bacio la

mano & prego ogni prosperità.

   Di Venetia alli 10 Aprile. 1593.

      Di V. Sig. Reverendiss.

                  Servitore obligatissimo

                          Filippo di Monte.

17. The dedication of the Seventeenth Book for Five Voices (1595).

AL SERENISSIMO PRENCIPE / DI TRANSILVANIA, / SIGISMONDO BATHORI,

CONTE DI SICULIA. / Et Prencipe del Sacro Romano Imperio, Signor & /

Padron mio Colendissimo.

E un pezzo, che havendo io inteso, quanto l'Altezza Vostra fra le

Heroiche sue ationi, & cure del governo de suoi popoli frammette

volentieri il diletto della Musica, ho desiderato di mostrare qual-

che publico segno della devotione, che insieme con tutti gli amatori

d'essa io porta al suo gloriosissimo nome, il che nondimeno per certo

mia natura amica di rispetto, & per reverenza, non ho havuto ardire

di esequire, fin che dal Sig. Gio. Battista Mosto Maestro di Capella

di V. S. non me n'è stato fatto non pur animo ma instanza ancora,

con assicurarmi che le compositioni mie non le siano discare. La

quale cagione come, che per se fosse bastante ad invitarmi a pre-

sentarlene alcuna; tuttavia il fo hora anco piu volentieri nel comune

applauso, con che da tutti i buoni vien celebrata la singulare sua

Religione, Prudenza, Magnanimità, Fortezza, & Valore. Si che l'Europa

tutta rivolta à V. A. quasi à splendidissimo lume nuovamente apparso,

tanto maggiormente l'ammira, poi che vede fiorire si perfette virtù

in età si fresca, & tenera, che la reputa mandata da Dio in questi

tempi calamitosi della Christianità, per uno de principali Campioni

della santa fede; & della salute universale. La supplico adunque

ad accettare benignmente come spero, nella sua Clemenza, questo

quantunque picciolo dono, se non degno dell'A. V. certo offertole da animo devotissimo, & desideroso d'ogni sau esaltatione, quale

augurandole da Dio N. Sig humilmente me l'inchino.   Di Venetia il

di 24 Novembre. 1595.

Di V. A. Sereniss.

Humiliss. & Devotiss. Servitore

Filippo de Monte.

Notes

Preface

1. "Schwierigkeit ein so umfassendes Thema in gedrängtesden Form zu behandlen. Monte der fruchtbarste aller Madrigalisten."

2. These *Notes* are only a small part of a large collection of Einstein's papers now in the University of California Music Library. They include, among the material related to the Italian madrigal, the German typescript of *The Italian Madrigal*, and Einstein's own heavily annotated copy of Vogel's *Bibliothek*.

3. Alfred Einstein, "Filippo di Monte als Madrigalkomponist," *International Society for Music Research, Report of the First Congress* (Liège, 1931): 102-8.

4. Alfred Einstein, "Italienische Musik und italienische Musiker am Kaiserhof und an den erzherzoglichen Höfen in Innsbruck und Graz," *Studien zur Musikwissenschaft* 21 (1934): 3-52.

5. Alfred Einstein, *The Italian Madrigal,* trans. Alexander H. Krappe, Roger Sessions, and Oliver Strunk, 3 vols. (Princeton, 1949). (Hereafter *The Italian Madrigal.*)

6. These transcriptions, and all of Einstein's transcriptions of early music, are now in the Werner Josten Library, Smith College, and are available on microfilm.

7. Filippo di Monte, *Opera Omnia,* ed. Charles van den Borren and Julius van Nuffel, 31 volumes (1927-39); reprint ed., New York, 1965). Only vols. 14, 19 and 25 contain secular madrigals.

8. Filippo di Monte, *New Complete Edition,* general editor René Lenaerts (Leuven, 1975 -).

9. See, in chapter 1, The Sources of Monte's Madrigals.

10. *The Italian Madrigal,* vol. 2, p. 511.

11. Gustave Reese, *Music in the Renaissance* (New York, 1959) pp. 406-8.

12. Edward J. Dent, "The Sixteenth-century Madrigal," *The New Oxford History,* vol. 4 (London, 1968), pp. 33-95.

13. Jerome Roche, *The Madrigal* (London, 1972).

14. Georges van Doorslaer, *La Vie et les Oeuvres de Philippe de Monte* (Bruxelles, 1921), hereafter cited as *La Vie.* Doorslaer offered further biographical findings in "Die Musikkapelle Kaiser Rudolfs II im Jahre 1582 unter der Leitung von Ph. de Monte," *Zeitschrift für Musikwissenschaft* 13 (1931): 481-91; and "La Chapelle musicale de l'Empereur Rudolphe II, en 1594, sous la direction de Philippe de Monte," *Acta Musicologica* 5 (1933): 148-61.

15.   Piet Nuten, *De "Madrigali Spirituali" van Filip de Monte* (Bruxelles, 1958).

16.   The following studies, either unpublished or in progress, may be mentioned: Hal Simmons, "Philippe de Monte, *Il terzodecimo libro delli madrigali a cinque voci, 1558:* a modern edition" (The American University, 1972); Robert Lindell, "Die sechs und siebenstimmige Madrigale von Filippo di Monte" (University of Vienna, 1972); Raymond Gobin, "The Late Madrigals of Philippe de Monte" (Northwestern University, in progress).

Chapter 1

1.   See Seld's letter, given on p. 4 .

2.   Doorslaer, *La Vie,* p. 19.

3.   Ibid., p. 219.

4.   Ibid., p. 32.

5.   Ibid., pp. 247-48, which gives the original Italian. See also the Appendix of this study.

6.   Ibid., pp. 33-34.

7.   Craig Wright, "Musiciens à la cathédrale de Cambrai," *Revue de Musicologie* 62 (1976): 204-28.

8.   Ibid., p. 219 (translation mine).

9.   Ibid., footnote 44 (translation mine).

10.   He is referred to in two of these archival entries as "Philippo de Monte," and "Philippo du Mont."

11.   Doorslaer, *La Vie,* pp. 36-38.

12.   Filippo di Monte, *Madrigali a cinque voci libro primo,* ed. Othmar Wessely and Erika Kanduth (Leuven, 1977), p. v.

13.   Ibid., p. viii, which gives a facsimile of Bruno's dedication. The original Italian reads: "i primi, e più maturi frutti delle compositioni à cinque; pur hora date in luce, de L'Eccelente Musico Philippo di Monte. . . . "

14.   Doorslaer, *La Vie,* pp. 248-49. The original Italian reads: "Essendomi risoluto di mandare in luce alcune mie fatiche per levare altrui l'occasione di publicarle senza mia saputa, come d'una parte de miei madrigali a cinque intervenne. . . . " See also the Appendix of this study.

15.   The madrigal is entitled *Colonna di smeraldo,* with a *seconda parte* entitled *In ferm'alta colonna.*

16.   Doorslaer, *La Vie,* p. 252. The original Italian reads: "La molta humanità mostratami da Vostra Sig. Molto Illustre, & in Anversa gli anni 1554 & 55 & ultimamente l'anno passato in Augusta. . . . " A more exact transcription of this dedication is given in Nuten, *De "Madrigali Spirituali" van Filip de Monte (1521-1603),* pp. 84-85.

17.   Doorslaer, *La Vie,* pp. 217-18 gives the original German text of this letter. It is also given in a more careful diplomatic reading in Horst Leuchtman, *Orlando di Lasso: Leben* (Wiesbaden, 1976), pp. 305-6.

18.   Doorslaer, *La Vie,* pp. 221-22. The original Italian reads: "In Aversa, mentre io mi truovavo in qualche difficoltà, & bisogno dell'aiuto, & favore de gli amici, & miei Signori V. S. Illustre da se stessa si mosse con tanta prontezza à dichiararmi la liberalità . . . " See also Appendix.

19. Doorslaer, *La Vie*, p. 45.

20. Ibid., pp. 248-49.

21. The fact that the opening madrigal cycle, *La dolce vista* appeared in an anthology of 1568, *Gli amorosi concenti* (RISM 1568[13]) strengthens this hypothesis.

22. Doorslaer, *La Vie*, pp. 223-24 and pp. 235-36. Doorslaer's transcription of the dedication of the Fourth Book for Six Voices inexplicably omits the date.

23. Ibid., p. 219.

24. Ibid., pp. 48-49.

25. In his recent study, *Musik und Musiker am Hof Maximilians II* (Tutzing, 1980), Walter Pass mentions that in September of 1567, Gabriel Martinengo was being considered for the position; Pass also mentions that Cornelio Celso, a bass in the Imperial Chapel, acted as a kind of agent in the negotiations with Monte (p. 72, p. 92). We know that Monte was in Rome at this time from his dedication to Flavio Orsini of the Fourth Book of Motets for Five Voices (1575); see *La Vie*, pp. 263-64.

26. For some detailed information on archival material pertaining to music at the Imperial Court, see Albert Smijers, "Die kaiserliche Hofmusik-Kapelle von 1543-1619," *Studien zur Musikwissenschaft: Beihefte der Denkmäler der Tonkunst in Osterreich* 6 (1919): 139-86; 7 (1920): 102-42; 8 (1921): 176-216; 9 (1922): 43-81. For this particular information see 9 (1922): 48: *"Die Khay. Mtt. etc. haben derselben capelmaister Philipp de Monte, umb daz er Jrer Mt. etc. ain mess componiert 50 fl. zu geben verordnet."* Hereafter this article is referred to as Smijers, "Die kaiserliche Hofmusik-Kapelle."

27. Doorslaer, *La Vie*, pp. 280-97.

28. Ibid., pp. 279-80.

29. Smijers, "Die kaiserliche Hofmusik-Kapelle," 9 (1922): 48.

30. The dedication of this book (in Latin) is given in *La Vie*, pp. 262-63.

31. Monte dedicated the following books to Maximilian: The Second Book of Madrigals for Six Voices (1569); the Fourth Book of Madrigals for Five Voices (1571); the First Book of Motets for Five Voices (1572); and the Third Book of Motets for Five Voices (1574). In 1574, he received a payment of 200 guilders "for two songbooks which he already dedicated to His Majesty in [15] 72 . . . " (See Smijers, "Die kaiserliche Hofmusik-Kapelle," 9 (1922): 48: "wegen zweyer gesangbucher, so er Jhr Mt. etc. noch im zwayundsiebenzigisten jarr . . . dedicert.") It is not clear which books are being referred to here.

32. See W. Richard Shindle, "Giovanni de Macque," *New Grove* (Vol. 11, pp. 450-51). See also Shindle, "The Madrigals of Giovanni de Macque" (Ph.D. dissertation, Indiana University, 1970).

33. See Walter Pass, "Giovanni della Gostena," *New Grove* (Vol. 5, pp. 345-46).

34. The dedications of all of these books are discussed in chapter 4 and given in the Appendix of this study.

35. The quotation comes from the Eighth Book for Five Voices (1581).

36. Smijers, *"Die kaiserliche Hofmusik-Kapelle,"* 9 (1921): 49: "auf sein . . . anhalten, auch in ansehung seiner viel jar hero gelaisten treuen und vleissigen dienst willen . . . "

37. Ibid., p. 49: "wegen ainer Jr. Mt. etc in gedruckten puechern mit funf stimen presentierten music . . . "

38. Monte's *Super flumina Babylonis* can be found in the old *Opera Omnia*, Vol. 15, pp. 57-68. Byrd's *Quomodo cantabimus* appears in the *Byrd Collected Vocal Works*, Vol. 9, pp. 99-129. Joseph Kerman accepts the authenticity of this exchange of motets in his article, "Byrd's Motets: Chronology and Canon," *Journal of the American Musicological Society* 14 (1961): 359-82.

39. Among the most prominent of English Catholics in Bohemia at this time was Edmund Campion, fresh from Rome. He was sent to Prague by the Society of Jesus, and was ordained deacon and priest by the archbishop of Prague in 1578. In 1580, he returned to England, where he was tried for sedition in the following year, and executed. Whether Monte had any contact with Campion is not known. Byrd's *Why do I use my paper, ink and pen? (Psalmes, Sonets and Songs,* 1588) is an elegy on Campion's death.

40. Joseph Kerman offers this interpretation in his article, "The Elizabethan Motet: a Study of Texts for Music," *Studies in the Renaissance* 9 (1962): 273-308.

41. These letters are given in J.A. Stellfield, *Bibliographie des Éditions musicales Plantiniennes* (Brusells, 1949), pp. 95-106.

42. Monte's report is given in Smijers, "Die kaiserliche HofmusikKapelle," 7 (1920): 117.

43. Doorslaer, *La Vie,* p. 293. The original Italian reads: "Sono entrato nella compagnia de podagrosi et questo ha causato ch'io non ho prima risposto a V. S. . . . "

44. Doorslaer, *La Vie,* pp. 269-70. Felis was in Prague from 1585 to 1590, in the service of the Papel nuncio, Antonio Puteo. In his dedication of this Sixth Book, which contains Monte's *Al discoglier d'un gruppo,* Felis states that he composed its madrigals while in Prague, and that Monte praised them ("furno da esso commendati . . . ").

45. Massaino's Latin dedication is given in full in Doorslaer, "Vereerende opdracht aan Ph. de Monte in 1592," *Musica Sacra "Sancta Sancte"* 37 (1930): 241-44.

46. Massaino's Latin phrase extolling Monte's virtues reads: "propter suavissimos candidae Vitae tuae mores."

47. See Lodovico Zacconi, *Prattica di musica* (Venice, 1622; reprint edition, Bologna, n.d.). The reference to Lasso and Monte comes in the *Seconda Parte, Libro Primo, Capitolo XII,* p. 13.

48. Horst Leuchtmann, *Orlando di Lasso: Leben* (Wiesbaden, 1976), p. 225.

49. *The Italian Madrigal,* p. 501.

50. Doorslaer, *La Vie,* p. 293, gives the entire Latin poem.

51. Smijers, "Die kaiserliche Hofmusik-Kapelle" 10 (1922): 51.

52. This book was unknown to Doorslaer; its dedication (in the original Italian) is given in Piet Nuten, *De "Madrigali Spirituali" van Filip de Monte* (Brussels, 1958), on p. 298.

53. Doorslaer, *La Vie,* pp. 299-305, gives the entire will in the original Latin.

54. The patrons of Monte's Italian years to whom he later dedicated his publications are: Fabio Boccamazzi (The Fifth Book of Madrigals for Five Voices, 1574); Cardinal Flavio Orsini (the Fourth and Fifth Books of Motets for Five Voices, 1575 and 1579); and Isabella de'Medici (the Sixth Book of Madrigals for Five Voices, 1575).

55. Doorslaer, *La Vie,* pp. 237-38. The original Italian reads: "in quello più vivace & allegro stile, . . . accio che porghino altrui materia d'esser allegramente cantati." See also the Appendix.

56. Ibid., pp. 241-42, gives the dedication to Alfonso in its entirety.

57.   Ibid., pp. 224-25. The original Italian reads: "vedo che V. Sig. Illustriss. sente molto gusto & piacere non solo in comporre, quanto le sue occupatione il permettono, alcuna cosa per trestullo, ma in ascoltar ancho & guidicare i componimenti altrui...."

58.   Ibid., pp. 243-45. The original Italian reads: "... non ho potuto di non mandarlo[questo mio Libro de Madrigali a Cinque voci] sotto l'honoratissimo nome di lei, percioche sonandose questi Madrigali le mesi adietro con le viuole da gamba, mostrò che piacessero tanto a V. Sig. Illustriss...."

59.   This list is based on the following sources: (1) Emil Vogel, *Bibliothek der gedruckten weltlichen Vocalmusik Italiens aus den Jahren 1500-1700, mit Nachträgen von Prof. Alfred Einstein.* 2 vols. (Berlin, 1892; reprint ed. Hildesheim, 1962), hereafter called *Vogel.* This reprint edition includes Einstein's revision of Vogel's section devoted to anthologies; this revision, hereafter called *Vogel-Einstein,* first appeared in *Music Library Association Notes,* vols. 2-5 (1944-48). (2) Alfred Einstein, François Lesure, Claudio Sartori, Emil Vogel, eds., *Bibliographia della musica Italiana vocale profana: publicata dal 1500 al 1700.* 3 vols. (Staderini, 1977), hereafter referred to as the *New Vogel.* (3) *International Inventory of Musical Sources: Einzeldrücke vor 1800* [Series A]. Volume 6 (Kassel, 1976). Vol. 6 gives all of Monte's integral publications which survive, omitting mention of any books which have disappeared (at any time) since their publication. Hereafter referred to as *RISM:A.* (4) Ignace Bossuyt, "Newly-discovered Part Books of Early Madrigal Collections of Philippus de Monte (1521-1603)," *Fontes Artis Musicae* 26 (1979): 295-97.

60.   Hereafter, unless the context is unclear, the titles of Monte's madrigal books will be translated into a regular English form, which omits the unnecessary "of madrigals."

61.   *New Vogel,* vol. 1, p. 522, states: *"Un esempl. comp. esisteva nella Collezione Heyer di Köln."*

62.   This transcription is in the Einstein Collection of the Smith College Music Library.

63.   This inventory is given in Franz Waldner, "Zwei Inventarien aus dem XVI. und XVII. Jahrhundert über hinterlassene Musikinstrumente und Musikalien am Innsbrucker Höfe," *Studien zur Musikwissenschaft* 4 (1916): 128-47.

64.   Ibid., p. 142.

65.   Einstein was apparently convinced of this book's authenticity, mentioning it in his article of 1934, and again in *The Italian Madrigal,* p. 501. His assertion (in the 1934 article) that this was Monte's last work is mystifying: I cannot see how it can be determined whether the book (if it ever existed) was published before or after the Ninth Book for Six Voices.

66.   *The Italian Madrigal,* p. 510.

67.   It is possible that the lost first edition of the Third Book for Four Voices came out in one of these two years; it must have appeared, in any case, between 1569 and 1576.

68.   These three motet books have recently appeared in the *New Complete Edition,* in (respectively) Series A, vol. 1 (1975), vol. 2 (1975), and vol. 3 (1978), all edited by Milton Steinhardt.

69.   There are only two major publications not printed in Italy. These are the *Missa ad Modulum Benedicta Es,* published in 1579 by Plantin, and the *Liber I Missarum...,* also published by Plantin, in 1587, containing seven masses. Four of these are now available in the *New Complete Edition,* Series B, vol. 1, edited by Chris Maas (Leuven, 1976).

70.   This dedication is given in Doorslaer, *La Vie,* p. 251, and in the Appendix.

71.   It is not clear whether or not this constituted an act of literary piracy, though Scotto's reputation was not high in these matters. See Claudio Sartori, "Scotto," *MGG,* vol. 12, cols.

435-37: "Girolamo, finally, was the typical printer-thief, who compelled Gardano frequently to protect his rights and his authors, so that he (Gardano) emphasized in his title pages that his editions alone were authentic."

72.   In 1586, for example, Scotto reprinted three quite different publications: the First Book for Four Voices, the Second Book for Five Voices, and the Eighth Book for Five Voices. Similarly, in 1592, Gardano reissued three of their earlier publications: the First Book for Six Voices, the Fifth Book for Five Voices, and the Fourth Book for Six Voices.

73.   This partbook, unknown to *RISM:A* and the *New Vogel,* has the following title page:

> BASSO / DI FILIPPO DI MONTE / MAESTRO DI CAPELLA / DELLA S. C.
> MAESTA' DELL' IMPERATORE / RODOLPHO SECONDO / Il secondo Libro
> de Madrigali, a quattro voci. / NOVAMENTE RISTAMPATI. [emblem] IN
> VENETIA, Appresso l'Herede di Girolamo Scotto. / MDCVII.

74.   This change was not part of any larger change in Gardano's "house style"; Gardano continued to print madrigal books in oblong quarto format after 1600. The remarkably settled quality of Monte's collaboration with Angelo Gardano can be seen in a telling bibliographical detail: all but two of the twenty-two madrigal books (sacred and secular) which Gardano published between 1582 and 1603 have exactly 29 pages of music (the two exceptions are the Second and Third Books of Spiritual Madrigals for Six Voices, of 1589 and 1590). These twenty-nine pages, taken together with a title page, dedication page, and index, produce a book of thirty-two pages—exactly the number of pages (and no more) which four sheets of paper in quarto format can produce. To judge from the *New Vogel,* few composers' publications exhibit so predictable and regular a format as this.

75.   *The Italian Madrigal,* p. 511.

76.   In view of the prominence given to Monte in these two anthologies, it seems odd that at least two of the four-voice pieces in *Musica divina* are not by Monte. *Da bei rami scendea* is by Arcadelt (see chart), and *Quando dagli occhi* is from Sessa d'Aranda's First Book for Four Voices (1571). I am grateful to Watkins Shaw of the Royal College of Music (London) for sending me a copy of the four voice-parts of Sessa's composition, thus making this identification possible. In view of these false ascriptions, it does not seem unreasonable to question the authenticity of the two remaining four-voice pieces—*Alma ben nata (Musica divina)* and *Io son sì vago (Harmonia celeste)*—for which there are no previous sources.

77.   In *Harmonia celeste,* the following Marenzio pieces appeared: *Tirsi morir volea, Frenò Tirsi, Cosi moriro, Che fa oggi* (all from I.5; 1580); *Madonna poi ch'uccider* (III.5; 1582); and *Qual vive Salamandra* (I.6; 1581). In *Musica divina,* only *Liquide perle* (I.5; 1580) appeared, among the anonymous pieces.

78.   The English anthologies tell a similar story; only two pieces from the 1570s are included in *Musica transalpina* of 1588, and the three later anthologies (*Italian Madrigals Englished,* 1590[4]; *Musica transalpina,* 1597[3]; and Morley's *Selected madrigals,* 1598[3]a) avoid Monte's music entirely.

79.   This anthology is cited in Doorslaer, *La Vie* (p. 192), yet somehow eluded *RISM:B.* It still exists, and has been consulted by Milton Steinhardt, in preparation for the *New Complete Edition.* I am grateful to Professor Steinhardt for sending me the incipits of the pieces in *Florilegium musicum* attributed to Monte.

80.   In his Fourth Book for Five Voices (1571), Monte set Guarini's sonnet *Hor che'l mio vivo sole;* this setting is mentioned briefly in *The Italian Madrigal,* p. 509.

81. *The Italian Madrigal,* p. 509.

82. I know of no exhaustive bibliographical study of these large mid-century anthologies. My information on both this two-volume anthology and the two-volume anthology discussed below is derived from the following sources: (1) Nicolo Haym, *Biblioteca Italiana o sia Notizia de' Libri rari* (Venice, 1736); (2) Jacques-Charles Brunet, *Manuel du Libraire et de L'Amateur de Livres,* 6 vols. (Berlin, 1922); (3) *Short-list of Books Printed in Italy and of Italian Books printed in Other Countries from 1465 to 1600 now in the British Museum* (London, 1958); (4) *Catalogue of Books printed on the Continent of Europe: 1501-1611, in Cambridge Libraries* (Cambridge, 1967).

83. I am grateful to Mr. William Clubb (Berkeley, California) for graciously supplying me with a photocopy of the index of this publication, and also for placing at my disposal a microfilm of six other large poetic anthologies of this period. Close scrutiny of these confirms my hypothesis that Monte drew his texts from the *Primo* and *Secondo Volume.*

84. This bibliographical unfolding extends back to at least 1545, when the *Rime diverse di molti eccelentiss. auttori nuovamente raccolte* appeared, published in Venice by Gabriel Giolito. I have been able to consult this book in the Bancroft Library; much of its material appears in the later anthologies.

85. A good example of Monte's attitude towards these chains of ottavas can be seen in his treatment of *Danzava con maniere.* In its original state, it has eleven stanzas; Monte extracts the first, second, fifth and seventh, to make his brief cycle (II.4; 1569). In 1584, he returned to the poem, setting the last stanza (*Mi havete amor,* in V.6). An even more remarkable example of this kind of thing can be seen in Monte's use on three occasions of a nine-stanza ottava chain by Matteo Androvandi. In the *Scelta di Rime di diversi eccellenti Poeti* (Genoa, 1579), I find the poem with the stanzas in the following order: (1) *Dolor, lagrime,* (2) *Oime cuor mio,* (3) *Mentre lontan da i vostri chiari lumi,* (4) *Deh foss'almen,* (5) *Piangi mi dice,* (6) *Ombra son io sepolto,* (7) *Deh dove e l'alma,* (8) *Ma sia che vol,* (9) *Facciami quanto.* In *Il terzo libro delle fiamme* (1568[12]), Monte set six of these as a cycle, but with his stanzas in the following order: nos. 1, 7, 2, 4, 5 and 8. In his Third Book for Five Voices (1570), Monte set stanza 6; finally, in his Fifth Book for Five Voices (1574), he set stanza 3.

86. To pick only one example from many: Rainieri's *Questa fera gentil* (Monte's Ninth Book for Five Voices; 1580) was also set by Hubert Waelrant (*Madrigali et Canzoni Francesi,* 1558), Marc'Antonio Pordenon (IV.5; 1573), and by Orazio Angelini (I.5; 1583).

87. See Angelo Solerti, *Le Rime di Torquato Tasso: Edizione critica su i Manoscritti e le antiche Stampe,* 4 vols. (Bologna, 1898-1902). Volume 1 *(Bibliographia)* is an exhaustive investigation of the printed and manuscript sources.

Chapter 2

1. See chapter 1, p. 5.

2. *The Italian Madrigal,* p. 503.

3. This text is taken from Alfredo Obertello, *Madrigali Italiani in Inghilterra* (Milan, 1949), pp. 250-51.

4. For an exhaustive study of sixteenth-century modal polyphony, see Bernhard Meier, *Die Tonarten der Klassischen Vokalpolyphonie* (Utrecht, 1974).

5. Ibid., pp. 192ff.

6.   It is Meier's central thesis that the vast majority of sixteenth-century polyphony conforms with contemporary theoretical injunctions concerning modal propriety.

7.   Vicentino's book (Rome, 1550; reprint edition, with postface by Edward Lowinsky, Kassel, 1959) discusses cadences and ways of avoiding them in the *Libro Terzo, Capitoli XXIV - XXXV,* 51 verso - 58 recto.

8.   Zarlino's discussion of the cadence can be conveniently consulted in Zarlino, *The Art of Counterpoint: Part Three of Le Istitutioni Harmoniche,* trans. Guy Marco and Claude Palisca (New Haven, 1968), pp. 141-53.

9.   Ibid., p. 151.

10.   *The Italian Madrigal,* p. 503.

11.   Filippo di Monte, *Madrigali a cinque voci libro primo,* ed. Othmar Wessely and Erika Kanduth (Leuven, 1977), p. v.

12.   Lasso's First Book for Five Voices is available in Orlando di Lasso, *Sämtliche Werke: Zweiter Band* (Leipzig, n.d.).

13.   Giaches de Wert, *Collected Works,* Volume 1, ed. Carol MacClintock (n.p., 1961).

14.   Ibid., pp. 66-80.

15.   Ibid., pp. 103-24.

16.   Ibid., p. 21, mm. 17-21, for its extraordinary turn to the triad of E♭ major, in an E Phrygian-mode piece.

17.   Ibid., p. 22, mm. 34-38; mm. 50-52.

18.   *The Italian Madrigal,* p. 505.

19.   See *Vogel* under Rore, nos. 47 and 51. The entire contents of these two four-voice books are given in Rore, *Opera Omnia,* ed. Bernhard Meier, Volume 4 (n.p., 1969).

20.   All of these pieces first appeared in the Second Book for Four Voices (1557); see Volume 4 (cited above) for *O Sonno,* pp. 66-69, and *Mia benigna fortuna—Crudele acerba,* pp. 79-81.

21.   Rore's setting of *Alla dolce ombra* appeared in the First Book for Four Voices (1551); see Volume 4, pp. 7-15.

22.   See *Vogel* under Rore, nos. 15 and 21. Rore's *Vergine* cycle appears in Volume 3 of the *Opera Omnia,* pp. 1-33. Palestrina's cycle *Da fuoco così bel* first appeared in Rore's Second Book for Four Voices (1557); for a modern edition see Ioannis Petraloysii Praenestini, *Opera Omnia,* ed. F.X. Haberl (Leipzig, 1862-1907), Volume 30.

23.   Lasso's *Standomi un giorno* (a setting of a Petrarch canzone) appeared as the first piece in his Second Book for Five Voices (1559); Wert's cycle in his First Book for Five Voices has already been mentioned; Nasco's *Madrigali a cinque voci* (1548) opens with a setting of *A qualunque animal* (a Petrarch sestina). For a full-length study of the cyclic madrigal, see Patricia Myers, *An Analytical Study of the Italian Cyclic Madrigals Published by Composers Working in Rome ca. 1540-1614* (Ph.D. diss. University of Illinois, 1971).

24.   The *New Vogel* gives a false picture of the original layout of this book by silently correcting its various mistakes. (*Vogel* leaves them as they are in the original.)

25.   Parabosco's *I Diporti* (Venice, 1550) has, in its *Giornata terza,* a number of poems later set by madrigalists, among them *Voi volete ch'io moia; Donna, s'io resta viva;* and *Donna gentile per farvi più perfetta.* (See also *The Italian Madrigal,* pp. 184-85).

26. James Haar, "*Pace non trovo:* A Study in Literary and Musical Parody," *Musica Disciplina* 20 (1966): 117-18. For more on the *note nere* madrigal, see Haar, "The *Note Nere* Madrigal," *Journal of the American Musicological Society* 18 (1965): 21-41.

27. Don Harrán, "Rore and the *Madrigale Cromatico,*" *The Music Review* 34 (1973): 66-81.

28. All of Rore's First Book for Five Voices appears in the *Opera Omnia*, Volume 2, ed. Bernhard Meier (1963). In *Cantai, mentre ch'i arsi,* Rore's use of vivid tempo contrasts can be seen in the varied treatment of *pieno di dolce aspro martire* (p. 3, mm. 73-81) and the following line, *Ov'hora in libertà piango e sospiro* (pp. 3-4, mm. 81-89).

29. The *New Vogel* lists fourteen settings of this text, to which the two by Monte and Striggio (the latter published in *Il primo fiore della Ghirlanda musicale,* 1577[1]) can be added. Monte's setting is by far the earliest; the last known setting appeared in 1598, in Luca Bati's Second Book for Five Voices. For a recent discussion of several of these settings, see Anthony Newcomb, *The Madrigal at Ferrara: 1579-1597* (Princeton, 1980), Volume 1, pp. 123-25.

30. Myers, op. cit., pp. 171-73.

31. *The Italian Madrigal,* p. 505.

32. Ibid., p. 502.

33. These are: *In me tanto l'ardore* (Amaltheo), *Quando muovo le luci a mirar voi* (Ariosto), *Occhi, se voi pur sete* (Amanio), *Occhi sereni* (Corfini), and *Tra bei rubini* (Amaltheo).

34. *The Italian Madrigal,* p. 506.

35. The text is taken from Obertello, *Madrigali Italiani in Inghilterra* (Milan, 1949), p. 405. For a discussion of Morley's piece, which is based on Lasso's setting, see Joseph Kerman, *The Elizabethan Madrigal* (New York, 1962), pp. 187-88.

36. The *New Vogel* lists sixteen settings of the text, ranging in date from Monte's (apparently the first setting to appear in an integral publication) to Antonio il Verso's Fifteenth Book for Five Voices (1619). Undoubtedly, more settings could be culled from *Vogel-Einstein.*

37. *The Italian Madrigal,* p. 506.

38. Both the madrigal and the parody mass appear in the old *Opera Omnia,* Volume 14.

39. *The Italian Madrigal,* p. 506.

40. *Nov'angeletta* is the basis for one of Lodovico Balbi's curious imitations in his *Musicale Esercitio* (*Vogel,* under Balbi, no. 2); *Voi volete ch'io moia* appears in *Florilegium musicum* of 1631 (see Table 1.3).

41. For an index of this manuscript, see Guglielmo Barblan and Agostino Zecca La Terza, "The Tarasconi Codex in the Library of the Milan Conservatory," *The Musical Quarterly* 60 (1974): 195-221.

42. These three lute transcriptions, along with the original madrigals, appear in Volume 25 of the old *Opera Omnia.*

43. *The Italian Madrigal,* p. 508.

44. Ibid., pp. 507-8.

45. Both *Che fai* and *Cari scogli* appeared in *Spoglia amorosa* (1585), and both were copied into the Tarasconi Codex. *Che fai* also appeared in *Harmonia celeste* (1583), and was adapted as a spiritual piece in the *Scielta de madrigali... accommodati in motetti* (1604).

46. Paston's adaptation of *Che fai,* with the words *Crowned with flow'rs and lilies, I saw the muses* is discussed and quoted in Philip Brett, *The Songs of William Byrd* (Ph.D. diss. Cambridge University, 1965), p. 122. Byrd later set these same words to new music, unrelated to Monte's *Che fai.* Paston's adaptation of another Monte madrigal (*Dolce mio duol,* from the Third Book for Five Voices, 1570) is also quoted and discussed, p. 87. The text of this adaptation is *Crowned with flow'rs, I saw fair Amaryllis.*

47. *Carlo, che'n tenerella* is available in *Italienische Musiker und das Kaiserhaus: 1567-1625,* ed. Alfred Einstein (Volume 77 of *Denkmäler der Tonkunst in Österreich,* Vienna, 1934), pp. 1-3. Rore's *Tu piangi e quella* is published in the *Opera Omnia,* Volume 2, ed. Bernhard Meier (1963), pp. 40-44.

48. *The Italian Madrigal,* pp. 508-9.

49. The six-voice *Parce mihi* (with a *seconda pars* entitled *Peccavi quid faciam*) appeared in *Thesauri Musici Tomus Tertius,* a motet collection published in Nuremberg (*RISM* 1564[3]).

Chapter 3

1. Doorslaer, *La Vie,* pp. 279-80. The letter is quoted more fully in chapter 1, p. 6.

2. The term was apparently first used in 1555, in the anthology *Primo Libro delle Muse a Quattro Voci: Madrigali Ariosi de Ant. Barre et altri...,* published in Rome by Barre. Monte contributed to both of the two known later numbers in this series: 1558[1] and 1562[3] a (see chapter 1, Table 1.3). *Dolorosi martir* of 1558[1], is discussed in chapter 2.

3. See Stefano Rossetti, *Il Primo Libro de Madrigali a Quattro Voci,* ed. Allen B. Skei (*Recent Researches in the Music of the Renaissance,* vol. 26; Madison, 1977).

4. Wert, *Collected Works,* vol. 15. The pieces in this book most in the *madrigale arioso* style are *Ma di che debbo lamentarmi, Era il bel viso,* and *O cameretta.*

5. See *The Italian Madrigal,* vol. 3, nos. 33-34, 53, 54, 58, 60, 70-75, 77, 78, 87, 88; these are all examples of the lighter forms. The more pointed rhythmic style alluded to here can be seen in any of these.

6. *The Italian Madrigal,* p. 509.

7. It appears that no more than ten Monte madrigals appeared in printed instrumental intabulations or versions in the sixteenth and early seventeenth centuries. In the following list, subscripted numbers before 1600 refer to Howard Mayer Brown, *Instrumental Music Printed Before 1600: A Bibliography* (Cambridge, Mass., 1965). Superscripted numbers after 1600 refer to *RISM:B.*

BROWN AND *RISM* NUMBERS	MADRIGAL TITLE	SOURCE IN MONTE'S PUBLICATIONS
1583[4]	*Alma de amor*	IV.6 (1580)
1584[1]	*Cantai un tempo*	II.6 (1569)
1584[3]	*In me tanto l'ardore*	I.6 (1563-69)
1584[5]	*In qual parte* *Per divina bellezza 2p*	IV.5 (1570)

BROWN AND RISM NUMBERS	MADRIGAL TITLE	SOURCE IN MONTE'S PUBLICATIONS
1593₇	*Ahi chi mi rompe* *Di ch'ella mosse 2p*	III.5 (1570)
1594₅	*Veramente in amore*	V.5 (1574)
1600⁵a	*Ahi chi mi rompe* *Di ch'ella mosse 2p* *Occhi vaghi (not the 2p)* *Poi che'l mio largo pianto*	III.5 (1570) X.5 (1581) I.6 (1563-69)
1600⁶	*Veramente in amore* *Leggiadre ninfe* *Il dolce e desiato 2p* *Amorosi pensieri*	V.5 (1574) I.6 (1563-69) III.6 (1576)
1601¹⁸	*Occhi vaghi (not the 2p)* *La dolce vista*	X.5 (1581) I.6 (1563-69)

8.   Thus Gerald Abraham in *The Concise Oxford History of Music* (London, 1979), p. 265.

9.   By Romanesca-like harmonies, I refer to the following four-chord progression (and its transpositions): C major, G major, a minor, E major. These are the first four harmonies of the Romanesca pattern, and occur often in the lighter forms; see, for example *The Italian Madrigal,* vol. 3, no. 53 (*E la morte di marito,* by Perissone Cambio), mm. 37-51.

10.   See chapter 2, p. 136, where Monte's first use of this triple-time dance was noted, in his First Book for Six Voices.

11.   Gabrieli's *Ecco l'aurora* (Alfred Einstein, ed., *The Golden Age of the Madrigal,* New York, 1942) and Nanino's *Donna gentil* (Luigi Torchi, ed., *L'arte Musicale in Italia: Volume Secondo*) are both more attractive and successful essays in a lighter style than either of the Monte pieces just discussed.

12.   Perhaps Monte had Rore's setting of *Mia benigna fortuna* and *Crudele acerba* in mind when he wrote *I'piansi; Crudele acerba* has a signature of one flat in the Canto and Tenore, and two flats in the Alto and Basso, and is in the Phrygian mode on D.

13.   This piece is the only one in his entire madrigalian output which uses A♭ and D♭.

14.   The extent of Monte's restraint in word-painting here is particularly evident if one compares Monte's opening with Willaert's settings of both *I'piansi* and *Cantai or piango* from his *Musica Nova.* Willaert makes more of the poetic contrasts, yet even here Einstein finds moderation and restraint (*The Italian Madrigal,* pp. 335-37). Perhaps Monte's own restraint derives in part from Willaert's treatment of the words in such instances as these.

15.   The chord of resolution in an authentic cadence can either be major or minor; the preceding chord must (of course) be a major one. In a plagal cadence the harmonic sequence can be: major to major (*I'piansi,* mm. 26-27); minor-major (*I'piansi,* mm. 38-39); or minor-minor (*I'piansi* lacks this type).

16.   Antonio Molino, who also called himself Manoli Blessi, is discussed in *The Italian Madrigal,* pp. 527ff., and also in Beatrice Pescerelli, *I Madrigali di Maddalena Casulana* (Florence, 1979), pp. 10-14.

17. Doorslaer, *La Vie*, p. 229. The original Italian reads: "La onde essendomi capitato alle mani i presenti Madrigali dell' Eccellentissimo Musico M. Filippo di Monto, ne havendo potuto mancare a requisitione di molti miei signori di darli alla stampa, hò voluto dedicargli à lei. . . . "

18. The dedication to Maximilian is given in Doorslaer, *La Vie*, pp. 220-21, and in the Appendix of this study.

19. Monte's dedication to Rudolf is given in Doorslaer, *La Vie*, pp. 233-34, and in the Appendix of this study.

20. Quintilian, in his *Institutio Oratoria*, states: "As regards Latin teachers of rhetoric, of whom Plotius was the most famous, Cicero informs us that they came into existence towards the end of the age of Crassus." Suetonius, in his *De Rhetoribus*, gives a brief account of Lucius Voltacilius Plotus, telling us that he began as a slave, was set free for his great talent, becoming a teacher of rhetoric. Neither author gives the anecdote Monte adduces.

21. The most recent (and balanced) treatment of Rudolf's patronage of the arts and his obsession with the occult appears in R.J.W. Evans, *Rudolf II and His World: A Study in Intellectual History, 1576-1612* (Oxford, 1973).

22. The "great lord of Delos" is Phoebus; Thetis is another name for Aphrodite, in her manifestation as sea-goddess. The image in lines 1-3, then, is of the sun setting in the ocean.

23. The opposition of Cnidus and Paphos with Scythia and Pontus is intended to symbolize the contrast between a civilized environment and a wild, uncivilized one.

24. Of the many available editions of this work, I have used the following: Michele Scherillo, ed., *Arcadia di Jacobo Sannazaro* (Turin, 1888). The *Prosa duodecima* (not so titled) appears in this edition on pp. 272-91.

25. Ibid., p. 276.

26. Ibid., p. 289.

27. The rather odd figure of "voluntary exile" (stanza 16) also comes from the pastoral tradition; the phrase *volontario exilio* appears in the *Arcadia*, as well as in Boccacio's *Filostrato*.

28. *Orlando Furioso*, Canto 7, stanza 29. A translation reads:

    > Never did ivy press or cling so close,
    > Rooted beside the plant which it embraced,
    > As now in love each to the other does; . . .

    A useful translation of the entire *Orlando Furioso* by Barbara Reynolds has recently been published in two paperback volumes by Penguin Books (1975-1977).

Chapter 4

1. Both the First Book of Spiritual Madrigals for Five Voices, and the First Book of Spiritual Madrigals for Six Voices are not discussed in this chapter. Monte's spiritual madrigals are the subject of a full-length monograph of Piet Nuten, *De "Madrigali Spirituali" van Filip de Monte* (Brussels, 1958).

2. See the Appendix for the Italian text of this dedication.

3. *The Italian Madrigal*, p. 510.

4. See the Appendix for the Italian text of this dedication.

5.   For the best discussion of Rudolf's patronage of the arts, see R.J.W. Evans, *Rudolf and his World: A Study of Intellectual History, 1576-1612* (Oxford, 1973).

6.   Ibid., p. 71.

7.   See the Appendix for the Italian text of this dedication.

8.   See the Appendix for the Italian text of this dedication.

9.   See *Calendar of State Papers, Foreign Series: of the Reign of Elizabeth,* Volume 14 (London, 1907), p. 284.

10.   *The Italian Madrigal,* p. 509.

11.   Ibid., p. 502.

12.   Regnart's book is entitled *Il Secundo Libro delle Canzone Italiane a cinque voci* (Nuremburg, 1581). Filippo Duc dedicated his *La Vergini* (Venice, 1574) to Monfort and his brother.

13.   The dedication is given in full in Doorslaer, *La Vie,* pp. 250-51.

14.   For a recent biography of this woman, see Beatrice Pescerelli, *I Madrigali de Maddalena Casulana* (Florence, 1979).

15.   See the Appendix for the Italian text of this dedication.

16.   Gabrieli's First Book for Three Voices, printed in 1575, apparently lacks a dedication in this first edition, leading Einstein to wonder whether this edition is indeed actually the first (*The Italian Madrigal,* p. 545). Gardano reprinted it in 1582, the same year he brought out Monte's new book.

17.   See the Appendix for the Italian text of this dedication.

18.   In contrast, nearly every one of Marenzio's books published before 1586 has either a Tasso or a Guarini poem.

19.   The *New Vogel* identifies the seven-voice canzone entitled *Coppia gentil* as by Rinuccini. I know of no print or manuscript source which supports this ascription.

20.   It is possible, for instance, that Monte found several texts in Gabrieli's two six-voice books. From the First Book (1574) Monte may have drawn *Quando nel cor m'entrassti* (which he set in the Eighth Book), *Tu mi piaghasti a morte,* and *Quand'io tal'hor mi doglio* (both of which he set in the Tenth Book). For *Quando nel cor m'entrassti* and *Quand'io tal'hor mi doglio* there are no other known previous settings. Likewise, Monte may have taken *Che piangi, alma* (which he sets in the Tenth Book) from Gabrieli's Second Book for Six Voices (1580); this is the only known previous setting.

21.   The Tenth Book ends with a very serious and melancholy chain of eight ottava stanzas; this is the last time we encounter so large a dose of this kind of lyrics in Monte's books. Yet the book typically includes a number of much lighter poems as well, *Occhi vaghi amorosi* and *Dolci amorose parolette,* for example. The two other five-voice books display a similar variety.

22.   Marenzio's favored mensuration is, of course, C. Yet he regularly includes pieces in ₵ in his publications; the anomaly is the single book for four, five and six voices of 1588, entirely notated in ₵, a book remarkable for the seriousness of its poetry and musical style.

23.   Wert, too, favors C after 1580, but includes pieces in ₵ in his last publication, the Eleventh Book for Five Voices (1595).

24.   *The Italian Madrigal,* p. 823-24.

25.   Ibid., p. 824.

26.   These pieces are: *Liquide perle* (1); *Spuntavan già* (3); *Che fa oggi il mio sole* (7); *Cantava la più vaga pastorella* (11); *Questa di verd'herbette* (12); and *Partirò dunque* (12). Einstein's list (see the preceding note) is not quite correct.

27.   See Angelo Solerti, *Le Origine del Melodramma* (Turin, 1903), p. 170. Della Valle, writing ca. 1640 in his *Della musica del l'età nostra,* states: "Quando io era giovanetto mi piacevano assai quei del Marenzio, e particolarmente per certe sue grazie quel tanto cantato *Liquide Perle.*"

28.   This poem is ascribed to Celiano in the *New Vogel;* this may be correct, though I have not been able to verify this independently.

29.   See Jacobi Arcadelt, *Opera Omnia,* ed. Albert Seay, Vol. 2 (1970), pp. 38-40.

30.   Einstein's words are: "an der Grenze der Schlüpfrigkeit," and "Alte Herr, wo bist du geraten?"

31.   Einstein devotes a brief section at the conclusion of chapter 8 to this topic (*The Italian Madrigal,* pp. 606-7): " . . . The setting in which this harmonic clarification took place was not so much the lofty madrigal, . . . but rather the canzonetta, the canzone, the balletto, and that anacreontic, pastoral variety of the madrigal created by Andrea Gabrieli."

32.   Berkeley, 1961.

33.   Einstein's comments read: "Wirklich hat M. sich den neuen, leichten Stil anbequemt: der erste Teil fast ganz homophon; der zweite mit jener behenden, luftigen, kleingliedrigen Motivik der neuen Oberitaliener; es scheint als ob. M. schon Madrigale Marenzios gekannt hätte. *Ein Stück das auch Erfolg hatte!*"

34.   This is not *the* Scipio Africanus, but another in this illustrious line, who may have been murdered. (See *A Dictionary of Greek and Roman Biography and Mythology,* ed. William Smith [London, 1902], vol. 3, p. 750). Why this Scipio would be the subject of a cinquecento poem is another matter.

35.   The Don Juan of Austria hypothesis is highly conjectural, and based on the following facts. The Emperor Charles V captured Tunis in 1535, and like Scipio of ancient Rome, took the title "Africanus." (See Hugh Trevor-Roper, *Princes and Artists: Patronage and Ideology at four Habsburg Courts, 1517-1633* [New York, 1976], p. 29 for a reproduction of an emblem celebrating Charles' victory at Tunis, inscribed, *"CAROLUS IMP. AUG. AFRICANUS.'*) Charles' illegitimate son, Don Juan of Austria (1547-1578), looking for fresh battlefields after his victory at Lepanto, also conquered Tunis. Like his father, he too considered himself a modern Scipio. He died (age 31) in the Netherlands, where he had gone as Governor General. He was not murdered or killed in action, though it might have been thought in some quarters that he was. Until a printed source for *Scipio, l'acerbo caso* is found, it may prove impossible to interpret it satisfactorily.

36.   Soriano's dedication is dated *"Di Roma li 15 Febraro 1581,"* not April 20 as given in *Vogel* and the *New Vogel.* Clearly, Monte might well have had the opportunity to see Soriano's setting.

37.   Monte's Tenth Book and Soriano's First Book have one more text in common, *Questi gigli novelli.* Both are set in the Mixolydian mode, with a high vocal scoring. Yet Monte's version of the poem is different from Soriano's and there is another setting in Pordenon's Fifth Book for Five Voices (1578).

38.   See Cipriani Rore, *Opera Omnia,* ed. Bernhard Meier, Volume 4 (1969), pp. 28-30.

39. For Marenzio's setting, see Luca Marenzio, *Sämtliche Werke,* ed. Alfred Einstein (in *Publikationen Älterer Musik* 6), Leipzig, 1931. Marenzio's setting begins with the words *"Filli, l'acerbo caso";* otherwise the text is identical with the others. I have transcribed Ingegneri's from microfilm; the other settings have not been available to me.

40. The style of these eight ottava stanzas suggests that they may be the work of the same poet who wrote the eighteen ottava stanzas in the Seventh Book of 1578.

41. For a modern edition, see Sir John Harrington, trans., *Lodovico Ariosto's Orlando Furioso,* ed. Robert McNulty (Oxford, 1972). In Harrington's scheme, *Sweet dream did promise me a quiet peace* is stanza 57 of the thirty-third book (p. 376 of this edition).

42. James Haar, *"Pace non trovo:* A Study in Literary and Musical Parody," *Musica Disciplina* 20 (1966): 95-149.

43. Ibid., p. 96.

44. Ibid., p. 100.

45. See Giuseppe Agnelli and Giuseppe Ravegnani, *Annali delle Edizione Ariostee,* 2 vols. (Bologna, 1933).

46. Ibid., vol. 2, pp. 202-204. On this kind of Ariostean centonization, see also Louise George Clubb, "The Making of the Pastoral Play: some Italian Experiments between 1573 and 1590," in *Petrarch to Pirandello: Studies in Italian Literature in honour of Beatrice Corrigan,* ed. J.A. Molinaro (Toronto, 1973), p. 64: "The playwrights' recognition of Ariosto's importance to the genre is expressed in their including him in prefatory genealogies and in their plundering of *Orlando furioso.* Della Valle places Ariosto with Petrarch in the first rank of pastoral authority by using them to make his plays partial centos: his rule in *Fillide* [pub. 1584] is 'È sempre obligo di chiudere il terzetto, e le stanze delle canzoni con un verso del Petrarca'. . . and in *Gelosi amanti* he quotes Ariosto by the same rule in Acts I and III, Petrarch in II and IV, and both alternately, in Act V."

47. I quote here from *Aretino: Selected Letters,* trans. George Bull (Harmondsworth, 1976), p. 102.

48. This episode occurs in Part 2, Chapter 18.

49. Once again, this is Harrington's translation (see note 41 above).

50. Egon Kenton, "A Faded Laurel Wreath," in *Aspects of Medieval and Renaissance Music: A Birthday Offering to Gustave Reese,* ed. Jan LaRue (New York, 1966), pp. 500-518.

51. Anthony Newcomb, "The Three Anthologies for Laura Peverara, 1580-1583," *Rivista Italiana di Musicologia* 10 (1975), 329-45.

52. Ibid., p. 331.

53. Ibid., pp. 333-34.

Chapter 5

1. This dedication is given in the original Italian in the Appendix.

2. Alfred Einstein, "Filippo di Monte as Madrigalkomponist," *International Society for Musical Research* (1930), pp. 102-8. The original German (pp. 107-8) reads: ". . . alles muss kurz, leicht, behend sein; die gehäuften Siebensilver verändern Montes Thematik und Motivik von Grund aus."

3. It seems likely that at least some singers of the period would have slightly altered the syncope pattern to achieve the proper accentuation, substituting:

    si   pie - to - se   for   si   pie - to - se   (as in m. 10).

4. Anthony Newcomb, "Madrigal II,8: 'The 1580s: The Ornamented Style; Dissemination of the Hybrid Madrigal'," *New Grove* (vol. 11), p. 470.

5. Joseph Kerman, *The Elizabethan Madrigal: A Comparative Study* (New York, 1962).

6. Friedrich Blume discusses the extent of Marenzio's influence upon Leonhard Lechner in *Protestant Church Music: A History* (New York, 1974), pp. 153ff. A set of parody magnificats was published by Michael Praetorius in 1611; the models include some very serious pieces by Marenzio and Wert. The Czech nobleman and dilettante composer Krystof Harant composed a parody mass on Marenzio's *Dolorosi martir* (from his I.5; 1580). More examples of the German appropriation of the serious Italian madrigal could be adduced.

7. The evidence suggests that Monte always received a special payment for a work dedicated to the Emperor; this seems to be the case with Zanotti, and most likely with other figures who were patient enough: Orologio received 60 *Gulden* "wegen seiner... dedicierten Mardrigal..." in May 1587; he had signed the dedication to Rudolf on 20 May of the preceding year.

8. Einstein reported his findings in "Italienische Musik und italienische Musiker am Kaiserhof und an den erzherzoglichen Höfen in Innsbruck und Graz," *Studien zur Musikwissenschaft* 21 (1934): 3-52. Hereafter called "Italienische Musik."

9. Einstein transcribed the following works (volume numbers refer to the Smith College Collection):

Luyton:	I.5 (1582)	Vol. 28
Orologio:	I.5 (1586)	Vol. 48
Orologio:	II.5 (1595)	Vol. 48
Regnart:	I.5 *(Canzone italiane)* (1574)	Vol. 53
Regnart:	II.5 *(Canzone italiane)* (1581)	Vol. 53
de Sayve:	I.5 *(Canzoni a la Napolitan)* (1582)	Vol. 58
Zanotti:	I.5 (1587)	Vol. 69
Zanotti:	I.6 (1589)	Vol. 69
Zanotti:	III.5 *con alcune Villotte* (1589)	Vol. 69
Zanotti:	*Madrigali tam italica*	Vol. 69

    From these transcriptions, Einstein selected representative samples, and published them in *Italienische Musiker und das Kaiserhaus: 1567-1625* (Vol. 77 of *Denkmäler der Tonkunst in Österreich*, Vienna, 1934). Hereafter called *DTO 77*.

10. See Walter Pass, "Regnart," in *New Grove* (Vol. 15), pp. 691-93. See also Walter Pass, *Thematischer Katalog Sämtlicher Werke Jacob Regnarts (ca. 1540-1599)* (Vienna, 1969). This is Volume 5 of the series *Tabulae Musicae Austriacae*.

11. Lasso's *Libro de Villanelle, Moresche, et Altre Canzoni* (Paris, 1581) appears in the *Sämtliche Werke*, Vol. 10. In his dedication to Duke William V, Lasso apologizes for the book, saying: "It would have been more fitting had I published these villanelle in my youth, when I wrote them, than in this my mature age...." Einstein (*The Italian Madrigal*, pp. 496-97) suggests that, while Lasso may have written the pieces in his youth, he "must have revised them about 1580."

12. All of Regnart's three-voice pieces, together with Lechner's reworkings of them, were published in *Jacob Regnart: Deutsche dreistimmige Lieder nach Art der Neapolitan nebst Leonhardt*

Lechner's fünfstimmiger Bearbeitung, ed. Robert Eitner (Leipzig, 1895). (This is Volume 19, *Publikation älterer praktischer und theoretischer Musikwerke.*)

13. See Walter Pass, "Zanotti," *New Grove* (Vol. 20), p. 643.

14. Zanotti's dedication is given in *DTO 77* (p. 98), where the composer states, "... havendo V. M. C. mostrato di gradir molto quel mio Primo Libro di Madrigali à Cinque voci, ch'io volsi già mandar fuore sotto il suo Augustissimo nome."

15. See note 13.

16. This dedication is given in full in *DTO 77*, pp. 100-101.

17. *DTO 77*, pp. 20-21.

18. Einstein, "Italienische Musik," p. 44.

19. *DTO 77*, pp. 60-62.

20. *DTO 77*, pp. 62-65.

21. See Walter Pass, "Della Gostena," in *New Grove* (Vol. 5), pp. 345-46. An excerpt from della Gostena's dedication to Rudolf of his First Book for Five Voices is given in the *New Vogel* (p. 466), and reads: "... Havendomi maggiormente questo talento qual si sia in quella Corte acquistato nella servitù de la Felice Memoria di Massimiliano Secondo, per opra di M. Filippo di Monte...."

22. See Robert Eitner, *Biographisch-Bibliographisches Quellen-Lexicon 7*, pp. 246-48 (Leipzig, 1903).

23. Einstein, "Italienische Musik," pp. 39-42.

24. For the most recent "one Orologio" view, see Keith Polk, "Orologio," *New Grove* (Vol. 13), p. 868.

25. Ibid.

26. *DTO 77*, pp. 58-59.

27. See Hellmut Federhofer, "Galeno," *New Grove* (Vol. 7), p. 95. More detailed information on Galeno is given in *Niederländische und Italienische Musiker der Grazer Hofkapelle Karls II: 1564-1590,* ed. Hellmut Federhofer and Robert John (Vienna, 1954). (This is Volume 90 of the *Denkmäler der Tonkunst in Österreich,* hereafter called *DTO 90.*)

28. Galeno's dedication (given in full in *DTO 90*, p. 105) reads: "Quella servitù, invittissimo Cesare, che sino da i primi anni della mia giovanezza dedicai a la Serenissima Casa d'Austria...."

29. *DTO 90*, p. 90. The original Italian reads: "... la supplico adunque humilmente, che la piaccia di aggradire l'affetto, & accettare l'effetto della mia volontà porgendo l'orecchie tal volta benignamente à l'armonia di quelle voci, che favoriranno questi Madrigali...."

30. Hellmut Federhofer *(New Grove)* states that following Rudolf's death in 1612, "there is no record of his [Galeno's] subsequent activities, though a reference to him in 1626 in the Prague court records relating to his service under Rudolph II suggests that he was alive then."

31. *DTO 90* includes, *inter alia,* works by Lambert de Sayve, Galeno, Pietro Antonio Bianco, and Matthia Ferrabosco. De Sayve, who served the Habsburgs in a number of places, published his *Primo Libro delle Canzoni a la Napolitan* in 1582; it is dedicated to Michel Zacchel, a chamberlain of the Archduke Karl. (Einstein includes three pieces from this publication in *DTO 77*, pp. 48-53.) Lambert's brother Mathias was "Monte's deputy choirmaster" in 1593, according to José Quitin, "Sayve," *New Grove* (Vol. 16), p. 540. One further composer must be

mentioned here: Karl Luyton, organist to the Imperial Chapel. He published a single madrigal book in 1582 (I.5), dedicating it to Johann Fugger in Augsburg, to whom Monte dedicated his First Book of Spirtual Madrigals for Six Voices in the following year. Three pieces from Luyton's book are given in *DTO 77*, pp. 37-47. One of these, a sonnet beginning *Sacro monte,* is evidently a tribute to the composer, cast in allegorical language.

32. Monte dedicated his Twelfth Book to "F. Ottavio Spinola," whom Monte describes as occupying a "loco principale" in Rudolf's court (see the Appendix for the full text of this dedication).

33. Zanotti's setting is given in *DTO 77*, pp. 65-66.

34. The dedication is given in full in the Appendix.

35. This correspondence between Plantin and Monte is given in J.A. Stellfeld, *Bibliographie des Editions Musicales Plantiniennes* (Brussels, 1949). A letter from Plantin to Monte (pp. 99-100) reads in part: "Monsieur, j'ay faict delivrer les vostres [lettres] a qui elles estoyent addressées, vous certifiant qu'oncques je ne vy personnes plus joyeuses que se sont montrés les Père et Mère de ma damoyselle Clara Gabri avec elle pour l'honneur que tous trois recognoissoyent recevoir de vous par le contenu de vosdictes lectres. . . . "

36. *Opera Omnia,* Vol. 20, pp. 66-79.

37. In Cornet's publication, the poem is titled, *"A L'Honneur de Vertueuse Damoyselle Claire Gabri,"* and the text is printed separately, a rare occurence in the prints of the period. The Berkeley Music Library has the Contra and the Sesto partbook for this publication; though Cornet's piece is in the same mode as Monte's (G Dorian), there seem to be no further musical connections.

38. The presence of several languages here is reminiscent of Wert's *Il Primo Libro delle Canzonette Villanelle a cinque voci,* which contains pieces in Italian, French, Spanish and Greek.

39. *The Italian Madrigal* (Vol. 3), pp. 297-300.

40. Einstein, "Filippo di Monte als Madrigalkomponist," *International Society for Musical Research* (1930), pp. 102-8. The original German reads: "Vom 16. Buch an, 1593, hat Monte denn auch die allzuleichte Haltung seiner letzten Werke bereut. Er kehrt einigermassen zu sich selbst zurück. Er pflegt wieder eine reichere Belebung im Imitatorischen, ohne den 'stil vivace' aufzugeben; die Wendung ist unverkennbar."

41. The dedication is given in the Appendix; the original Italian here reads: " . . . Musica, laquale come con maravigliosa armonia risplende ne suoi Reali costumi, cosi vuole spesso udire, compartita fra angeliche voci, & cantata da cosi spiriti che chi vi si trova si crede haver certa caparra della beata vita."

42. See Anthony Newcomb, *The Madrigal at Ferrara, 1579-1597,* chapter 7, "The New Ferrarese Style of the 1590s."

43. See Vittorio Rossi, *Battista Guarini ed il Pastor Fido* (Turin, 1886), p. 103: " . . . il tanto tormentato poema vide finalmente la luce in Venezia verso la fine del 1589, colla data 1590." For a discussion of the polemical reception of Guarini's play, see Bernard Weinberg, *A History of Literary Criticism in the Italian Renaissance* (Chicago, 1961), vol. 2, chapter 21: "The Quarrel over Guarini's *Pastor Fido,*" pp. 1074-1105.

44. Both books were dedicated to highly placed figures at court, the Sixth to Imperial Vice-Chancellor Jacob Kurz, the Seventh to Albert von Furstenberg. In both dedications, Monte refers to the delight which these men took in music. The dedication to Kurz is given in the Appendix; the dedication to Albert (unavailable to me) can be read in Doorslaer, *La Vie,* pp. 225-26.

45. In its listing of the contents of the Seventh Book, the *New Vogel* ascribes *Ahi chi mi rompe il sonno* and *Per far una leggiadra sua vendetta* to Veniero and Petrarch, respectively. Yet an examination of Einstein's transcription of the Basso partbook makes it clear that both of these poems merely cite the opening lines of the two poems in question (Veniero's oft-set sonnet and Petrarch 2).

46. The dedication is given in the Appendix.

47. The dedication is given in the Appendix. Einstein (*The Italian Madrigal*, p. 675) refers to de Campo as "the major-domo of the Pope." Patricia Myers, in her recent introduction to a new edition of Marenzio's Seventh Book for Five Voices (Luca Marenzio, *The Secular Works*, Vol. 14, New York, 1980, pp. xviii and xx) states that de Campo apparently held only an unofficial position in the Pope's court.

48. The original Italian reads: "Mando a V. S. Reverendissima il Sestodecimo Libro de' miei Madrigali à Cinque, si per sodisfar al suo desiderio di veder alcuna cosa nuova delle mie. . . . "

49. A facsimile of Marenzio's dedication to de Campo is available on p. xix of Patricia Myers' edition of this publication, cited in note 47. Marenzio begins: "L'obligo grande in che m'ha posto l'affetto, col quale V. Sig. Reverendiss. hà mostrato sempre di favorir l'opere mie, si con la cortesia del sentirle volentieri, come con l'amorevolezza di lodarle, sopra i meriti loro, richiede, che levandomisi co'l partirmi di Roma l'occasione di poterla con la presenza servire, io le lasci qualche testimonio dell'osservanza. . . . "

50. The dedication is given in the Appendix. The original Italian here reads: " . . . in questi tempi calamitosi della Christianità, per uno de principali Campioni della santa fede. . . . "

51. The dedication is given in the Appendix.

52. The dedication of *La Fiammetta* is given in its entirety in *DTO 77*, p. 101.

53. See Ruth de Ford, *Ruggiero Giovanelli and the Madrigal in Rome, 1572-1599* (Ph.D dissertation Harvard University, 1975), Appendix I, pp. 241-42, which lists all the known madrigal books dedicated to Cardinal Pietro Aldobrandini, and includes a list of three other publications dedicated to "Cardinal Aldobrandini" which do not make clear which cardinal was intended.

54. Einstein, "Italienische Musik," p. 27: "Es ist ein Wiener, ein Kaiserliches Werk. . . . "

55. My reading of *Niuna sconsolata* is taken from Giovanni Boccaccio, *Decameron,* ed. Enrico Bianchi, Carlo Salinari, Natalino Sapegno (Milan, n.d.), pp. 272-73.

56. Monte's last contribution to an anthology appears in *I diporti della villa in ogni stagione* (Venice, 1601). Whether Monte went on to compose a *third* book for seven voices (as Einstein believed) cannot be proven. His Ninth Book for Six Voices (1603) is his last known publication, and now survives only in Einstein's transcription.

57. Of this piece, Einstein wrote: "Es ist, am Ende der Blüte der a cappella-Kunst, noch ein Gipfel, ein letztes Aufleuchten, ein herrlicher Abschied" ("Italienische Musik," p. 26).

58. *The Italian Madrigal,* p. 511.

59. "Filippo di Monte als Madrigalkomponist," p. 108. The German reads: "Er ist auf seine alten Tage ein Schäfer geworden wie Don Quixote, nachdem ihm heroische Taten versagt waren . . . [elipsis in original]. Es ist tragisch, dass trotzdem auch jetzt seine Madrigalbücher keine Auflagen mehr erleben."

60. "Filippo di Monte als Madrigalkomponist," p. 108. The German reads: "Mann kann sich nicht vorstellen, was nach diesen grossen Zeugnissen der Meisterschaft noch hätte kommen können. Sie waren unzeitgemass. . . . Aber es gibt kein Stuck von ihm, aus keiner Periode seines

Schaffens, das nicht ein Meisterstück des Stils gewesen wäre; und für uns Heutige ist vollends die Unzeitgemässheit seines späteren Schaffens kein Hindernis mehr, die Höhe seiner Kunst zu erkennen und zu bewundern."

Bibliography

Abraham, Gerald. *The Concise Oxford History of Music*. London, 1979.

Agnelli, Giuseppe, and Ravegnani, Giuseppe. *Annali delle Edizioni Ariostee*. 2 vols. Bologna, 1933.

Arcadelt, Jacobi. *Opera Omnia*. Edited by Albert Seay. *Corpus Mensurabilis Musicae* 31. American Institute of Musicology, 1965-.

Aretino, Pietro. *Selected Letters*. Translated by George Bull. Harmondsworth, 1976.

Ariosto, Ludovico. *Orlando Furioso*. Edited by Marcello Turchi and Edoardo Sanguineti. 2 vols. n.p., 1974.

Ariosto, Ludovico. *Orlando Furioso*. Translated by Barbara Reynolds. 2 vols. Harmondsworth, 1975-79.

Barblan, Guglielmo, and Zecca La Terza, Agostino. "The Tarasconi Codex in the Library of the Milan Conservatory." *The Musical Quarterly* 60 (1974): 195-221.

Blume, Friedrich. *Protestant Church Music: A History*. New York, 1974.

Boccaccio, Giovanni. *Decameron*. Edited by Enrico Bianchi, Carlo Salinari, and Natalino Sapegno. Milan, n.d.

Bossuyt, Ignace. "Newly-discovered Part Books of Early Madrigal Collections of Philippus de Monte (1521-1603)." *Fontes Artis Musicae* 26 (1979): 295-97.

Brett, Philip. "The Songs of William Byrd." Ph.D. dissertation, Cambridge University, 1965.

Brown, Howard Mayer. *Instrumental Music Printed before 1600: A Bibliography*. Cambridge, Mass., 1965.

Brunet, Jacques-Charles. *Manuel du Libraire et de L'amateur de Livres*. 6 vols. Berlin, 1922.

Byrd, William. *The Collected Works of William Byrd*. Edited by Edmund H. Fellowes. 20 vols. London, 1937-50.

Calendar of State Papers, the Foreign Series: of the Reign of Elizabeth. Vol. 14. London, 1907.

Catalogue of Books printed on the Continent of Europe: 1501-1611, in Cambridge Libraries. Cambridge, 1967.

Cerone, Pietro. *El Melopeo y maestro, tractado de musica theorica y practica*. Naples, 1613.

Clubb, Louise George. "The Making of the Pastoral Play: some Italian Experiments between 1573 and 1590." In *Petrarch to Pirandello: Studies in Italian Literature in honour of Beatrice Corrigan*, edited by J.A. Molinaro. Toronto, 1973.

De Ford, Ruth. "Ruggiero Giovanelli and the Madrigal in Rome, 1572-1599." Ph.D. dissertation, Harvard University, 1975.

Dent, Edward. "The Sixteenth-century Madrigal." In *New Oxford History of Music*, vol. 4, edited by Gerald Abraham. London, 1968.

Doorslaer, Georges van. "Die Musikkapelle Kaiser Rudolfs II. im Jahre 1582 unter der Leitung von Ph. de Monte." *Zeitschrift fur Musikwissenschaft* 13 (1931): 481-91.

————. "La Chapelle musicale de l'Empereur Rudolphe II, en 1594, sous la direction de Philippe de Monte." *Acta Musicologica* 5 (1933): 148-61.

_____. *La Vie et les Oeuvres de Philippe de Monte.* Brussels, 1922.

_____. "Vereerende opdracht aan Ph. de Monte in 1592." *Musica Sacra "Sancta Sancte"* 37 (1930): 241-44.

Durling, Robert M., trans. *Petrarch's Lyric Poems: The "Rime sparse" and other Lyrics.* Cambridge, Mass., 1976.

Einstein, Alfred. *Einstein Collection of Manuscript Scores.* In the Werner Josten Library, Smith College, Mass.

_____. "Filippo di Monte als Madrigalkomponist." *International Society for Musical Research* (1930): 102-8.

_____. "Italienische Musik und italienische Musiker am Kaiserhof und an den erzherzoglichen Hofen in Innsbruck und Graz." *Studien zur Musikwissenschaft* 21 (1934): 3-52.

_____. "Notes." Uncatalogued manucript, headed "Filippo di Monte als Madrigalkomponist." University of California, Berkeley, Music Library.

_____. *The Italian Madrigal.* Translated by Alexander H. Krappe, Roger Sessions, and Oliver Strunk. 3 vols. Princeton, 1949.

_____, ed. *Italienische Musiker und das Kaiserhaus: 1567-1625.* Vol. 77, *Denkmäler der Tonkunst in Osterreich.* Vienna, 1934.

_____, ed. *The Golden Age of the Madrigal.* New York, 1942.

Einstein, Alfred; Lesure, François; Sartori, Claudio; Vogel, Emil; ed. *Bibliographia della Musica Italiana vocale profana: pubblicata dal 1500 al 1700.* 3 vols. Staderini, 1977.

Eitner, Robert. *Biographisch-Bibliographisches Quellen-Lexicon.* 10 vols. Leipzig, 1900-1904.

Evans, R.J.W. *Rudolf II and his World: A Study in Intellectual History, 1576-1612.* Oxford, 1973.

Federhofer, Hellmut. "Galeno." *The New Grove Dictionary of Music and Musicians.* Vol. 7, p. 95. London, 1980.

Federhofer, Hellmut and John, Robert, ed. *Niederländische und Italienische Musiker der Grazer Hofkapelle Karls II: 1564-1590.* Vol. 90, *Denkmäler der Tonkunst in Osterreich.* Vienna, 1954.

Gobin, Raymond. "The Late Madrigals of Philippe de Monte." Ph.D. dissertation, Northwestern University. In progress.

Haar, James. *"Pace non trovo:* A Study in Literary and Musical Parody." *Musica Disciplina* 20 (1966): 95-149.

_____. "The *Note Nere* Madrigal." *Journal of the American Musicological Society* 18 (1965): 22-41.

Haar, James, et. al. "Madrigal." *The New Grove Dictionary of Music and Musicians.* Vol. 11, pp. 462-83. London, 1980.

Harrán, Don. "Rore and the *Madrigale Cromatico." The Music Review* 34 (1973): 66-81.

Harrington, John, trans. *Lodovico Ariosto's Orlando Furioso.* Edited by Robert McNulty. Oxford, 1972.

Hartmann, Arnold. "Battista Guarini and *Il Pastor Fido." The Musical Quarterly* 39 (1953): 415-25.

Haym, Nicolo. *Biblioteca Italiana o sia Notizia de' Libri rari.* Venice, 1736.

International Inventory of Musical Sources: Einzeldrücke vor 1800 [Series A]. Vol. 6. Kassel, 1976.

Kenton, Egon. "A Faded Laurel Wreath." In *Aspects of Medieval and Renaissance Music: A Birthday Offering to Gustave Reese.* Edited by Jan La Rue. New York, 1966.

Kerman, Joseph. "Byrd's Motets: Chronology and Canon." *Journal of the American Musicological Society* 14 (1961): 359-82.

_____. *The Elizabethan Madrigal: A Comparative Study.* New York, 1962.

_____. "The Elizabethan Motet: A Study of Texts for Music." *Studies in the Renaissance* 9 (1962): 273-308.

Lasso, Orlando di. *Sämtliche Werke.* Edited by Adolf Sandberger and F.X. Haberl. 21 vols. Leipzig, 1894-1927.

Lenaerts, René B. "Contribution à l'Histoire de la Musique Belge de la Renaissance." *Revue Belge de Musicologie* 9 (1955): 103-21.

Leuchtmann, Horst. *Orlando di Lasso: Leben.* Wiesbaden, 1976.

Lindell, Robert. "Die sechs und siebenstimmige Madrigale von Filippo di Monte." University of Vienna, 1972.

Lowinsky, Edward. *Tonality and Atonality in Sixteenth Century Music.* Berkeley, 1961.

Marenzio, Luca. *Sämtliche Werke.* Edited by Alfred Einstein. 2 vols. *Publikationen älterer Musik.* Leipzig, 1929-31.

Marenzio, Luca. *The Secular Works.* Edited by Steven Ledbetter and Patricia Myers. New York, 1977-.

Meier, Bernhard. *Die Tonarten der Klassischen Vokalpolyphonie.* Utrecht, 1974.

Monte, Philippi De. *Opera: New Complete Edition.* General Editor, Rene Lenaerts. Leuven, 1975.

Monte, Philippi De. *Opera Omnia.* Edited by Charles van den Borren, Julius van Nuffel, and Georges van Doorslaer. 31 vols. Bruges, 1927-39. Reprint: New York, 1965.

Myers, Patricia. "An Analytical Study of the Italian Cyclic Madrigals Published by Composers Working in Rome ca. 1540-1614." Ph.D. dissertation, University of Illinois, 1971.

Newcomb, Anthony. *The Madrigal at Ferrara: 1579-1597.* 2 vols. Princeton, 1980.

———. "The Three Anthologies for Laura Peverara, 1580-1583." *Rivista Italiana di Musicologia* 10 (1975): 329-45.

Nuten, Piet. *De "Madrigali Spirituali" van Filip de Monte (1521-1603).* Brussels, 1958.

Obertello, Alfredo. *Madrigali Italiani in Inghilterra.* Milan, 1949.

Palestrina, Giovanni da. *Le Opere Complete.* Edited by R. Casimiri. 32 vols. Rome, 1939-.

———. *Opera Omnia.* Edited by F.X. Haberl. 33 vols. Leipzig, 1862-1907.

Pass, Walter. "Della Gostena." *The New Grove Dictionary of Music and Musicians.* Vol. 5, pp. 345-46.

———. *Musik und Musiker am Hof Maximilians II.* Tutzing, 1980.

———. "Regnart." *New Grove Dictionary of Music and Musicians.* Vol. 15, pp. 691-93.

———. *Thematischer Katalog Samtlicher Werke Jacob Regnarts (ca. 1540-1599).* Vienna, 1969.

———. "Zanotti." *The New Grove Dictionary of Music and Musicians.* Vol. 20, p. 643.

Pescerelli, Beatrice. *I Madrigali di Maddalena Casulana.* Florence, 1979.

Polk, Keith. "Orologio." *The New Grove Dictionary of Music and Musicians.* Vol. 13, p. 868.

Quitin, José, "Sayve." *The New Grove Dictionary of Music and Musicians.* Vol. 16, 540-41.

Reese, Gustave. *Music in the Renaissance.* New York, 1959.

Regnart, Jacob. *Deutsche dreistimmige Lieder nach Art der Neapolitan nebst Leonhardt Lechner's fünfstimmige Bearbeitung.* Edited by Robert Eitner. Leipzig, 1895.

Roche, Jerome. *The Madrigal.* New York, 1972.

Rore, Cipriano de. *Opera Omnia.* Edited by Bernhard Meier. *Corpus Mensurabilis Musicae* 14. American Institute of Musicology, 1959-.

Rossetti, Stefano. *Il Primo Libro de Madrigali a Quattro Voci.* Edited by Allen B. Skei. In *Recent Researches in the Music of the Renaissance,* Vol. 26. Madison, 1977.

Rossi, Vittorio. *Battista Guarini ed il Pastor Fido.* Turin, 1886.

Sannazaro, Jacopo. *Arcadia.* Edited by Michele Scherillo. Turin, 1888.

Sartori, Claudio. "Scotto." *Die Musik in Geschichte und Gegenwart* Vol. 12, cols. 435-37.

Shindle, William R. "Macque, Giovanni de." *The New Grove Dictionary of Music and Musicians.* Vol. 11, pp. 450-51.

———. "The Madrigals of Giovanni de Macque." Ph.D. dissertation, Indiana University, 1970.

Short-list of Books printed in Italy and of Italian Books printed in other Countries from 1465 to 1600 now in the British Museum. London, 1958.

Simmons, Hall. "Philippe de Monte, *Il terzodecimo libro delli madrigali a cinque voci,* 1588; a modern edition." Master's thesis, The American University, 1972.

Smijers, Albert. "Die kaiserliche Hofmusik-Kapelle von 1543-1619." *Studien zur Musikwissenschaft: Beihefte der Denkmaler der Tonkunst in Osterreich* 6 (1919): 139-86; 7 (1920): 102-42; 8 (1921): 176-216; 9 (1922): 43-81.

Smith, William, ed. *A Dictionary of Greek and Roman Biography and Mythology.* London, 1902.

Solerti, Angelo. *Le Origine del Melodramma.* Turin, 1903.

_____. *Le Rime di Torquato Tasso: Edizione critica su i Manoscritti e le antiche Stampe.* 4 vols. Bologna, 1898-1902.

Stellfeld, J.A. *Bibliographie des Editions Musicales Plantiniennes.* Brussels, 1949.

Torchi, Luigi, ed. *L'Arte Musicale in Italia.* 7 vols. Milan, 1897-1908.

Trevor-Roper, Hugh. *Princes and Artists: Patronage and Ideology at Four Habsburg Courts, 1517-1633.* New York, 1976.

Van der Linden. "Note sur les dédicaces de Philippe de Monte." *Académie royale de Belgique: Bulletin de la Classe des Beaux-Arts* 50 (1968): 13-25.

Vicentino, Nicola. *L'antica musica ridotta alla moderna prattica.* Rome, 1550. Facsimile edition, with postface by Edward Lowinsky: Kassel, 1959.

Vogel, Emil. *Bibliothek der gedruckten weltlichen Vocalmusik Italiens aus den Jahren 1500-1700.* 2 vols. Berlin, 1892.

_____. *Bibliothek der gedruckten weltlichen Vocalmusik Italiens aus den Jahren 1500-1700, mit Nachträgen von Prof. Alfred Einstein.* 2 vols. Hildesheim, 1962.

Waldner, Franz. "Zwei Inventarien aus dem XVI. und XVII. Jahrhundert über hinterlassene Musikinstrumente und Musikalien am Innsbrucker Höfe." *Studien zur Musikwissenschaft* 4 (1916): 128-47.

Weinberg, Bernard. *A History of Literary Criticism in the Italian Renaissance.* 2 vols. Chicago, 1961.

Wert, Giaches de. *Collected Works.* Edited by Carol MacClintock. *Corpus Mensurabilis Musicae* 24. American Institute of Musicology, 1961-.

Willaert, Adrian. *Opera Omnia.* Edited by Walter Gerstenberg and Hermann Zenck. *Corpus Mensurabilis Musicae* 3. American Institute of Musicology, 1950-.

Wright, Craig. "Musiciens à la cathédrale de Cambrai." *Revue de Musicologie* 62 (1976): 204-28.

Zacconi, Lodovico. *Prattica di Musica.* Venice, 1622. Facsimile edition: Bologna, n.d.

Zarlino, Gioseffo. *The Art of Counterpoint: Part Three of "Le Istitutioni Harmoniche."* Translated by Guy Marco and Claude Palisca. New Haven, 1968.

General Index

Index of Pieces Cited

Unless otherwise noted, Monte is the composer. RISM, not Vogel-Einstein, superscripts are given. Pieces cited only in tables are not indexed.